Explaining Economic Growth

To Pang Shuk Chin and Wong Oi Henn

Explaining Economic Growth
A New Analytical Framework

David Lim
Professor of Economics
Griffith University

Edward Elgar
Cheltenham, UK•Brookfield, US

Published by
Edward Elgar Publishing Limited
8 Lansdown Place
Cheltenham
Glos GL50 2HU
UK

Edward Elgar Publishing Company
Old Post Road
Brookfield
Vermont 05036
US

British Library Cataloguing in Publication Data
Lim, David
    Explaining Economic Growth: New
    Analytical Framework
    I. Title
    338.9

Library of Congress Cataloguing in Publication Data
Lim, David
    Explaining economic growth: a new analytical framework / David
Lim.
    1. Economic development. I. Title.
HD75.L55 1996
338.9—dc20   95–42410
                                                        CIP

MIX
Paper from
responsible sources
FSC
www.fsc.org   FSC® C013604

ISBN 978 1 8589 8119 2

Printed and bound by CPI Group (UK) Ltd, Croydon, CR0 4YY

Contents

Preface

There are many explanations of economic development and therefore of the different development performances of countries. However, none is totally satisfactory because the predictions do not always accord with the facts. And yet there is enough in each of the explanations, when introduced at the right time and place, to suggest that they are important pieces in solving the jigsaw puzzle.

This book presents a new analytical framework for presenting these explanations. This is the stepwise and backtracking framework, which begins by identifying the sources of output growth and goes on to identify the factors behind these sources. It next identifies the economic policies needed to produce the factors and ensure their efficient use. It then examines the political and social values that facilitate the introduction of such economic policies, and ends by suggesting how the next stage should proceed in the search for the holy grail of development studies.

The advantage is using this framework is that it enables the strengths of the existing explanations to be highlighted. For example, the popular argument that economic growth owes a great deal to the presence of Confucian values explains everything and nothing at the same time. Yet we know that the presence of some of these values do help. The use of the stepwise and backtracking analytical framework allows the Confucian explanation to be introduced at the appropriate place, where it comes into its own to show that certain cultural values help in introducing the often unpopular and harsh economic policies required for sustained economic growth.

The new framework has another advantage. In tracking the path of economic growth logically from inputs to output to policies, it provides decision-makers with an operational framework to identity the policies needed to produce greater output growth.

I have not proposed a new hypothesis for explaining growth but rather a new analytical framework which can help in the systematic and efficient search for a hypothesis which is more powerful than the existing ones. Thus the book is a cross between a research monograph and a textbook. The research part is in the introduction of the stepwise and backtracking framework. The textbook part is in the presentation of the large literature on economic development within this new framework.

The ideas behind the book first appeared in late 1991 when I gave Griffith University's Research Lecture for that year. An amended version of this lecture was published in the July 1994 issue of *Economic Development and Cultural Change*.

As will be seen, I am indebted to many individuals in the evolution of my thinking on the subject matter of the book. On a more immediate level, I would like to thank Robyn White, Lea-Anne Moscoso and Susan Lockwood-Lee for the skilful, efficient and cheerful production of the camera-ready copy of the manuscript. I am also grateful to Dee Koster for her support and to Edward Elgar for encouraging the project through to the publication stage.

David Lim
Griffith University
Brisbane, Queensland
Australia 4111

List of Tables

List of Figures

PART I

Introduction

1. Development Performances of Developing Countries

1.1 A BRIEF HISTORY

In the 1950s when most of the newly independent developing countries began their search for greater economic growth, most observers of the development scene despaired of seeing much progress. Many of the developing countries had registered no growth at all for thousands of years. Most were experiencing rapid population growth and decreases rather than increases in their per capita income were seen as more likely. Even the industrialized nations, blessed with far more favourable initial conditions of growth, could only manage to increase their per capita income by no more than 2 per cent per year for any length of time (Kuznets, 1967).

Indeed this gloomy picture of what could be hoped for was reflected in the very terms which were used then to describe the developing countries[1]. First, they were called 'backward', the most unpleasant and pessimistic term of all, but widely used, as seen from the titles of the early works on development economics. An example is the excellent collection of readings edited by Agarwala and Singh (1963), which was a popular volume for students back in the days when economic development emerged as a burning issue for public debate and as a subject fit for study in universities. The editors came from India, a political and economic leader and giant of the developing world then, but chose to describe countries such as India as backward.

Many of the students using the book came from former colonies in Africa, Asia and Latin America and could be expected to have been politically conscious and sensitive, but they also raised no objection. It was as if the poverty was so extensive and permanent that teachers and students alike were numbed into meek acceptance of the word.

The next term used, 'underdeveloped', is not that much better. It is certainly less derogatory but still carries with it the sense of stagnation and despair. Yet all the major studies (e.g. Myrdal, 1957; Bauer and Yamey, 1957; Reddaway, 1963) used it without qualm. It was not until the term 'less developed' became fashionable that a note of optimism was introduced because it indicated that such countries could become more developed. The term most commonly used now is 'developing' which conveys the most hope. Somewhere along the way the term 'the Third World' crept in (e.g. Todaro, 1994). This is meant to distinguish the developing countries from the advanced capitalist countries (the First World) and the socialist countries (the Second World) but is a throwback to the early days as it bears the connotation that the Third World is inferior to the First World and the Second World. None of the terms used describes the countries concerned well but what is striking is the sense of hopelessness that characterizes the early description of what are now commonly known as developing countries.

This sense of despair was also reflected by the distinct lack of faith by some in the relevance and usefulness of the existing social sciences for solving the problems of the developing countries. Take, for instance, the case of economics. In an influential series of lectures given in Egypt in the early 1950s, Myrdal exhorted the 'young economists in the underdeveloped countries ... to throw away large structures of meaningless, irrelevant and sometimes blatantly inadequate doctrine and theoretical approaches' (1957, p. 101), if they wanted to help their countries. The economies implicitly dealt with in popular economics textbooks used in the West are industrialized market economies, which make up only a handful of the world's economies. The economic analysis presented, so argued Myrdal, would therefore have little relevance to developing countries, which are different to developed ones not only in degree but also in kind.

Even for those who believed that the likes of Myrdal were overstating the case, there was much soul-searching. For example, in his professorial lecture at the London School of Economics and Political Science for one of the first chairs created in the economics of developing countries, Myint (1967) argued that there is a need for the existing economic theory to be more dynamic in dealing with developing countries if it is to remain both relevant and realistic. Likewise, Reddaway, whose chair at Cambridge University was for his contribution to development economics, pointed out that even though the problems confronting developed and developing countries were the same, in dealing with the latter one has to 'make the right instinctive assumptions and to realize instinctively what things were likely to be quantitatively important ...' (1963, p. 2) because the context is so different.

There could have been many true believers among European economists specializing in development issues in those early days. But few of them chose to speak out in defence of their beliefs and convictions in the way Bauer (1976) so defiantly and consistently did. The silence was also deafening in the USA.

Against this background of low historical economic growth rates for developing countries, low expectations of what could be achieved, and low esteem for the theoretical literature, it was not surprising that the projection exercises carried out at that time predicted rather low growth rates for the per capita income of developing countries. For example, in 1960 Rosenstein-Rodan (1961), of the Massachusetts Institute of Technology's major centre of research on developing countries, forecasted that none of the 66 developing countries studied would have a growth rate in their per capita income of more than 3 per cent per year over the 1961-71 period. A similarly pessimistic picture was provided by Chenery and Strout (1966) in their study of expected growth performances over the 1962-75 period.

1.2 GROWTH PERFORMANCES, 1950-90

What was actually achieved over the 1950-75 period exceeded all expectations. Table 1.1 shows that the per capita GNP of developing countries as a group grew at an average of 3.4 per cent a year. This not only surpassed the growth rate of the developed countries over the same period but also that achieved by the developing and developed countries over any comparable period before 1950. As far as Rosenstein-Rodan's predictions were concerned, Morawetz (1977) pointed out that the average annual growth rates of the per capita GNP of 17 of the sample of 66 developing countries exceeded the 3 per cent said to be not achievable. Table 1.2 shows that 65 per cent of the sample of countries grew faster than predicted. The forecasts of Chenery and Strout were equally off the mark.

Table 1.3 takes the story of growth performances up to more recent times, when international economic conditions have become very difficult. While the growth rate of developing countries has slowed in the years since 1975 it still exceeded or kept pace with that of developed countries. The growth performances of countries in East Asia and the Pacific were particularly impressive.

The use of official exchange rates to convert estimates of the GNP per capita in national currencies to a single common denominator, usually the US dollar, does not give an accurate picture of the relative domestic purchasing powers of the converted incomes.

Table 1.1   GNP per capita and its annual growth rate, 1950-75

Region	Population 1975 (millions)	GNP per capita		
		1950 (1974 US$)	1975 (1974 US$)	Annual growth rate 1950-75 (%)
South Asia	830	85	132	1.7
Africa	924	170	308	2.4
Latin America	304	495	944	2.6
East Asia	312	130	341	3.9
China	820	113	320	4.2
Middle East	81	460	1,660	5.2
Developing countries	2,732	160	375	3.4
Developed countries	654	2,378	5,238	3.2

Source: Morawetz (1977, p. 13).

Table 1.2   Outcome of projections for GNP per capita and GNP growth rate for developing countries, 1962-76

Projection	Number of countries			
	Projections			
	too high	correct	too low	Total
Rosenstein-Rodan (1961) projections of GNP per capita in 1976	17	6	43	66
Chenery-Strout (1966) projections of annual GNP growth rates for 1962-75				
• Plan-based projections[a]	12	13	20	45
• Upper-limit projections	20	11	14	45

Note: [a] Based on the development plans.
Source: Morawetz (1977, p. 21).

Table 1.3   GNP per capita and its annual growth rate, 1965-90

Region	Population 1990 (millions)	GNP per capita	
		1990 (US$)	Annual growth rate 1965-90 (%)
Sub-Saharan Africa	495	340	0.2
East Asia and Pacific	1,577	600	5.3
South Asia	1,148	330	1.9
Europe	200	2,400	–
Middle East and North Africa	256	1,790	1.8
Latin America and the Caribbean	433	2,180	1.8
Developing countries	4,146	840	2.5
Developed countries	816	19,590	2.4

Note: – not available.
Source: World Bank (1992, p. 219).

This is largely because the prices of non-traded goods, mainly personal services, are higher in rich countries than in poor ones. The per capita GNP figures of Table 1.1 and Table 1.3 would therefore exaggerate the income gap between the rich and the poor countries. To produce meaningful comparisons of the income gap and of the growth rates of the income levels, purchasing power parities instead of exchange rates have to be used in the conversion exercise. The purchasing power parity conversion factor is simply the number of units of a country's currency that is required to buy the same amounts of goods and services in the domestic market that could be bought with one dollar in the United States. By using it, cross-country comparisons of GNP and its growth rate will reflect differences in the quantity of goods and services and in its rate of change, free of any price-induced differences.

Table 1.4 gives the unweighted average of the annual growth rates of the per capita GNP for different groups of countries, converted by the purchasing power parity factor, for 3 different periods. For the 1960-73 period, it shows, contrary to Table 1.1, that the developing countries grew less rapidly than the developed ones. But the growth rate achieved by the former was considerably better than most observers at that time were prepared to believe possible and for the 1973-80 period the developing countries did better than the developed countries. In the most recent period, 1980-88, the growth performances of the developing countries were significantly below those of the developed countries, but if a weighted average had been taken, the rapid growth rates of the highly populated East Asian and South Asian countries would have produced a vastly different result.

Table 1.4   Average annual growth rates of GNP per capita measured in purchasing power parity dollars (%)

Region	1960-73	1973-80	1980-88
Sub-Saharan Africa	1.90	-1.51	-0.50
East Asia	5.04	5.26	4.14
South Asia	0.57	1.93	2.52
Europe, Middle East and North Africa	3.47	2.87	-0.60
Latin America and the Caribbean	2.91	2.41	-1.45
Developing countries	2.77	2.19	0.82
Developed countries	3.95	2.02	1.84

Source: Summers and Heston (1991, pp. 356-8).

In summary, then, output in developing countries has grown faster than the population to produce significant increases in income per head since 1950. This performance generally matched or surpassed that of developed countries, bettered that achieved by developed and developing countries alike in the pre-1950 period and exceeded the expectations of most observers.

1.3 POVERTY

In spite of these achievements, abject poverty still exists in many countries. In some, the GNP per head has grown only very slowly, the incidence of poverty (the percentage of the population living below the poverty line) remained high, the level of labour utilization low and the provision of infrastructural facilities inadequate. In the more extreme cases, the living standards today are actually lower than they were during the colonial period.

The poor economic performances of some developing countries led the World Bank (1991) to begin its *World Development Report* of 1991 with the following dramatic statement:

> Development is the most important challenge facing the human race. Despite the vast opportunities created by the technological revolutions of the twentieth century, more than one billion people, one-fifth of the world's population, live on less than one dollar a day – a standard of living that Western Europe and the United States attained two hundred years ago. (p.1)

Table 1.5, taken from the World Bank's *World Development Report* of 1992, shows that there was only a negligible reduction in the incidence of poverty in developing countries in the second half of the 1980s. The number of poor had increased at almost the same rate as the population, with the result that the incidence of poverty declined only from 30.5 per cent in 1985 to 29.7 per cent in 1990. The absolute number of poor increased from 1.051 billion to 1.137 billion.

Table 1.5   Poverty in developing countries, 1985-2000

Region	Percentage of population below the poverty line[a]			Number of poor (m.)		
	1985	1990	2000	1985	1990	2000
All developing countries	30.5	29.7	24.1	1,051	1,133	1,107
South Asia	51.8	49.0	36.9	532	562	511
East Asia	13.2	11.3	4.2	182	169	73
Sub-Saharan Africa	47.6	47.8	49.7	184	216	304
Middle East and North Africa	30.6	33.1	30.6	60	73	89
Eastern Europe[b]	7.1	7.1	5.8	5	5	4
Latin America and ...the Caribbean	22.4	25.5	24.9	87	108	126

Notes: [a] The poverty line is an annual income per head of $370 in 1985 purchasing power parity dollars.

   [b] Does not include the former USSR.

Source: Ravallion, Datt and Chen (1992).

The World Bank believes that the prospects for future poverty alleviation for developing countries are somewhat better, as it forecasts that by 2000 the incidence of poverty will drop to 24.1 per cent. However, this is rather optimistic as it has been obtained on the assumption that economic growth will not change the distribution of income within countries. Available evidence suggests that income inequality tends to worsen with economic growth in most developing countries, if not in the long run, then certainly in the short run.

Table 1.5 shows that the problem of poverty is most daunting in South Asia and sub-Saharan Africa. In 1985 there were 532 million people living below the poverty line in South Asia. This amounted to 50.6 per cent of the total number of poor people in the world and 51.8 per cent of its own population. By 1990 the number of poor had increased to 562 million or 49.6 per cent of the total and 49 per cent of its own population. The relative performance of sub-Saharan African developing countries was even worse. Over the period the number of poor increased from 184 to 216 million, which increased its share of the world's poor from 17.5 to 19.1 per cent and did nothing to change the percentage of its population living below the poverty line.

The East Asian countries have the best record in eliminating poverty, especially if the projected performances to the year 2000 are taken into account. Over the period 1985-90 the number of poor was reduced from 182 to 169 million and in the process its share of the world's poor went down from 17.3 to 14.9 per cent and the share of their population living below the poverty line declined from 13.2 to 11.3 per cent. By 2000 the number of poor is forecasted to be only 73 million, or 6.6 per cent of the world's poor and 4.2 per cent of their own population.

In large part, the better performances of the East Asian economies in reducing poverty has been due to their higher rate of economic growth. Table 1.1 shows that the average annual growth rate of their real GNP per capita over the 1950-75 period of around 4 per cent was well above that recorded for South Asia, Africa, Latin America and developing countries as a whole and only exceeded by that registered by the Middle East. The economic performance of East Asia was even more impressive in more recent times. Table 1.3 shows the average annual growth rate of its real GNP per capita to be 5.3 per cent over the 1965-90 period, by far the highest among all the regional groupings and well in excess of that recorded by developed countries as a group. The same picture is obtained when the performances are measured in purchasing power parity dollars (Table 1.4). The East Asian GNP per head grew by 5.0, 5.3 and 4.1 per cent per year for 1960-73, 1973-80 and 1980-88 respectively, rates which exceeded very markedly those recorded by the other regional groupings and by the developed countries as a whole.

Why have the East Asian economies done so much better in increasing their rate of economic growth and in reducing their incidence of poverty? In more general terms, why has development performance differed between countries? If an answer can be provided, then the economic strategies, programmes and policies behind the development success of the East Asian economies can be identified and used for bringing about greater economic growth with equity in the other economies. Before this can be attempted, there is a need to identify the sub-group in East Asia to be used as the exemplar of successful development, as the East Asian group consists of the newly industrializing economies of Hong Kong, Singapore, South Korea and Taiwan and the Southeast Asian economies of Indonesia, Malaysia, the Philippines and Thailand.

1.4 DEVELOPMENT PERFORMANCES OF ASIAN DEVELOPING COUNTRIES

Table 1.6 gives the average annual growth rates of the GNP per head of 15 developing economies of Asia over varying periods, using figures converted by using the official exchange rates and the purchasing power parities. The economies are presented in 4 groups: newly industrializing, Southeast Asian, South Asian and China. No matter which series is used, the growth performances of the newly industrializing economies (NIEs) stand out. The Southeast Asian countries, with the exception of the Philippines, have also done well, as has China. The South Asian economies have tended to lag significantly behind the others, except when purchasing power parity figures were used for the 1980-88 period, when some of them did better than the Southeast Asian ones.

The NIEs have also done well in income distribution and the quality of life, two other important indicators of economic development. In a study of 34 developing countries, Riedel (1988) ranked them according to the household income shares of successive cumulative quintile aggregates and found that Taiwan has the best income distribution, surpassing even that of Sri Lanka, while Singapore, South Korea and Hong Kong are placed in the top third of the sample. Table 1.7 shows that the NIEs are well ahead of the other countries in the percentage of the age-group enrolled in secondary education and in the life expectancy at birth, two significant measures of the quality of life. The Philippines and Sri Lanka are the exceptions to this observation.

Thus the NIEs have not only grown much faster than other Asian developing economies, especially the South Asian ones, but have also produced a more equitable distribution of income and a better quality of life. Other measures of economic performance (e.g. employment and

Table 1.6   *Average annual growth rates of GNP per capita of Asian developing economies, 1950-90 (%)*

Region	Converted by official exchange rate		Converted by purchasing power parity		
	1950-75	1965-90	1960-73	1963-85	1980-88
Newly industrializing economies					
Hong Kong	5.0	6.2	7.0	5.9	6.0
Singapore	6.4	6.5	6.4	6.1	4.9
South Korea	5.1	7.1	6.7	5.2	6.9
Taiwan	5.3	–	7.5	6.3	5.3
Southeast Asia					
Indonesia	2.0	4.5	–	6.7	2.3
Malaysia	2.6	4.0	3.9	6.0	0.8
Philippines	2.8	1.3	2.5	3.2	-0.5
Thailand	3.6	4.4	3.8	4.2	3.8
South Asia					
Bangladesh	–	0.7	-1.0	3.1	0.8
India	1.5	1.9	0.2	0	2.8
Myanmar	2.3	–	2.2	3.2	3.2
Nepal	0.7	0.5	0.2	1.9	1.2
Pakistan	–	2.5	1.9	1.3	4.0
Sri Lanka	1.6	2.9	-0.1	2.1	3.1
China	4.2	5.8	2.3	3.7	7.8
Developing countries	3.4	2.5	2.8	2.2	0.8

Note: – not available.
Sources: Morawetz (1977, pp. 77-80); World Bank (1992, pp. 218-19); Summers and Heston (1991, pp. 356-8).

wages growth), equity performance (e.g. reduction in the incidence of poverty) and quality-of-life performance (e.g. the number of doctors per head) could have been used in the comparison but they would have shown the same thing: the development performances of the NIEs are better than those of Southeast Asia, which are, in turn, better than those of South Asia.

Table 1.7   Indicators of quality of life for Asian developing economies, 1990

Region	Quality of life	
	Per cent of age-group enrolled in secondary education	Life expectancy at birth (years)
Newly industrializing economies		
Hong Kong	73	78
Singapore	69	74
South Korea	86	71
Taiwan	–	–
Southeast Asia		
Indonesia	47	62
Malaysia	59	70
Philippines	73	64
Thailand	28	69
South Asia		
Bangladesh	17	52
India	43	59
Myanmar	24	61
Nepal	30	52
Pakistan	20	56
Sri Lanka	74	71
China	44	70

Note: – not available.
Source: World Bank (1992, pp. 218-9 and 274-5).

The results from the United Nations Development Programme's *Human Development Report 1992* bear this out. Four sets of data were presented: the composite Human Development Index (HDI) for 1990, changes in the HDI over the 1970-90 period, the HDI adjusted for income distribution and the HDI adjusted for male-female disparities.

The HDI has three components. The first is longevity, which is measured by life expectancy at birth. The second is knowledge, which is measured by adult literacy and the mean years of schooling. Educational achievement is calculated by assigning a weight of two-thirds to adult literacy and one of one-thirds to the mean years of schooling. The third is the income per head. The three components are then combined in a three-step process to produce an average deprivation index, whose difference from unity produces the HDI. The lower the deprivation index, and therefore the higher the HDI, the higher is the level of human progress (UNDP, 1991, pp. 88-9).

Table 1.8 shows that the NIEs have much higher values for the HDI in 1990 than the other Asian economies. The magnitude of the NIEs' achievement is perhaps better seen from the fact that its best performing member, Hong Kong, is ranked twenty fourth out of a sample of 160 developed and developing countries, placing it ahead of such countries as Greece, Hungary and the USSR. The table also gives, for comparative purposes, the HDI value for the highest ranked country, which is 0.982 for Canada.

The NIEs have also done better than most of the Asian economies in increasing the values of their HDI over the 1970-90 period. Malaysia, Indonesia and Thailand have performed better than the NIEs because they had a low base and the NIEs an already high one in 1970. The significance of the achievement of South Korea, the best performing NIE, can be seen from the fact that it is ranked only second to Saudi Arabia in a sample of 110 countries.

The HDI is a national average and cannot show the marked differences in the distribution of its components among the population. Equity considerations therefore require that the HDI be adjusted for inequality in the distribution of its components. The UNDP has produced HDI values adjusted for distribution in income, though not for distribution in longevity and knowledge because these are naturally much less unevenly distributed than income. The results given in Table 1.8 show that the NIEs have also outperformed the other Asian countries in this more severe measurement of human progress. The same conclusion can be drawn if the HDI figures were made gender-sensitive and adjusted for discrimination against the female part of the population, such as lower wages and longer hours of work for women.

A recent World Bank study (1993a) also shows that the NIEs have performed better in increasing economic growth and decreasing income inequality over the 1965-89 period. Economic growth was measured by the per capita real GDP growth and was defined as rapid when this rate exceeded 4 per cent per annum. Income inequality was measured by the ratio of the income shares of the richest 20 per cent and the poorest 20 per cent of the population. The higher the ratio the more unequal the income distribution, with countries having a ratio of less than 10

Table 1.8   *United Nations Development Programme's Human Development Index (HDI), 1990*

Region	HDI 1990	Change in HDI 1970-1990	HDI adjusted for income distribution 1990	HDI adjusted for male-female disparities 1990
Newly industrializing economies				
Hong Kong	0.913	0.151	0.871	0.649
Singapore	0.848	0.119	0.835	0.601
South Korea	0.871	0.282	0.884	0.571
Taiwan	–	–	–	–
Southeast Asia				
Indonesia	0.491	0.176	0.495	–
Malaysia	0.789	0.251	0.731	–
Philippines	0.600	0.058	0.572	0.472
Thailand	0.685	0.150	0.644	–
South Asia				
Bangladesh	0.185	0.011	0.168	–
India	0.297	0.039	0.278	–
Myanmar	0.385	0.000	–	0.285
Nepal	0.168	–	0.136	–
Pakistan	0.305	0.079	0.297	–
Sri Lanka	0.651	0.078	0.623	0.518
China	0.612	–	–	–
Highest ranked country				
(Canada)	0.982	0.301	0.979	0.938

Note: – not available.
Source: UNDP (1992, pp. 19-22 and 94).

defined to have low relative income inequality. The study covered 9 developed and 31 developing economies. One developed economy (Japan) and 6 developing economies fell into the category of countries which registered rapid economic growth and low income inequality, the best possible combination of results. The NIEs were among the 6 developing economies, the other two being Indonesia and Thailand.

This finding of the superior development performances of the NIEs is not new and is generally accepted. If there are valuable lessons to be learned from the experiences of successful development cases, most would probably argue that those of the NIEs should be examined first.

NOTE

1. In this context, it will be interesting to read the fascinating account by Arndt (1987) of how and when the term 'economic development' entered the English language and the literature on development economics.

2. Explanations of Different Growth Performances

2.1 DIVERSITY OF VIEWS

Unfortunately it is not clear what lessons other developing economies can learn from the NIEs because there appears to be no generally accepted explanation of their economic success. There is a large but often contradictory literature on the determinants of economic growth and therefore on the reasons for the different growth performances of the different countries.

Take, for example, the conflicting positions taken by exogenous and endogenous explanations of economic growth. The former sees economies, including the NIEs, growing rapidly largely because they have been fortunate enough to have good things bestowed upon them by nature, history, chance or friendly powers. Thus a country blessed with abundant natural resources will do well, as will one located in a strategic position and showered with largesse by a friendly superpower. On the other hand, endogenous explanations point out that the NIEs and other performing countries have done well principally because they have put their houses in order. Having abundant natural resources will help but the government of the country concerned will still have to introduce and implement appropriate policies to turn potential into reality.

The same degree of disagreement may be seen by examining the explanations according to the academic disciplines they are presenting. Each disciplinary advocate clearly argues for the primacy of the discipline concerned and when another discipline is admitted grudgingly to have something useful to say, it is usually allocated a secondary role. Thus while economists might differ on the role of the public/private sector in generating economic growth, they would point out that it is economic policies which matter. On the other hand, political scientists would stress that the necessary economic reforms cannot be formulated, implemented and sustained without having the appropriate political system (authoritarian or democratic) in place. Likewise, sociologists will emphasize the crucial role played by cultural values such as the Confucian emphasis on frugality and education and some give religion a central role in the rise and fall of civilizations.

The picture is confused further by the different positions taken by different paradigms within a discipline and by the different explanations which arise from appealing to a number of disciplines in a straightforward multi-disciplinary way or in the more difficult interdisciplinary fashion.

In sum, there is a diversity of views on the reasons behind the different growth performances of developing economies and on the spectacular economic successes of the NIEs. The rest of this chapter will present the more important of these hypotheses and briefly assess their ability to explain the growth performances of developing countries. The hypotheses examined are those which emphasize the importance of a lack of natural resources, the availability of foreign aid, the presence of Confucian values and the adoption of market-friendly and internationally competitive policies.

2.2   SOME EXISTING EXPLANATIONS

2.2.1   Lack of natural resources

Not so long ago, most would have argued that the lack of natural resources would have constrained economic growth very significantly. However, in recent times it has been pointed out that having abundant natural resources could bring with it unexpected economic problems, resulting in the so-called Dutch disease. Having little natural resources would be an advantage and could explain the economic success of the NIEs as these lack natural resources.

The Dutch disease refers to the phenomenon where the existence of a buoyant primary export sector is a bane rather than a boon in the long run. The massive inflow of foreign exchange from the export earnings increases the value of the local currency and reduces the international competitiveness of the traditional exports. This compounds the problems faced by a sector whose costs of production have been increased and which has lost resources to the booming sector.

This phenomenon was first noticed in the Netherlands in the 1960s when the discovery of abundant gas supplies in the North Sea led to huge export earnings. This affected adversely the traditional Dutch exports of dairy and manufacturing products as their competitiveness was eroded by the appreciation of the guilder, an increase in the costs of non-tradable services, which produces an effect equivalent to the appreciation of the currency, and the loss of resources to the more profitable gas sector. The result was a decline in its dairy and manufacturing activities, a rise in the inflation rate, a fall in savings and investment and an increase in the level of unemployment.

A similar phenomenon was observed in the United Kingdom when North Sea oil started to be produced and in Australia with its mining boom from the middle of the 1960s to the early part of the 1970s. Among the developing countries which suffered from the same problems are Nigeria, Mexico, Indonesia, Ivory Coast, Cameroon, Gabon and Venezuela. As the phenomenon was first observed in the Netherlands, it is now widely known as the Dutch disease. For those countries with large oil exports and very small populations, the phenomenon is known as the Kuwait effect.

There is quite a large and sophisticated literature on the Dutch disease. For our purpose, the easiest way of showing its adverse effects formally is to use an early model of it developed by Corden (1984). This has three sectors. First is a booming sector, which could be any primary export industry facing buoyant prices, the exploitation of an important discovery of a natural resource, or a cost-reducing technological change. Second is a lagging tradable sector, which could include other export items and import substitutes in manufacturing and agriculture. Third is a non-tradable sector, which consists of such activities as transport, services and utilities. In Corden's 'core model' covering the medium term, only labour is mobile between the three sectors, the other factors being specific to each of the sectors. Capital is assumed to be immobile internationally, and while the stocks of all factors of production are fixed, their prices are seen to be flexible.

Growth in the booming sector, whether it be based on investment expenditure or an increase in export earnings, produces a spending effect and a resource movement effect. The spending effect refers to the increase in the demand for products of the non-tradable sector and the lagging sector. In the short run, this raises the prices of non-tradable services because their supply is inelastic and produces an effect equivalent to a real appreciation of the domestic currency. The prices of the products of the lagging sector do not rise because the increase in demand is met by additional imports. The increase in the relative price of non-tradable items will encourage labour to move from the lagging sector to the non-tradable sector and reduce the output of the trading sector.

The resource movement effect describes the movement of labour from the lagging and non-tradable sectors to the booming sector, in response to the rise in the marginal revenue product of labour in that sector. For the lagging sector, both the spending and the resource movement effects reduce its labour force and produce an unambiguous drop in its output. If the lagging sector produces largely manufactured goods, this results in 'direct de-industrialization'. If it produces agricultural exports and import-competing food and manufacturing items, as is likely for developing countries, 'direct de-agriculturalization' will take place.

The impact on the output of the non-tradable sector is not clear. The resource movement effect will reduce its supply of labour and therefore its output. However, the spending effect will increase its output and the net result will depend on the relative strengths of the two opposing movements. If the former is smaller than the latter, the output of non-tradables will increase and this can only come about by moving labour from the lagging sector to the non-tradable sector. This produces the so-called 'indirect de-industrialization' and/or 'indirect de-agriculturalization' in the lagging sector.

The increase in the prices of non-tradable products will most likely lead to an increase in the level of nominal wages. This would produce an inflationary spiral, making the production of tradables less profitable as the cost of labour and non-tradable products increases.

Damage to the lagging sector will be continued by the rise in the value of the currency as a result of the large inflow of foreign exchange. The competitiveness of its most efficient activities, the export products, will be reduced. This destruction of the industrial and agricultural sectors is a problem if the growth industry happens to be a non-renewable resource such as oil because there is a need to plan for the time when the supply of the resource runs out. This is not an easy exercise as the large export earnings encourage excess spending and waste, which prevent the effective development of replacement activities.

Apart from causing the problems associated with the Dutch disease, an abundant supply of revenue can reduce the taxing and spending efficiency of the government. Difficult tax reforms can and will be postponed and many private and public investment programmes undertaken that would not have passed the normal project evaluation processes.

It is generally accepted that the NIEs lack natural resources. This is evident whether the measure is the land area per capita or the share of exhaustible natural resources, defined to exclude imports for re-exports, in total exports. Given such shortages, it would have been natural to argue that the NIEs and similar economies will begin their development process under a huge handicap. However, this argument has been stood on its head. The shortage is seen to have spared the NIEs the debilitating effects of the Dutch disease and has enabled them to grow much faster than their better endowed counterparts.

On the surface, there appears to be empirical support for this recent and unexpected explanation of the economic success of the NIEs and other resource-poor economies. Many of the developing economies generally accepted as being resource-rich have done much less well in economic terms. For example, the average annual growth rates of the real GNP per capita over the 1965-90 period for Nigeria (0.1 per cent), Ivory Coast (0.5 per cent), Cameroon (3.0 per cent), Mexico (2.8 per cent), Venezuela (-1.0 per cent), Gabon (0.9 per cent) and Indonesia (5.0 per cent) were significantly below those recorded by the NIEs and some like Mexico have done much worse after they have become major oil producers.

However, a more careful analysis shows that sudden increases in export revenue from oil do not inevitably lead to the Dutch disease and slower economic growth in the long run. First, the presence of disguised unemployment, assumed away in the Corden model, and the introduction of labour-saving devices in the lagging sector will reduce or eliminate the resource movement effect, especially if the booming sector is highly capital-intensive, as is the case with the production of oil (Yukawa, 1988; Tan, 1988).

Second, while it may not be possible to totally sterilize the adverse impact of the Dutch disease, much of it can be contained by sensible economic management. There will certainly be severe pressure on the government to spend its new-found wealth quickly and if this is on domestic goods and services, wage increases and welfare payments, it will lead to an increase in money supply and the rate of inflation. Together with an appreciated currency, this will result in the stagnation of the non-oil sector of the economy. However, there is nothing inevitable about these consequences. Holding a sizeable proportion of the government oil revenue in deposits overseas and/or spending a large part of it on imports to diversify the production base of the economy and to increase its efficiency will do much to reduce the severity of the problem. The appreciation of the domestic currency can be countered by a series of periodic mini-devaluations to preserve the competitiveness of traditional exports and prevent the artificial cheapening of imports (Gillis et al., 1988, p. 534). Such a strategy of devaluation is preferred to one which opts for the occasional major devaluation as it is less traumatic and introduces the element of certainty necessary to maintain business confidence.

There is no question that having abundant natural resources does bring with it its own set of problems. However, resource-rich countries do have more policy options than resource-poor ones and sensible use of them will maximize the benefits and minimize the problems of resource largesse. Thus it would be difficult to argue that the NIEs have performed well because they lack natural resources. It could just as well be argued that they would have done even better if they had been more generously endowed by nature.

It is easy to forget that the NIEs do have booming manufacturing sectors but there is, for example, no Singaporean or South Korean disease. This is because sensible economic policies have been put in place to counter the forces which reduce the competitiveness of the other sectors. It is true that a country with a booming oil sector does not have to be very concerned with these forces because its enclave nature, with its small reliance on local labour and materials, will not lead to a significant increase in its costs of production. International reserves can continue to be built up without reducing its competitiveness. However, there is nothing to say that action need not and cannot be taken to ensure the competitiveness of the other sectors. The ability to get the most out of the situation depends more on the nature of the macroeconomic policies pursued than on the size and the type of the booming sector.

2.2.2 Abundant foreign largesse

If physical deprivation cannot account for the success of the NIEs, then international politics and their geographical location can, so runs another exogenous explanation. More specifically, South Korea and Taiwan were only able to initiate their growth process and to sustain it at a high level because of massive foreign aid from the United States of America and other friendly and rich anti-communist countries. The aid produced an investment ratio and a human resource management level which would have taken a much longer time to materialize had the two economies been dependent on domestic savings and the local educational system. At the same time the backing of a superpower gave them the status and stability to attract direct foreign investment.

Unfortunately this explanation raises more questions than it answers. The empirical evidence that foreign aid leads to faster economic growth is mixed. Some developing countries such as Cuba and Papua New Guinea receive significant aid but grow very slowly, if at all, while others such as Malaysia and Thailand receive little aid but grow very rapidly.

A recent study has shown that the availability of large quantities of aid in a generous form has not helped the growth of the South Pacific economies (Lim, 1993a). In 1988 the per capita levels of aid received were $74 for Fiji, $88 for Papua New Guinea, $243 for Kiribati, $192 for

Solomon Islands, $186 for Tonga, $260 for Vanuatu and $182 for Western Samoa. These are very large absolute figures by international standards. So are they when presented as a percentage of central government revenue, with the exception of that for Fiji, where it was only 4 per cent. For the others they ranged from 32 per cent for Solomon Islands to 84 per cent for Vanuatu (World Bank, 1991). Most of this aid is also in the form of grants.

In spite of such generous aid, the economic performances of the recipients have been disappointing. Table 2.1 shows that their GDP grew very slowly over the 1980-88 period and in some cases (Fiji, Kiribati and Solomon Islands) below the rate of population growth to produce decreases in the per capita GDP. The same fate would have befallen Tonga and Western Samoa if large-scale emigration had not taken place. The domestic savings rates were low and in the cases of Kiribati, Solomon Islands and Western Samoa consumption actually exceeded output. The domestic investment ratios were high and sustained but this was made possible only by remittances and foreign aid, the exception being Fiji. Also the investment programme must have been carried out inefficiently as it did not produce rapid economic growth. Export performances in the 1980s were also poor.

It has often been argued that the South Pacific economies have not been able to make effective use of their aid receipts and achieve faster economic growth because they are small, remote and open. That size can be a constraint on efficiency and growth is well recognized, especially if it is accompanied by a small natural resource base. The unit cost of production will be high because of the limited size of the domestic market. Remoteness, together with a very fragmented land mass, can lead to high transport costs and difficult access to the major international markets. The cost of imported inputs will be high which will further increase the cost of exports, already burdened by the high cost of locally produced inputs and the high cost of being transported to the metropolitan markets. The openness of the South Pacific economies makes them vulnerable to external forces outside their control and produces export instability which may be detrimental to economic growth. The net effect of being small, remote and open is to make development of the South Pacific economies beyond the stage of 'primitive affluence' inherently difficult. The situation would have been worse if the governments had no foreign aid to counter these constraints to growth. In much the way that the availability of massive foreign aid had brought about or facilitated economic growth in South Korea and Taiwan, it would have produced a similar effect on the South Pacific economies, if these had not been handicapped by the geographical

Table 2.1   Selected growth indicators for South Pacific economies, 1970-88

	Average annual growth rate of real per capita GDP 1985-88 (per cent)	Gross domestic savings/ GDP 1985-88 (per cent)	Gross domestic investment/ GDP 1985-88 (per cent)	Average annual growth rate of real exports	
				1970-79 (per cent)	1980-88 (per cent)
Fiji	-0.9	18.6	16.1	17.3	3.6
Kiribati	-0.6	-37.6	31.0	–	12.7
Papua New Guinea	-0.7	11.0	23.0	14.1	6.4
Solomon Islands	-1.7	-0.3	29.8	33.0	1.6
Tonga	3.7	–	–	21.8	4.9
Vanuatu	0.1	4.7	30.8	26.8	-6.2
Western Samoa	0.1	-6.3	31.3	26.0	6.0

Note: – not available.
Source: Lim (1993a, pp. 46-7).

24

features of smallness, remoteness and openness. Having abundant foreign largesse would have produced rapid growth if only nature had been more accommodating.

However, the evidence to support this argument is weak (Lim, 1993a). The small island economies of the Caribbean and the Indian Ocean, which are more or less handicapped and receive less foreign aid, have performed much better. The Caribbean group, excluding Trinidad and Tobago and Barbados, increased its per capita GNP by over 4 per cent over the 1980-88 period, while Maldives and Mauritius increased theirs by over 5 per cent. According to the World Bank (1991), this better economic performance was achieved in spite of these economies being less well endowed in land area, sea area, arable land per person and forest area than the South Pacific economies. Moreover, the terms of trade of the Caribbean island economies deteriorated significantly in the 1980s whereas those of the South Pacific economies remained more or less the same. The instability of export earnings and imports for the South Pacific economies is also not significantly higher than that for small island economies elsewhere. In any case, it is by no means certain that export instability is bad for economic growth (Lim, 1991).

The reasons for slow economic growth in the South Pacific lie elsewhere, most probably with the policies pursued by the governments of the countries. Of particular importance are the policies which have increased the size of the public sector, inhibited the development of the private sector and produced a poor human resource development base. If the share of central government expenditure in GDP is used as the measure of the size of the public sector, the South Pacific economies have large public sectors by the standards of developing countries. For the 1985-89 period the average share for developing economies with low and middle income levels was 21 per cent (Lim, 1992a). For Kiribati it was 85 per cent, for Tonga, Vanuatu and Western Samoa 50 per cent and for Fiji and Papua New Guinea 30 per cent. An important reason for the large public sector in these countries is the growth of public enterprises in directly productive activities. These have been managed inefficiently and have been operating at a loss. They have not only caused a drain on the budget but encouraged rent-seeking and disadvantaged private investors.

The development of the private sector has also been retarded by policies which have directly reduced its level of competitiveness. For example, the real effective exchange rates of some countries (e.g. Tonga, Kiribati and Papua New Guinea) have been kept too high because of the concern for price stability rather than competitiveness. The average level of real wages is well above that in countries with similar or higher per capita incomes because of the implementation of minimum wage legislation, a high degree of unionization, generous wage awards to civil servants which flow on to the rest of the labour force and a centralized wage fixing system. Industrial and trade policies shield producers from outside competitive forces and the complex licensing systems, regulations and procedures appear to be designed to control rather than promote new investment. At the same time, policies to develop the financial system have been inadequate.

The human resource development programme has been successful in producing a high level of literacy but much less so in the supply of skilled workers. There is a severe shortage of skilled and experienced technical and vocational personnel, which has acted as a major constraint on economic growth. Expatriates continue to fill key positions.

It would thus appear that the policies pursued by the governments of the South Pacific countries have played the crucial role in slowing their rate of economic growth. Of all the explanations which emphasize the role of exogenous factors, the only one which has strong empirical support is the adverse impact of natural disasters. Easy access to foreign aid has contributed to the poor economic performance because most of the policies pursued by the governments have been encouraged by the availability of abundant foreign aid. Thus the presence of high levels and generous forms of aid has helped to increase the size of the public sector by underwriting its high wages and keeping badly run and unprofitable public enterprises in business. It has been responsible for the overvaluation of the real exchange rates, directly by the inflow of foreign exchange and indirectly through raising wages and prices in the non-tradable sector to create the equivalence of an appreciation in the domestic currency. The need to develop the financial system to raise funds for investment has been reduced by the easy access to cheap and/or free foreign exchange. Similarly the development of local training facilities for producing vocational and technical personnel has been hindered because the availability of such funds has enabled the employment of expatriates in areas of excess demand.

The development experiences of the South Pacific economies thus show that the availability of foreign aid has discouraged and not encouraged economic growth because the aid has been used badly. The principal lesson is that having easy access to foreign aid does not lead automatically to faster economic growth. It also depends crucially on what is done with it. Detailed studies of South Korea (Krueger, 1979; Mason et al., 1980) and Taiwan (Scott, 1979; Kuo 1983) show that foreign aid did play an important role in their development but this was because it was used mainly to control inflation, which helped significantly to produce the economic and political stability essential for economic growth.

In general, then, the availability of abundant and cheap foreign aid can give the recipients a headstart but this advantage can only be realized and sustained by pursuing sound macroeconomic policies. The explanation of the impressive economic performances of the NIEs must largely lie elsewhere. Even if the answer lies in foreign aid, it will only provide a counsel of despair because of the prevailing aid fatigue.

2.2.3 Confucian heritage

A popular explanation of the spectacular economic success of the NIEs is that they share a common Confucian heritage which gives them most of the important ingredients needed for rapid economic growth (Berger, 1988; Pye, 1988; O'Malley, 1988; Hofheinz and Calder, 1982; Kahn, 1979; Morishima, 1982). Hong Kong, Singapore and Taiwan are predominantly Chinese and heavily influenced by Confucian values, while South Korea has historically been influenced by Chinese and Confucian values. This cultural hypothesis has also been used to explain the economic success of Malaysia and Thailand, widely believed to be joining the ranks of the NIEs soon, and of Indonesia, as there is a significant Chinese influence in these three countries.

The Confucian values seen to promote economic growth are diligence, loyalty, hard work and respect for education. These arise from the importance of hierarchical relationships in Confucianism, where the duty of the subordinate is to show respect and loyalty, while that of the superior is to lead by example of high moral and intellectual standards. This applies to relationships between people from different generations, between members of a family and between the ruler and the ruled. The reverence for education is strengthened by the fact that entrance to the administrative corps of the government is by public examination that is open to all members of the public, regardless of background. The importance of the above traits is reinforced and enhanced over time as their possession provides the quickest way of promotion in the hierarchical system.

The Confucian value system can contribute to economic growth in a number of ways. First, it results in a hard-working, loyal and highly educated work force. Second, it produces a strong government and a meritocratic bureaucracy able to withstand the demands of pressure groups and thereby to reduce the level of rent-seeking activities. Third, it leads to an industrial organization which emphasizes team spirit and mutual respect. Fourth, it enables government and business to work closely together for the benefit of the country. All these produce a set of institutional arrangements which enables the formulation and implementation of coherent economic policies.

The Confucian explanation is not particularly convincing. It conveniently ignores the fact that in the 1950s Confucian values were blamed for the lack of economic progress in Taiwan and South Korea (Han, 1984; Baum, 1982) and for the economic decline of China in the past (Needham, 1954). It does seem strange that the same set of values is now being invoked to explain East Asian success (Pang, 1988; Papanek, 1988). Also the hypothesis clearly cannot explain the economic success of those developing countries without the Confucian connection.

The argument either does not believe or ignores the fact that people respond rationally to changes in the economic environment. Probably the workers in the NIEs work hard because they get paid well, remain loyal because they are treated fairly, value education because of the mobility and reward it gives them and save substantially because of high real interest rates. Certainly there is ample evidence to show that attitudes to work can be changed by the provision of incentives and by giving people room to move. For example, farmers in developing countries increase their output once agricultural pricing policies reward rather than punish their efforts. As pointed out by Arndt (1989), culture adapts to economic opportunity.

The presence of institutions seen to have promoted economic growth in the NIEs can be explained in economic terms without resorting to the Confucian value system (Chowdhury and Islam, 1993). Take, for example, the close government–business relationship in policy-making. Far from being a consequence of Confucian teaching, this co-operation has arisen because of economic factors. High business transaction costs and imperfect capital markets force firms to use their own internal funds to finance their operations. The underdeveloped capital market in most developing countries encourages the state to control and regulate the financial system in order to finance development activities. Thus both the private corporate sector and the state operate their own 'internal capital market' but clearly working closely together, with the state being the senior partner. This explanation of the close co-operation between government and business in the NIEs is based on the theory of the firm by Williamson (1975; 1985), which sees the state as a 'quasi-internal organization' (Lee, 1992; Lee and Naya, 1988; Wade, 1988; Zysman, 1983).

Another economic explanation of the close links between government and business is that members of the ruling elite share the same background, often coming from the same schools and universities. This enables the establishment of a subtle network of informal but binding long-term ties between key members of the state (politicians and civil servants) and the private sector (Okimoto, 1989; Lee and Naya, 1988). This creates, in effect, a 'quasi-internal organization' whose strength can be reinforced through a number of institutional arrangements such as the 'discussion councils', where key members of the private and public sectors meet to discuss important issues faced by society and the economy.

As all-embracing explanations of economic growth, the Confucian hypothesis or hypotheses which parade cultural determinism explain everything and nothing at the same time and 'smack of rationalization after the fact' (Chandavarkar, 1993, p. 22). There is little doubt that countries which possess the Confucian virtues of hard work, diligence, loyalty and an appreciation of education do have an advantage over other countries but 'cultural factors cannot be more than contributory factors, which may play their part, but only when other conditions are favourable' (Little, 1979, p. 463).

Even if the cultural explanation is valid, it would still offer little consolation to the less performing developing countries. It will take a long time for the necessary values to be inculcated and large-scale migration of the right people is not politically possible. This could encourage these countries to believe that they are doomed to poverty because their populations do not possess the necessary cultural values. Not so long ago Malaysians were urged to 'look east' and learn from the countries in northeast Asia. This they did with enthusiasm, only to find that cultural values could not be transplanted in a vacuum, even with prime ministerial exhortation. It must be accompanied by the adoption of appropriate policies.

2.2.4 Market-friendly economic policies

A recent explanation of the superior economic performances of the NIEs is that they have pursued market-friendly and internationally competitive policies. By allowing their governments and markets to work together to produce international competitiveness, they have grown much faster than those which persist with confrontation between the two and with the belief that they could operate outside the international trading system.

The phrase 'market-friendly' describes an approach where the government and the market each has an important role to play but with each recognizing its comparative advantage. Thus 'if markets can work well and are allowed to, there can be a substantial economic gain. If markets fail and governments intervene cautiously and judiciously in response, there is a further gain. But if the two are brought together, the evidence suggests that the whole is greater than the sum. When markets and governments have worked in harness, the results have been spectacular but when they have worked in opposition, the results have been disastrous' (World Bank, 1991, p. 2).

Governments are allowed to intervene in the market but do so to strengthen and not replace it. It is not a *laissez faire* strategy where the government plays only a minimal role in supplying public goods and the economy is guided primarily by the invisible hand of the market.

The phrase 'internationally competitive' refers to the need for market–government co-operation to produce goods and services at world prices. For example, if a private company cannot produce a 'socially desirable' manufactured good profitably without some protection initially, then government comes in to provide this assistance in a form which is transparent and which deals directly with the cause of the distortion or 'market failure'. The assistance should also be reduced as the industry moves from infancy to adolescence and picks up skills and experience. By the time the import-substituting market has been saturated, adulthood will have been reached and the firm able to compete without any more help. Macroeconomic, industry and trade policies should ensure such a transition and not one which encourages industries never to grow up and to require more and more protection as they become more and more inefficient. In other words, the policies should not encourage industries to go from infancy to second childhood straightaway and to become senile before their time. They should aim at producing international competitiveness, if not in the short run, then certainly in the long run. To achieve this, industry and trade policies should not, as much as is possible, discriminate between production for the domestic and export markets and between domestically produced goods and imports.

There is considerable support for this explanation. The evidence shows that the NIEs pursue a more market-friendly and internationally competitive approach to development than other developing countries. The governments of Singapore, South Korea and Taiwan did intervene in the running of the economy, often more so than governments of less successful developing countries, whether this be measured by the share of state enterprises in the GDP or the extent of regulatory control (Wade, 1988, 1990; World Bank, 1993a). However, this was intervention that was different to, and more sophisticated than, that favoured in the 1950s, in the heyday of planning when the so-called dirigisme syndrome dominated development thinking. First, the intervention was less on protecting domestic production because the effective rates of protection on manufacturing were significantly lower than those in most other developing countries. Second, the governments were more concerned that the intervention did not unduly distort prices down the line. For example, the anti-export bias created by protecting domestic producers was neutralized more quickly than elsewhere. Third, they subjected their intervention to the discipline of international and domestic competition. For example, in the 1970s the South Korean government increased the level of protection to encourage the development of the heavy chemicals industry. It also provided subsidized credit and tax rebates. When the industry performed badly the government withdrew its support and liberalized imports. In many other countries the response would have been the opposite. What the governments of South Korea and other NIEs did in such situations was to undo the harm quickly once they realized they had made a mistake. The first two examples illustrate the concern for being market-friendly, the third the concern for being internationally competitive.

This ability to intervene effectively in strengthening the market is enhanced by the presence of what has been called a 'strong, developmental state' (Vogel, 1979; Johnson, 1982; Dore, 1986), where decisions can be made more at arms' length to fulfil the long-term needs of society, insulated to a large degree from narrow sectional interests. This relative political autonomy is brought about by having an elite meritocratic bureaucracy backed by an authoritarian political system which also has close links with the private sector.

The existence of these conditions will produce intervention of a high quality and more efficient economic policies as they turn the state into a 'quasi-internal organization' which produces more interaction and co-operation between the main players. In Olsonian terms, this converts the negative rent-seeking activities of sectional interests into the positive 'collective action' more likely of a bigger or encompassing organization (Olson, 1982). In game theoretic terms, this reduces the number of times the players ('distributional coalitions') compete with each other and so reduces the number of paradoxical situations where the individual outcome from competition is worse than the one resulting from co-operation (Axelrod, 1984). In Williamsonian terms, it produces the equivalence of a multi-divisional (M) firm able to deal with 'market failure' arising from the presence of pervasive transactions costs, and with 'organizational failures' arising from managerial opportunistic behaviour, with the centralized policy-making body in the role of the head office and the business groups in the role of the divisions

(Williamson, 1975, 1985; Lee and Naya, 1988; Lee, 1992; Chowdhury and Islam, 1993).

Thus what has happened in Singapore, South Korea and Taiwan has taken the debate on the role of government in development well beyond the stage represented by studies by Rubinson (1977), Landau (1983) and Ram (1986). These attempted to examine the impact of government size on economic growth by simply regressing, for example, the share of government revenue or consumption in the GNP on the rate of economic growth, with no concern for how the government funds were generated or spent. It should come as no surprise that studies conducted in this vein have often produced contradictory results.

The pursuit of market-friendly policies is thus a plausible explanation of the impressive growth performances of the NIEs. It is certainly more acceptable than the views prevalent in the 1970s. This was that the NIEs did well because they adopted market-and export-oriented policies. There was no or only minimal government intervention because deviation from the market would have produced monopoly rents which encouraged the rise of 'distributional coalitions' or lobbying groups to capture them. These rent-seeking activities, which range from legal lobbying to the offer of bribes, are unproductive because they do not contribute to the long-run growth of the economy, even though they result in profits to private interests. They are also self-perpetuating because vested interests are loathe to give up their privileged positions. As a result of these views, the more zealous of the free marketeers claim that every successful country (e.g. Taiwan, South Korea, Singapore, Hong Kong and Japan) has relied primarily on private enterprise and free markets, while every country in trouble has relied primarily on government. The belief that it was unadulterated market forces that produced the economic success of the NIEs prompted some to argue that it represented a resurgence of neoclassical economics in the study of developing countries. It also led them to point out, but probably in jest, that intervention-infested economies only grow at night when the government is asleep.

Unfortunately these claims do not accord with what actually happened in Singapore, South Korea and Taiwan, where, more often than not, it was the long arm of the state and not the invisible hand of the market which was responsible for the rapid economic growth. The literature which warns of the dangers of rent-seeking has been, in reality, better in explaining failures than successes because there have been many cases of state-led industrialization and development success stories (Bardhan, 1990).

The market-friendly and internationally competitive hypothesis is also more acceptable than the pure 'statist' hypothesis, which sees the state as the engine of growth, albeit in a more sophisticated form than prevailed in the heyday of economic planning, and which dismisses the role of the market. The market-friendly explanation lies somewhere between the extreme versions of the statist and neoclassical explanations of East Asian economic success and presents a more accurate account of what actually happened.

However, it has not escaped criticism. Thus it has been argued that it tells only part of the story because unpopular market-reinforcing action against vested interests could only have been taken in economies such as Singapore, South Korea and Taiwan with authoritarian regimes. Such decisions could never have been made and implemented effectively if there had been a free press and open debate. In democracies it would have been all talk and no action.

Another criticism of the market-friendly and internationally competitive hypothesis is that the conditions needed to produce high-quality government intervention were not always present in all East Asian economies. For example, it is not generally accepted that a quasi-internal organization has ever operated in the internal capital market in Taiwan (Wade, 1988, 1990; Park, 1990) while in South Korea the operation has not been continuous.

Even if the quasi-internal organization were to have operated at all times, it is by no means clear that it will always produce efficient economic policies. In much the way that Williamson's multi-divisional firm will face more internal organizational failures as it expands (Hill, 1985, 1988), so will the economy as it grows because of the presence of more enterprises and business groups (Lee and Naya, 1988). At the same time, the targeting of industries to promote will become more difficult as the economy moves beyond the stage of producing simple labour-intensive and low-technology products.

2.3 COMPARATIVE ASSESSMENT

As all-embracing explanations of differing growth performances between developing countries, the hypotheses examined have not been totally satisfactory. The predictions they make do not produce results which are consistent with most of the facts, though there is enough in each of them not to warrant total rejection.

Thus, having little natural resources cannot explain to the satisfaction of all the economic success of the NIEs. From what is known about the

NIEs, their development performances would have been even more impressive if they had more natural resources. However, having abundant natural resources does present countries with some economic problems.

Having an abundant supply of foreign aid does not guarantee economic success. As with the natural resources argument, what matters is what is done with the available resources. Foreign aid, even if given for the implementation of projects, can be used for other purposes without the donors knowing, such is its 'fungibility'. It can also lead to wasteful spending behaviour and a lower savings ratio. However, there can be little doubt that a country which receives abundant aid and uses it effectively does have a significant headstart in the development process.

Cultural explanations of economic performances do not take the debate very far. Many developing countries have done well without having been influenced by Confucian values. For countries with a Confucian heritage, the argument was pushed when they prospered and shelved when they did not. Values such as hard work, loyalty and diligence can also be determined endogenously. Yet if these values had been present at the start of the development process, if there had existed a 'small inner voice' to begin with, it would have been easier to produce the economic ingredients for growth.

The market-friendly and internationally competitive hypothesis is built on a number of assumptions which do not hold at all times and in all countries. However, its eclectic approach has given it more credence than the extreme neoclassical and statist schools of thought. It also strikes the right balance in emphasizing that international factors, though important, are ultimately less so than domestic ones in determining economic growth.

Of all these all-embracing explanations of economic growth, the one which emphasizes the adoption of market-friendly and internationally competitive policies would appear to be the most acceptable. The others rely too much on the influence of exogenous factors on growth and not enough on the policies pursued by the developing countries themselves. The East Asian economies have put their houses in order and become internationally competitive. Other economies have done less well because they have not introduced the necessary policies. For a while they succeeded in convincing their populations and parts of the international community that this was all due to factors outside their control, that there was nothing much they could do themselves to get things going. For those which were generously endowed by nature, the debilitating Dutch disease was the culprit. For those which were less well treated by nature, the rich countries' lack of generosity was the main problem. For those whose populations were lulled into indolence by negative pricing policies, it was the absence of certain cultural values. For some of these countries massive amounts of foreign aid flowed in, failures were tolerated and the world went in search of alternative approaches to development.

But the results remained poor relative to those of East Asian economies and the world grew tired of hearing the same old excuses. Today there are encouraging signs that the practice of blaming the lack of progress on others is disappearing and that governments have recognized that alternative approaches to development still have to deal with scarcity and efficiency. Ultimately the answers to differing development performances between countries must be found in the economic policies they formulate and implement. There is no one else to blame and there is no substitute for getting the economic fundamentals right.

PART II

A New Analytical Framework

3. A New Framework of Analysis

3.1 WEAKNESSES OF EXISTING FRAMEWORK

Not everyone will agree that the market-friendly and internationally competitive hypothesis is the most acceptable all-embracing explanation of economic growth in East Asia. It still leaves many important questions unanswered. The search for a better explanation will continue so long as poverty exists and so long as there is academic curiosity on the reasons for the different growth performances of economies.

Enough has been learned from the literature on economic growth to suggest that to be fruitful the continuation of this search should take into account two considerations. The first is that for an explanation to be useful it must provide an operational framework for producing policy prescriptions to improve development performances. Some of the existing explanations are far too general and aggregative to provide decision-makers with a handle on the specific policies and instruments needed to promote growth. Take, for example, the argument that it was the presence of foreign aid which produced the rapid economic growth in some of the NIEs. Presumably its general policy prescription for the other countries is to seek more foreign aid but the specific policies for the receipt and efficient use of this aid are not spelt out in enough detail.

The second consideration is that for a new hypothesis to do better it must build on the strengths of the existing ones. While each of these on its own cannot reveal the whole picture, it does have something useful to say and these insights should be used.

This chapter presents an analytical framework which allows the existing hypotheses to be presented at the appropriate level, thereby enabling their strengths to be identified and used in the search for a more powerful explanation of economic growth. It also provides policy-makers with a better operational framework.

3.2   A STEPWISE AND BACKTRACKING FRAMEWORK

The new framework of analysis is the stepwise and backtracking framework, an earlier version of which has appeared in Lim (1994). This has four steps. Step 1 is to use production function analysis in its general or specific form to identify the sources of output growth and the contribution that each makes to the measured growth rate of output. Step 2 is to identify the factors responsible for these sources of output growth. Step 3 is to identify the economic policies needed to bring about the necessary factors and to ensure that they are used efficiently from the country's viewpoint. Step 4 is to identify the social and political values required for introducing the necessary economic policies.

Schematically, the framework can be presented as:

Step 1:   identifies the sources of output growth
Step 2:   identifies the factors behind the sources of output growth
Step 3:   identifies the economic policies needed to produce the necessary factors and to ensure their efficient use
Step 4:   identifies the social and political values needed to introduce the necessary economic policies.

This method thus backtracks logically and stepwise the growth sequence: from output growth to input requirements, the economic policies needed to increase input supply and the efficiency of input use, and the social and political values conducive to the introduction of the economic policies.

The following hypothetical example illustrates how the stepwise and backtracking approach can be used. Suppose Step 1 establishes that capital contributes the most to the output growth of developing countries. Step 2 finds domestic savings to be the most important factor behind capital accumulation. Step 3 identifies prudent monetary and fiscal polices to be the most important determinants of domestic savings. It also establishes that less distorted prices for capital, labour and foreign exchange are more likely to lead to a more socially efficient use of the capital attracted. Step 4 finds that countries with authoritarian regimes are better placed to introduce the harsh and unpopular economic policies and programmes needed.

What is obtained is the identification of capital as the most important input for output growth, domestic savings as the main source of capital accumulation, prudent monetary and fiscal policies as the most likely to ensure the supply and efficient use of domestic savings, and authoritarianism as the most effective type of political regime to introduce these economic policies. The analysis begins by identifying the sources of economic growth and ends by identifying the causes of economic growth.

The same procedure is adopted for the other contributors to output growth (for example, labour and technical progress). After Step 3 has been completed separately for all the contributors to output growth and if there are, say, three of these, then three sets of economic policies will be produced. Some of these policies will complement each other in increasing the supply of inputs. For example, a high real interest rate will encourage domestic savings, by making it more attractive, and the greater use of labour, by not artificially reducing the price of capital. However, there can be conflicts and choices have to be made. For example, reducing the percentage of the population below 15 years, that is, the youth dependency ratio, will decrease consumption and increase domestic savings but will reduce the future supply of labour. If capital contributes more than labour to output growth and a high level of labour underutilization already exists, then the choice is to introduce or continue programmes which reduce the population growth rate and the youth dependency ratio. Thus Step 3 can be used to identify and co-ordinate the economic policies needed to increase output from the use of all factor inputs.

The stepwise and backtracking framework of analysis can be used to trace the growth process not only at the national level, but also at the sectoral level. For example, it can be used to trace the growth process of the agricultural sector. When conducted at this level for a number of sectors (e.g. agriculture, industry and services), the co-ordination of the economic policies to be introduced becomes significantly more complicated. There will be a socially optimum set of co-ordinated economic policies for each sector and the overall co-ordination and management of these in a consistent and efficient manner will not be easy. As this is the first time that the stepwise and backtracking framework is used, it will be attempted only at the national level in this study.

It is important to point out that the stepwise and backtracking framework of analysis is not another all-embracing explanation of differing growth performances between countries. It only provides the framework for a more systematic and efficient search for a more powerful and more widely acceptable explanation. Its use enables the existing explanations to be presented at the appropriate level, thereby highlighting their strengths and enhancing their value. For example, as an all-embracing explanation, the Confucian hypothesis has been accused of explaining everything and nothing at the same time. However, there is little doubt that the Confucian values of loyalty and respect for education are helpful in implementing some of the economic policies necessary for increasing the supply of inputs (for example, an increase in the number of educated and committed workers). The value of the Confucian hypothesis will become more evident if it were presented at Step 4 of the sequence. Its value as an all-embracing explanation may be limited but it can make a useful contribution at this level.

The criticism of the hypothesis which sees the absence of resources as a blessing rather than a curse will likewise be less strident if the hypothesis were presented at Step 3. This will highlight the special problems encountered in having abundant resources and the economic policies needed to deal with them.

The weakness of the argument that the availability of foreign aid will lead automatically to greater economic growth will become more obvious when presented in the new framework. Step 2 shows that foreign aid will become a factor input only if it were used as such and not for the purchase of fleets of Rolls Royce and Mercedes Benz or the fattening of unnumbered Swiss bank accounts. If foreign aid contributed to the supply of factor inputs, Step 3 shows the economic policies needed to attract more foreign aid and to use it more effectively. The new framework shows that foreign aid will promote economic growth only if used properly and that it will be continued only if correct economic policies are introduced.

The usefulness of the market-friendly and internationally competitive hypothesis can also be judged more effectively. The efficiency of the economic policies it recommends in increasing the required factor inputs can be assessed at Step 3, while the political and/or social systems needed to implement these policies can be identified at Step 4.

It is generally accepted that none of the existing hypotheses on its own can provide all the answers, though each has something to offer. By enabling these hypotheses to be presented at the appropriate level, the new framework will enable their strengths to be used more effectively to build new and more powerful hypotheses to explain economic growth.

Another advantage is that, in tracking its path logically and sequentially from input requirements to the economic policies needed to attract such inputs and to use them efficiently, it provides decision-makers with an operational framework to identify these policies and to introduce them at the appropriate time and level. This ability brings out the weaknesses of some of the existing explanations of economic growth in their policy prescription. Take, for example, the Confucian argument. Clearly its recommendation is for the Confucian values of hard work, loyalty, diligence and respect for authority and education to be introduced. However, the needed economic policies have not been spelt out unless it be that workers have to be paid well in order to be encouraged to work hard. But this would be carrying it too far. In any case, it is not necessary to resort to the teachings of Confucius to arrive at this. Any good first-year economics textbook will do.

The use of the stepwise and backtracking framework will also force the foreign aid explanation of rapid economic growth to spell out its economic policy prescription. It will then be noticed that the availability of aid on its own will not lead automatically to greater economic growth. Much depends on how it is used and on the macroeconomic policies pursued.

The economic policy prescription of the argument that the superior economic performance of the NIEs is due to their lack of natural resources cannot be that poor-performing natural resource-rich countries cease making use of these resources. The use of the new framework will make this obvious and point to the economic policies needed for these countries to cope effectively with their good fortune.

In an important sense, the stepwise and backtracking analytical framework is a policy-oriented one, but one which arrives at the policy prescription in a logical way and allows it to be introduced at the right time and level. This gives it a significant advantage over other frameworks of analysis.

For the new paradigm to be of use to the decision-makers in their search for growth-promoting policies, there must be consistency in the results across developing economies on the relationship specified in each of the four steps. Unless there is widespread agreement on the sources of output growth in developing economies, the factors behind these sources of output growth, the economic policies needed to produce these factors and to use them efficiently, and the social and political values conducive to the introduction of these policies, no meaningful advice can be derived from using the new framework.

It is also important to note that the framework has implicitly assumed that the social and political values identified at the fourth step are exogenous. This assumption can be criticised for taking far too simplistic and uni-directional a view of the role of social and political factors in economic policies, whose implementation they are said to help. For example, if the regulatory framework penalizes initiative, business will be reluctant to take risks. Over time, any entrepreneurial spirit there might have been to begin with, will be conditioned out of the business sector. It can also be argued that a succession of poor economic results can lead to the installation of a totalitarian regime keen and able to introduce harsh economic policies. If this turns the economy around, the regime may put its economic achievements to the test successfully and achieve political legitimacy in an election. In both cases, economic performances affect the political system, not the other way around.

There is substance to this criticism but it is not enough to invalidate the use of the new analytical framework. It can be argued that 'small inner voices' exist to produce growth-promoting social values, and while economic circumstances will affect their development over time, it cannot account for their presence in the first place. Even if there is no inner source of strength, economic factors may only be a small part of the tangible factors which influence social values. It is possible under these circumstances to talk of social values, the result largely of non-economic influences, affecting the ability of a country to introduce harsh economic policies.

The same may be said of the role of political systems in economic development. Many factors influence the choice of the political system. If the influence of economic factors is only minor, then it is possible to argue that the political regime adopted, the result largely of non-economic influences, will affect the ability of the government to push through economic reforms.

3.3 COMPARISON WITH MAINSTREAM TEXTBOOK APPROACHES

Since the economic plight of developing countries became a subject fit for academic study in the late fifties, many textbooks in development economics have been written. As these deal with the economic obstacles to development and the economic policies needed to overcome them, they are, in essence, attempts to use 'received doctrine' to explain economic development and, by implication, why this differs between countries. It would therefore be useful to compare the approaches used by the mainstream development textbooks with the stepwise and backtracking approach proposed.

The first generation of these textbooks can be divided into two groups. The first consists of those which concentrate very largely on presenting the grand and not so grand theories of development before delving into the policies needed to generate economic growth. The second comprises those which spend much less time on the theories of development and more on the factors of production.

Typical of the first group is Higgins (1959). This covers in great detail the general theories of development presented by the Classical School, Marx, Schumpeter, Harrod and Hansen, and the theories of underdevelopment such as geographic determinism, sociological and technological dualism, lack of the required cultural values, colonial exploitation and unfair trading, and the presence of small and disjointed domestic markets. It also discusses measures to increase private and public savings and the inflow of direct foreign investment and foreign aid and some aspects of development planning.

The analytical framework adopted is very different to the one suggested here but in searching the economic literature for ideas relevant for generating economic growth in developing countries and presenting them in the way of Higgins, this category of first-generation development textbooks has performed a useful task. It would have been even more useful if the policy discussion had been more focussed and related to the schools of thought examined.

There is more similarity between the framework adopted by the second category of first-generation development textbooks and the stepwise and backtracking one. Typical of this group is Hagen (1980). First published in 1968, it makes only passing reference to the theories of development and spends most of its time discussing the factors of growth, with separate chapters for land, labour, physical capital, scale of production, technical progress, entrepreneurship and institutions. Thus it may be argued that a production function framework has been used implicitly, even though there was no attempt to quantify the contributions of these factors to output growth. In fact, as far as Hagen's own presentation is concerned, the similarity to the stepwise and backtracking framework goes further because the section following that on factors of growth is on the possible sources of resources for capital formation. Thus Hagen's treatment has implicitly incorporated Step 1 and Step 2 of the stepwise and backtracking framework. Step 3 would have been there as well if more emphasis had been placed on the economic policies needed to attract the resources for capital formation.

Of all the texts in the second category of first-generation texts on development economics, perhaps the one whose framework comes closest to the one proposed here is Bruton (1965). The first part uses the production function in its general form to describe the process by which an economy increases its per capita output. The sources of growth are identified as capital, labour, technical progress, natural resources and appropriate social and cultural values. The second and third parts then examine the ways in which the supply of some of these determinants can be increased. Part four identifies the criteria for making efficient use of capital resources. The book concludes by examining the role of money and finance in the development process and the usefulness of a number of fashionable development strategies.

The first part of Bruton's book clearly coincides with Step 1 of the new framework. The only difference is the inclusion of social and cultural values as a determinant of output at this stage whereas the new framework has it at Step 4. The second, third and fourth parts deal with the issues tackled at Step 2 and Step 3, that is, the factors behind the sources of output growth and the economic policies needed to produce them and to ensure their efficient use.

Bruton believed that the subject matter of development was ill-defined and unwieldy, with no widely accepted set of principles that could be presented in the conventional textbook manner. As there was no received doctrine, his book attempted to shift through the vast literature in the search for a corpus of ideas that could form the basis for a textbook. In this exercise there is a need to provide a framework in which the search can be undertaken in some order. The framework used by Bruton would have provided this much needed order but unfortunately the book never attracted the attention it deserves.

The second generation of development textbooks has very largely dispensed with the discussion on theories of development and has paid a great deal more attention on the major domestic and international problems faced by developing countries and the economic policies needed to deal with them.

The change in the contents of the first and the second generations of textbooks is reflected in the different editions of the popular annotated collection of readings by Meier (1990). The first edition came out in 1964 and was concerned primarily with the prevailing conflicting hypotheses of development. By as early as the second edition, published in 1970, the 'leading issues' of economic development had become the important development problems facing developing countries.

The emphasis on development problems is seen in Todaro (1994), a popular second-generation development textbook. This first came out in 1977 and though it has gone through five editions its overall orientation and organization have remained the same. It is presented in four parts. Part I presents the characteristics of developing countries in the global context, examines the meaning of development and assesses the usefulness of leading theories of development and the relevance of the historical growth experiences of developed countries in achieving this. Part II examines the major domestic development problems facing developing countries and the economic policies needed to solve them while Part III does the same on the international front. Part IV reviews the possibilities and prospects for the economic development of developing countries. The treatment of alternative theories of development is cursory, taking up a mere 32 of 660 pages of text. The emphasis is very much on identifying real-world development problems and the policies needed to solve them, approached not only from the economic but also institutional and structural perspectives.

The analytical framework adopted by Meier and Todaro appears to be very different to the stepwise and backtracking one but is, in reality, indirectly related. The identification of development problems and of economic policies to solve them is partly the flipside of Step 3 of the new framework. The presence of development problems only reflects the fact that the factors of production have not been used efficiently. Step 3 attempts to identify not only the economic policies which will increase the supply of such factors but also those which will improve the efficiency with which these are used.

There is also similarity in the importance each framework attaches to policy-prescription. A useful pedagogical innovation of Todaro's textbook is the standard procedure provided for arriving at policies for solving development problems. The principal issues arising out of a development problem are first identified, the main goals and possible objectives then discussed, followed by the use of economic analysis to arrive at policy alternatives and to assess their consequences. In providing a useful methodology and operating procedure for analysing and reaching policy conclusions about a development problem, the Todaro approach is at one with the stepwise and backtracking approach.

Gillis et al. (1992) is another widely used textbook at the moment. It has gone through three editions, with the first one appearing in 1983, but the basic structure and thrust remain the same. Part I introduces the concept and measurement of economic development and the more important theories to explain it. Part II and Part III deal with the contributions of human resources and capital respectively to development. Part IV examines the ways in which international trade can contribute to development. Part V uses the lessons from the preceding analysis to understand the development of the major sectors of the economy.

Many elements of the stepwise and backtracking framework are present in this textbook. For example, the concept of the production function was introduced in Part I in the discussion on the use of one-sector and two-sector growth models to analyse the different growth rates and development patterns of countries. Its role is to identify the contributions of various inputs to growth and to facilitate later analysis on how such inputs can be mobilized. This use of the production function is similar to Step 1 of our approach. The next two parts, which deal with the contribution of the capital and labour inputs to output growth, would then correspond to Step 2 and Step 3. There is no separate equivalence to Step 4 but as the book deals explicitly with the political and institutional framework in which growth takes place, this step is implicit in the framework adopted.

Presented in this way, there is much similarity between the framework used in the textbook and the one proposed here. However, the textbook has not been presented in this way explicitly or implicitly. Thus the production function was used to identify the different sources of output growth only when the one-sector Harrod–Domar model of growth (Harrod, 1939; Domar, 1947) was seen to be deficient in subsuming all the sources under the capital input. It was not used to see what growth models, such as the two-sector Lewis model (1954, 1958), have to say about producing the inputs needed for output growth, as would be done under the stepwise and backtracking framework. It was alluded to (Gillis et al., 1992, p. 43) but not followed up explicitly.

Of all the second-generation development textbooks, the one whose analytical framework resembles most directly the stepwise and backtracking one is Thirlwall (1994). In the very first edition, which came out in 1972, and throughout the other editions, the book argues right at the beginning of Part I that if discussions of ways to reduce poverty in developing countries are to 'advance beyond the stage of anecdote, hunch and opinion, growth and development must be placed in an analytical framework so that hypotheses can be advanced subject to the possibility of testing' (1994, p. 67). The production function approach is proposed as a useful first step in this direction as it will facilitate the understanding of the sources of output growth and help to quantify the contributions of these sources to any measured output growth rate.

This is then followed in Part II by a presentation of the factors in the development process, identified as land, labour, capital and technical progress. However, this discussion is not linked to the production function analysis in a backtracking manner to identify the economic and non-economic policies needed to produce the factors of production and to use them in a socially efficient way. Take, for example, the chapter on land, labour and agriculture. The topics covered are the role of agriculture in development, the organization of agriculture and land reform, transforming traditional agriculture, the growth of the money economy, finance for traditional agriculture, the interdependence of agriculture and industry, economic development with unlimited supplies of labour, a model of the complementarity between agriculture and industry, rural–urban migration and urban unemployment, disguised unemployment, and incentives and the cost of labour transfers. What it does is to analyse the role of agriculture and surplus labour in the development process in the conventional way. There are references to the policies needed to increase the supply of land and labour and to use them efficiently but they are not done within a backtracking framework.

The same can be said of the other chapter in Part II, on capital and technical progress. The topics covered are the role of capital in development, the capital–output ratio, technical progress, capital- and labour-saving technical progress, how societies progress technologically, learning and education. Thus the chapter simply looks at the role of capital accumulation and technical progress in the development process. It does not discuss the policies needed to increase the stock of capital, this being left to a late section of the book on financing economic development. There is some discussion on the determinants of technical progress but this is done at a general level.

That Thirlwall does not use the production function approach in the analysis of economic growth in the stepwise and backtracking way can be seen from the comments in the preface to the third edition of the book. He said that the chapter on the production function approach

> stays unchanged, except that it is stressed more directly than hitherto that the approach cannot tell us *why* factor supplies and productivity grow at different rates between countries. The production function approach is essentially a supply-oriented approach to growth which treats the supply of factors of production as exogenous to an economic system. (1983, p. xiv)

This point was stressed later on in the text:

> Thus, while the production function approach can disaggregate any measured growth rate into various constituent growth-inducing sources and can 'explain' growth rate differences in terms of these sources, it cannot answer the more fundamental question of why labour supply, capital accumulation and technical progress grow at different rates between countries. (1983, p. 62)

The same points were made in the fifth edition of the book.

The essence of the stepwise and backtracking approach is that it makes use of production function analysis to go the next stage, which is to accept that the supply of most factors of production is endogenous to the economic system, and then goes on to identify the economic policies needed to encourage this supply and its efficient use, before finally identifying the political and social environment needed to implement the economic policies. Thirlwall's approach falls far short of this. It sets out in the same direction but then collapses and reverts to the conventional textbook approach of dealing with the important development issues such as obstacles to development (Part III), planning, the allocation of resources and the choice of techniques (Part IV), financing economic development (Part V), and international trade, the balance of payments and development (Part VI), but without direct and systematic reference to the production function approach to growth introduced earlier. However, even in using production function analysis in this truncated way, Thirlwall has gone much further than the authors of other textbooks.

In a study on the causes of development, Lim (1991) spent a great deal of time presenting and evaluating the general theories before using the production function framework to present his own theory. In this, output is seen to depend on economic leadership, government leadership, ordinary labour, infrastructural facilities and natural resources, with the first two being more dominant than the others. The acronym, EGOIN, is then used to describe the theory, which is seen to be eclectic, flexible and multi-causal.

This framework is different to the one introduced here. While the production function framework is used, its adoption does not conform to Step 1 of the stepwise and backtracking framework because economic leadership and government leadership have been included as determinants, alongside capital, labour and natural resources. Step 4 has thus been collapsed into Step 1. Step 2 and Step 3 have also been omitted because there is no explicit attempt to identify the policies needed to influence the determinants.

It would appear that the stepwise and backtracking analytical framework is linked to the ones adopted in many development economics textbooks. By adopting the production function framework and identifying the important factors of production, the approach resembles an older textbook approach, where it was used implicitly. By going the next logical step and identifying the economic policies needed to encourage the supply and efficient use of these factors of production, it resembles indirectly the modern textbook approach. This concentrates on identifying the major development problems and the economic policies needed to solve them but the presence of development problems simply reflects the fact that resources are absent or have been used inefficiently. By bridging the gap between the two generations of development textbooks, the stepwise and backtracking analytical framework may provide a more comprehensive and coherent way of studying the economic problems of developing countries.

4. Sources of Output Growth

4.1 THE PRODUCTION FUNCTION

Production function analysis will be used to identify the sources of output growth and to estimate the contribution of each of these to the measured growth rate of output. This analysis is based on the concept of the production function from the theory of the firm.

A firm's production function shows the technological relationship between the inputs of factor services it uses in production and the quantity of output obtained per period of time. It can be written as:

$$q = q (f_i, ..., f_m) \tag{4.1}$$

where q is the quantity of output produced by the firm and $f_i, ..., f_m$ the quantities of m different factors used in production over a period of time. Of the range of technologies available, the firm is assumed to use those which are most efficient, in the sense that they provide the greatest value of output for a given value of input. In general, technical progress will increase the output possible from given quantities of factors of production.

If a production function can be written for a firm, so can one be done for the economy as a whole. The output of the economy will then be a function of the factor inputs available for the country as a whole and the technology prevailing. It can be presented as:

$$Q = f(R, K, L, T) \tag{4.2}$$

where Q is aggregate output and R, K and L the total supply of land, capital and labour respectively, all expressed over a period of time, and T the prevailing technology. The production function analysis used to study the causes of aggregate output growth is thus derived from, and consistent with, the theory of the firm. It has therefore a microeconomic foundation, which is a most desirable property of any macroeconomic analysis.

In order to see how the aggregate production function can be used to identify the sources of output growth, it will be necessary to examine in more detail the properties of the production function. To simplify matters, land is subsumed into capital and technology is held constant over the period of analysis. There will be only two factors of production, capital and labour, and the aggregate production function can then be presented in a two-dimensional diagram such as Figure 4.1.

Figure 4.1   Production function curves

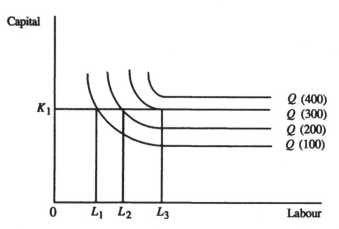

The vertical axis measures the amount of capital (K) and the horizontal axis the amount of labour (L). Each production function shows the same output level that can be produced with different combinations of K and L. For example, the function $Q(100)$ shows the combinations of K and L that lead to an output level of 100 units, and the function $Q(300)$ the factor combinations which produce 300 units of output. If the analysis had been conducted at the firm level, the function would be known as an isoquant.

The functions slope downward to the right to reflect the fact that capital and labour can be substituted for one another in the production process. If less of one is used, more of the other must be applied to compensate for the decrease in the first, if the output level is to remain constant. The functions are also convex to the origin of the diagram because the marginal productivities of factors decrease as more of them are used. Thus as the supply of one factor is decreased by one unit it has to be replaced by more and more of the other to keep output constant.

The functions do not intersect as an intersection point means that a single combination of capital and labour produces two different maximum outputs. This implies that an increase in output can be brought about with no increase in the amount of capital and labour used. It also implies that by decreasing the quantities of the two resources output can be increased. Both outcomes are economically nonsensical.

The level of the prevailing technology is shown by the position of the function. The more advanced the technology, the greater the output level per unit of the total inputs used. In terms of Figure 4.1, this will be reflected by the production function of a given output value lying closer to the origin of the diagram.

This brief analysis of the properties of the production function shows that there are three broad sources of output growth for the economy. First is the increase in the supply of the factors of production. Thus if the supply of both capital and labour were to increase, the example used in Figure 4.1 shows that this will lead to a new production function capable of a higher output level, as, for example, $Q(200)$, with an output level of 200 units. If capital and labour were to continue increasing, theoretically output should increase indefinitely. Output will also increase if the supply of only one factor were to increase but this will not be forever because the marginal product of the variable factor will eventually become zero. Take, for example, the common case of a developing economy with scarce capital and abundant labour. Suppose its capital stock is fixed at OK_1 (Figure 4.1). Increases in the supply of labour from its pool of disguised unemployed will increase the country's output but only to the 300-unit level. The marginal productivity of the variable factor, labour, will become smaller and smaller as it has to work with the same amount of capital resources. This is shown by the flatter slope of the production functions at successive employment levels OL_1 and OL_2. The limit is reached at OL_3 where the production function $Q(300)$ becomes horizontal and the marginal product of labour zero.

The second source of output growth is increasing returns to scale, which result when increases in the use of all the factors produce a more than proportionate increase in output. For example, a doubling in the use of capital and labour might triple the output produced so that output will have risen not only from an increase in the use of the two factors of production but also from the economies of scale generated. These economies may arise because of increasing possibilities of division and specialization of labour and greater possibilities of using more efficient technology. There could, of course, be decreasing returns to scale as increasing difficulties are faced in co-ordinating and controlling larger and larger operations, and also constant returns to scale. To depict diagrammatically increasing returns to scale, the production functions representing equal additional amounts of production must be drawn closer and closer together. For decreasing returns, they have to be drawn further and further apart and for constant returns equidistant from one another. In Figure 4.1 the production functions $Q(100)$, $Q(200)$ and $Q(300)$ exhibit constant returns to scale, and $Q(400)$ increasing returns to scale.

The third source of output growth is technical progress which increases the productivity of the factors of production. These technological economies of scale are different from the economies of scale generated by the use of more and more factors of production. The impact of technical progress on the production process will be reflected by either the same amount of factor inputs producing a higher output than before or the same output being produced by a smaller amount of factor inputs. On a production function diagram, such as Figure 4.1, if the functions and not the axes are relabelled, the impact will be captured by a shift in all the production functions towards the origin. If it were the axes which were relabelled, it will be reflected by these representing smaller quantities of factor inputs.

In short, production function analysis has identified three broad sources of output growth: increases in the supply of factor inputs, increasing returns to scale from large-scale operation, and technical progress. In order to make use of this analysis to estimate the contributions of these three sources to output growth, there is a need to choose a specific form of the aggregate production function which satisfies all the properties of a production function, fits the empirical data reasonably well and is easy to estimate. Such a production function is the Cobb–Douglas production function (Cobb and Douglas, 1928).

4.2 THE COBB–DOUGLAS PRODUCTION FUNCTION

The Cobb–Douglas production function may be written as:

$$Q_t = T_t K_t^{\alpha} L_t^{\beta} \tag{4.3}$$

where Q is real output, T an index of technology, K an index of the capital stock measured in constant prices and L an index of labour-time. The subscript refers to the period t.

The constant α measures the elasticity of output with respect to capital, when the supply of labour is held constant: a one per cent increase in capital will increase output by α per cent, if the supply of labour remains the same. Similarly the constant β measures the elasticity of output with respect to labour, when the supply of capital is held constant: a one per cent increase in labour will increase output by β per cent, if the supply of capital remains constant. If both capital and labour are increased by one per cent, then output will expand by $(\alpha + \beta)$ per cent. If the sum of α and β is greater than one, then increasing returns to scale will be present. If it is less than one, then decreasing returns, and when it is equal to one, constant returns.

Changes in technology are assumed to be determined exogenously and independent of changes in the supply of factor inputs. They are also assumed not to affect the factor-intensity of production, that is, the technical progress is neutral.

The identification of the three sources of output growth is best achieved by rewriting equation (4.3) so that the growth rates of the variables are presented. This can be done by taking the logarithms of the variables and differentiating with respect to time, to produce the following discrete approximation:

$$\dot{Q} = \dot{T} + \alpha\dot{K} + \beta\dot{L} \tag{4.4}$$

where $\dot{Q}$ is the growth rate of output, $\dot{T}$ the growth rate of total factor productivity or technical progress, $\dot{K}$ the growth rate of capital, $\dot{L}$ the growth rate of labour and α and β the partial elasticities of output with respect to capital and labour respectively, all measured over a period of time. The equation simply says that the growth rate of output is made up of the growth rate of total productivity, the growth rate of capital weighted by α and the growth rate of labour weighted by β.

Once the values of $\dot{Q}$, $\dot{K}$, $\dot{L}$, α and β have been obtained, the contributions of the three sources to output growth can be worked out. Suppose $\dot{Q}$, $\dot{K}$ and $\dot{L}$ are 10, 5 and 3 per cent per annum respectively and α and β are 0.25 and 0.75 respectively. The contribution of capital to output growth is $(0.25 \cdot 5)/10$, which is 12.5 per cent, while that of labour is $(0.75 \cdot 3)/10$, which is 22.5 per cent. The contribution of technical progress, obtained as a residual, then works out to be 65 per cent as in this example there is no contribution from increasing returns to scale, constant returns being assumed by the value of one given to the sum of α and β.

In actual empirical work to identify the separate influences of the three sources of growth, two methods are used to obtain the values of α and β. One is to adopt the constrained form of the Cobb–Douglas production function, with the sum of α and β made equal to one and their respective values determined by the shares of capital and labour in the national income. Such a method of deriving values for α and β assumes that perfect competition exists because under such conditions factors of production are paid the value of their marginal products and factor shares will reflect the elasticities of output with respect to the factors.[1]

There are problems with using this method to obtain the values of α and β. First, by making their sum to be equal to one the production function estimated will allow increasing or decreasing returns to scale only to be captured by T, the index for technology. This means that the measured contribution of technical progress to output growth will be overstated if there are increasing returns and understated if there are decreasing returns. The presence of this built-in bias will produce inaccurate estimates of the contribution of technical progress to output growth. Second, as perfect competition, the assumption behind the approach, does not exist, especially in developing economies, the results obtained may not be reliable.

The other method of obtaining values for α and β is to estimate them empirically, by fitting the estimating equation to the data for Q, K and L. The constant T will also be obtained in the process. The advantages of using the Cobb–Douglas production function in this unconstrained form are that the values for α and β are not presumed and the estimate for T will not be biased. As far as the first advantage is concerned, the values obtained for α and β often do not differ markedly from estimates of the shares of capital and labour in the national output, which this has led many to use the constrained version as a short-cut, thereby avoiding the trouble of making empirical estimates of α and β.

The use of the Cobb–Douglas production function to estimate the separate contributions of the three sources to output growth has certain limitations, even if the correct method has been used to obtain α and β. First, the contribution of technical progress is obtained only as a residual, as definitionally that part of output growth not accounted by increases in the factors of production and increasing returns to scale. It will therefore include the effects of the many factors which increase the productivity of capital and labour. In cases where technical progress is estimated in this way to contribute most to output growth, this is clearly not a satisfactory method of arriving at its contribution, especially as the estimate will also incorporate errors in the measurement of capital and labour.

Second, it is not possible to distinguish between shifts in the production function (technical progress) and movements along it (changes in factor-intensity) because the estimated function for a given period will capture only one combination of factors of production. This is unless technical progress is neutral. If it is not, then the results will be biased and inaccurate. The severity of this criticism may be reduced by the finding that technical progress, at least in developed countries, can be neutral.

Third, the use of the Cobb–Douglas production function assumes that capital can always be substituted for labour at the fixed ratio of one, that is, the elasticity of substitution is one.[2] This assumption can produce misleading results if the actual elasticity is significantly different from one and the growth rates of the factors of production also differ markedly. Take, for example, the case where the elasticity of substitution between capital and labour is significantly lower than one and capital grows much faster than labour. By forcing the elasticity data into a mould which only allows an elasticity of one, the exercise will overstate capital's contribution to growth. The problem in switching from labour to capital will make it more difficult to increase output simply by using more capital, the faster growing factor input, because its marginal productivity will fall with a relatively decreasing supply of labour. By assuming that the substitution possibility is greater than it is, the contribution of capital to output growth will therefore be exaggerated.

In reality this is not an important criticism. The use of the constant elasticity of substitution production function, where the elasticity is assumed to have a constant value between zero and infinity, produces values that are close to unity.[3] The Cobb–Douglas production function is therefore quite a good approximation of reality. Even if it is not, the factors of production will have to grow at vastly different rates for the elasticity of substitution to play a deciding role in arriving at accurate estimates of the three sources of output growth.

In addition to the criticisms which are specific to the Cobb–Douglas production function, there are those which refer to the use of aggregate production functions in identifying the sources of output growth. An important one is the difficulty in measuring the variables used. This is especially the case in aggregating capital goods for these have different vintages, costs and productivities. If the measurement of the variables is faulty, the results obtained will be inaccurate. As an important canon of empirical work has it, garbage in, garbage out, no matter how sophisticated the theory and technique. This is advice well worth following, especially in developing countries where the data collected is often poor.

It is generally accepted that, on balance, the conceptual and practical problems in using the Cobb–Douglas production function to identify the sources of output growth are not serious enough to invalidate its use. The next section will present the results obtained with its use. The results for developed countries will be given first, even though this study is mainly concerned with developing countries, because the first studies have been on developed countries and these have set the format for the later studies on developing countries. However, the presentation of the empirical results for developed countries will be kept to the minimum.

4.3 EMPIRICAL EVIDENCE

4.3.1 Developed countries

In introducing and then using their production function, Cobb and Douglas were only interested in testing the neo-classical marginal productivity theory that the partial elasticities of output would measure the shares of the factor inputs in total output. They were not concerned with identifying the sources of output growth as such. The results obtained show that there was strong support for the neo-classical position in American manufacturing over the 1899-1922 period.

Most of the succeeding cross-section and time-series studies were also concerned with testing the neo-classical model. The results from the cross-section studies reported in Walters (1968) also show that this has stood up well. The sum of the partial elasticities from most of the cross-section inter-firm and inter-industry studies is near to unity and the partial elasticity of output with respect to labour close to the share of labour in the total output. The few instances where this was not the case can be explained easily. For example, the decreasing returns to scale in Japanese agriculture in 1939 was caused by the negative value for the coefficient for labour. This could, in turn, be explained by a very high level of disguised unemployment, with farm workers getting into each other's way and reducing their marginal productivities below zero. This is a phenomenon which may be quite common today among those developing countries with rapidly growing populations. The case of increasing returns in the American railway industry in 1936 could be explained by the operation of relatively large plants, with their inherent indivisibilities, at a time when the level of utilization was quite low.

The results of the time-series studies reported by Walters were less supportive of the neo-classical theory. While those for periods before the depression of the 1930s were in line with its predictions, those for later years show increasing returns and a labour coefficient which exceeds the share of wages in the total output.

The use of production function analysis to identify the sources of output growth in developed countries only began with the discovery by Abramovitz (1956) that between 80 and 90 per cent of the growth of output per head in the United States over the 1870-1953 period could not be accounted for by increases in capital per head. A similar conclusion was reached by Solow (1957) in a study of the American non-farm sector over the 1919-57 period.

This finding, that capital accumulation mattered so little to output growth, was totally unexpected. It led to many attempts to reinstate capital's central role, in much the way that Leontief's empirical contradiction of the eminently plausible Heckscher–Ohlin prediction, that countries have a comparative advantage in producing goods which use relatively more of their abundant resources, led to many attempts to explain the so-called Leontief paradox.

Abramovitz began the process of rehabilitating capital's position by claiming that while factor inputs *per se* might not have been important for growth they did interact with other factors to produce the increase in total productivity, the so-called residual, which accounted for the bulk of output growth. This was followed by others who argued that if capital and labour were measured in the conventional way, then improvements in their quality would not be captured and subsequently their contribution to output growth would be understated. Attempts were thus made to measure the factor inputs so that they incorporate such improvements. Other researchers took the path of measuring the factor inputs in the conventional way but disaggregated the residual factor.

A number of ways have been used to adjust the time-series on capital stock to reflect the fact that existing equipment is less productive than new because of technical progress, that is, to measure what has been called embodied technical progress. One is to measure capital gross at current prices and not net at constant prices, with the price variable capturing the embodied technical change. The influence of technical change that is not dependent on capital accumulation, the so-called disembodied technical change, will be captured by the residual factor. Another is to add an exponential time trend to the production function to capture the disembodied technical change, which will then be assumed to proceed at a constant rate. Embodied technical progress will be reflected in the residual.

A third is to value each year's addition to the capital stock separately, with higher weights being given to the later and more productive additions. This is the so-called vintage approach to measuring capital, pioneered by Solow (1960) and Nelson (1964). Its use with the Cobb–Douglas production function to capture embodied technological progress will produce the following estimating equation:

$$\dot{Q} = \dot{T}' + \alpha\dot{K} + \alpha\dot{P} - \alpha\dot{P}\Delta A + \beta\dot{L} \tag{4.5}$$

where $\dot{T}'$ is the growth rate of the total productivity index after discarding the effect of technical progress embodied in new capital, $\dot{P}$ the growth rate of improvement in the quality of new capital, ΔA the change in the average age of the capital stock and the other variables are as defined previously. The contribution of disembodied technical progress will be captured by $\dot{T}'$, that of embodied technical progress by $\alpha\dot{P}$ and $\alpha\dot{P}\Delta A$.[4] Equation (4.5) can be used to obtain these contributions only by assuming that all technical progress is embodied. As this is clearly unrealistic and negates the reason for using the equation, different rates of embodied technical progress are experimented with. The rate chosen for use in the final estimating equation is the one which produces the best statistical fit for the equation.

Attempts to reduce the size of the residual factor were also made by adjusting the labour input for improvements in its quality. Such improvements can come about through a rise in the average quality of labour, from greater work experience, and through the higher productivity of new workers, from their greater formal education and training. If it were solely the latter, then a model which is analogous to the vintage one for capital is often used to produce the following estimating form of the Cobb-Douglas production function:

$$\dot{Q} = \dot{T}* + \alpha\dot{K} + \alpha\dot{P} - \alpha\dot{P}\Delta A + \beta\dot{L} + \beta\dot{E} - \beta\dot{E}\Delta W \qquad (4.6)$$

where $\dot{T}*$ is the growth rate of the total productivity index excluding the effect of technical progress embodied in both new capital and workers, $\dot{E}$ the growth rate of improvement in the average efficiency of the labour force and ΔW the change in the average age of the labour force.

Another factor which might have inflated the size of the residual factor and downgraded the contribution of capital and labour is the shift of resources from less to more productive activities. If the weights used for aggregating capital and labour are not 'continually revised to reflect their changing productivities in different occupations, the effects of resource reallocation will appear independent of the factors of production whereas, in practice, growth from this source is intimately bound up with factor endowments and the sectors in which the growth of factors of production takes place' (Thirlwall, 1994, p. 77).

Two main methods have been used to estimate the effect of resource shifts on measured output growth. One is to subtract from the aggregate measure of technical progress the weighted average of the rates of technical progress within different sectors. The difference will then measure the productivity increase due to the shift of resources between sectors (Massell, 1961; Denison, 1967). The second is to measure directly the contribution of each factor to output growth from its movement from a low to a high-productivity sector (Robinson, 1971). Suppose capital and labour have shifted from the low-productivity agricultural sector to the high-productivity industrial sector. The contribution to measured output growth of the shift of labour resources will then be measured by:

$$\left(MP_i - MP_a\right)\Delta SL_i \frac{L}{Q}$$

where MP_i and MP_a are the marginal revenue products of labour in industry and agriculture respectively, ΔSL_i the change in the share of the labour force in industry and L/Q the share of labour in the total output. The contribution of the shift of capital resources can be written in a similar way.

The result of all these attempts to adjust the data on capital and labour for changes in the quality of the inputs and to account for the effect of resource shifts is to increase the importance of capital and labour in the growth process and to downgrade that of the residual factor. However, most of these continue to show that capital accumulation remains a relatively unimportant contributor to output growth in developed countries. For example, Denison (1967), after adjusting the capital stock of the United States for quality improvements, found that capital could account for only 25 per cent of American output growth over the 1950-62 period. For Northwest Europe over the same period this contribution was even lower at around 20 per cent. In a study in which an embodied technical progress model was used, Solow (1960) found capital accumulation to be much more important for economic growth. However, this contribution was still significantly less than that of disembodied technical progress.

The same conclusion was reached in a recent study by Boskin and Lau (1990) on France, West Germany, Japan, the United Kingdom and the United States for the 1960-85 period. The contribution of capital accumulation to output growth varies from only 23 per cent for West Germany and the United States to 36 per cent for Japan, while that of growth in the total factor productivity ranged from 50 per cent for the United States to 87 per cent for West Germany.

The most striking exception to the conclusion that changes in total factor productivity are far more important than changes in factor inputs in explaining output growth is the study by Jorgenson and Griliches

(1967). This argues that there have been serious errors in measuring output and factor inputs and that without these growth in output will be largely explained by growth in factor inputs. For the American economy over the 1945-65 period, with the use of inaccurate output and input data, the growth in inputs explained 52.4 per cent of the growth in total output. However, after eliminating aggregation errors in combining investment and consumption goods, and labour and capital services, this contribution was increased slightly to 54.3 per cent. If errors in measuring the prices of investment goods were also avoided, the contribution went up to 61 per cent. Further adjustments for the rates of utilization of labour and capital stock increased this significantly to 71.6 per cent. When capital services were then aggregated properly, the share went up to 83.7 per cent. And lastly when labour services were aggregated correctly, it went up to 96.7 per cent. These results led the study to conclude that if quantities of the output and inputs were measured accurately, growth in total output might be largely explained by growth in total input.

However, on balance, the weight of the evidence suggests that technical progress is the most important source of output growth in developed countries. Increases in the supply of factors of production matter far less, when compared to the contribution of technical progress and to the primary role assigned to them. In general, growth in the labour force contributes as much as capital accumulation to output growth. Another important finding on the sources of output growth in developed countries is that increasing returns to scale are not important. The sum of the partial elasticities of output with respect to capital and labour approximates unity in most of the studies.

In summary, the majority of the empirical studies on sources of output growth in developed countries show that technical progress is by far the most important. The contributions of capital and labour cannot be ignored but they are far less significant. Increasing returns to scale play no part at all.

4.3.2 Developing countries

Thirlwall (1994) has given an excellent summary of the results from the empirical studies. The first study surveyed is the one by Maddison (1970) of twenty-two developing countries for the 1950-65 period. The labour variable in the production function analysis was the effective labour force, after adjustments were made for improvements in health and education and for the shift or migration of workers from the low-productivity agricultural sector to the high-productivity industrial one.

The capital variable was measured in the conventional way, without adjusting for improvements in its quality or taking into account the actual level of capital utilization.[5] The partial elasticities of output with respect to capital and labour were both assumed to be equal to 0.5.

The results, given in Table 4.1, show that for all countries capital accumulation was the most important source of output growth. For most countries, additions to the effective labour force came next, with technical progress a very distant third. In the more developed countries of the sample (Greece, Spain and Taiwan), the contribution of technical progress exceeded that of growth in the effective labour force. For the sample as a whole, capital accumulation accounted for over 55 per cent of the growth in output, with the growth in the effective labour force contributing 35 per cent and technical progress only 10 per cent.

Thirlwall then examined the study by Nadiri (1972), which is in itself a survey of a number of studies: Correa (1970) on nine Latin American countries for the 1950-62 period, Voloudakis (1970) on Greece for the 1951-61 period, Psacharopoulos (1969) on India for the 1950-60 period, Gaathon (1971) on Israel for the 1950-65 period, Chung (1970) on Japan for the 1952-67 period and Lampman (1969) on the Philippines for the 1947-65 period. For the Latin American countries, the labour input was adjusted for improvements in health and nutrition, and in education and their different effects were separately estimated. For all but three of the fourteen countries covered (India, Israel and the Philippines), the impact of resource shifts from agriculture to industry was also estimated separately but as part of the contribution of growth in total productivity.

The results, given in Table 4.2, differ from those of Maddison in two important areas. First, the growth in the effective labour input was more important than the growth in the capital input in promoting output growth. This will be even more so if the impact of resource shifts were counted, as done by Maddison, as part of the effect of the growth in labour. According to Thirlwall, this result was probably due to the smaller value given to the partial elasticity of output with respect to capital in the studies surveyed by Nadiri, to reflect the lower share of capital in the national income. If the value were estimated empirically, there would have been a downward bias as the capital input used would not have incorporated the actual level of capital utilization. Second, in six of the fourteen countries the contribution of total factor productivity growth exceeded that of capital input growth, even if the effect of resource shifts were taken out of total factor productivity growth. That is, the residual featured more prominently in these studies than it did the study by Maddison.

However, the two sets of results do agree in two important areas. One is that they show capital accumulation to be a much more important contributor to output growth in developing countries than in developed ones. The other is that growth in total factor productivity, the residual factor, matters much more for economic growth in developed countries than in developing ones.

Table 4.1 Contributions of growth in factor inputs and increased efficiency to output growth of selected developing countries, 1950-65 (%).

	Contribution to output growth of growth in:		
Country	Human resources	Non-residential capital	Efficiency
Argentina	32.8	87.5	-20.3
Brazil	45.2	58.7	-3.9
Ceylon	47.0	58.8	-5.8
Chile	26.2	61.2	12.6
Colombia	39.1	63.0	-2.1
Egypt	28.2	50.9	20.9
Ghana	35.7	71.4	-7.1
Greece	20.3	44.5	35.2
India	67.1	67.1	-34.3
Israel	29.9	52.3	17.8
Malaya	58.6	51.4	-10.0
Mexico	40.2	52.4	7.4
Pakistan	45.9	50.0	4.1
Peru	21.4	60.7	17.9
Philippines	48.0	51.0	1.0
South Korea	46.8	35.5	17.7
Spain	16.0	50.7	33.3
Taiwan	20.0	41.2	38.8
Thailand	42.8	54.0	3.2
Turkey	33.7	48.1	18.2
Venezuela	46.3	69.4	-15.7
Yugoslavia	23.9	68.3	7.8
Average	35.0	55.1	9.9

Source: Maddison (1970, p. 53).

Table 4.2 also shows that improved health and nutrition contributed quite significantly to output growth in a number of Latin American developing countries, exceeding considerably the role played by improvements in education. In some countries the contribution of resource shifts from agriculture to industry cannot be ignored.

The next study examined was Bruton (1967). This was an attempt to explain differences in productivity growth between Argentina, Brazil, Colombia, Chile and Mexico over the 1940-64 period. It concluded that the main reason was differences in the ability to exploit unused resources. Changes in total productivity accounted for only about 25 per cent of output growth in the five Latin American countries, which was well below that recorded for developed countries, a finding which supports those by Maddison and the other studies surveyed.

Another study examined is Robinson (1971), a cross-section analysis of thirty-nine developing countries with data that is the average for the 1958-66 period. Output was seen to originate from four sources – capital accumulation, additions to the labour force, resource shifts from agriculture and foreign borrowing – and the residual factor. The results show that the respective contributions were 32, 19, 18, 14 and 17 per cent. When the analysis was conducted without foreign borrowing as a source of output growth, the contribution of capital accumulation increased markedly to 52 per cent, that of additions to the labour input only very slightly to 20 per cent, while that of resource shifts fell slightly to 16 per cent and that of the residual to 12 per cent. These results are consistent with those of earlier studies and confirm the primacy of capital accumulation in the growth of output in the developing world.

The same conclusion was reached in a recent study by the World Bank (1991) for sixty-eight countries for the periods 1960-73, 1973-87 and 1960-87. Four of the countries (Japan, Greece, Spain and Portugal) are now high-income countries but the results have not been affected by their inclusion. Of the sixty-four developing economies, twenty-seven are in Africa, nine in East Asia, eight in Europe, the Middle East and North Africa, fifteen in Latin America and four in South Asia. The results are given in Table 4.3.

For the 1960-73 period and for the sample as a whole, growth in capital accounted for 56 per cent of the growth in output. The contribution of growth in labour was 18 per cent and that of total factor productivity growth 26 per cent. The importance of capital accumulation was even greater over the 1973-87 period (76 per cent) and for the entire 1960-87 period its contribution was 65 per cent, which was well ahead of those of the growth in labour (23 per cent) and the growth in total factor productivity (14 per cent).

Table 4.2   Contributions of growth in effective labour input, capital input and total factor productivity and of resource shifts to output growth of selected developing countries, 1947-65 (%)

| Country | Effective labour input growth | | | | Contribution to output growth of | Total factor productivity growth | |
	Total (1)	Employment growth (2)	Improved health and nutrition (3)	Improved education (4)	Capital input growth (5)	Total (6)	Resource shifts (7)
Argentina	49.5	29.1	3.8	16.6	44.8	5.7	0
Brazil	44.4	33.3	7.8	3.3	30.2	25.4	7.1
Chile	25.0	15.4	4.8	4.8	7.6	67.4	2.6
Colombia	49.0	34.6	10.2	4.2	21.7	29.3	6.9
Ecuador	31.1	19.5	6.8	4.8	22.7	46.2	-7.4
Honduras	48.0	23.5	18.1	6.4	21.0	31.0	30.5
Mexico	40.4	24.0	15.6	0.8	47.2	12.4	7.4
Peru	24.9	11.9	10.1	2.9	24.9	50.2	6.4
Venezuela	33.4	28.3	2.7	2.4	26.4	40.2	7.2
Greece	52.9				30.8	16.3	11.3
India	31.6				34.7	23.7	
Israel	31.8				37.3	30.9	
Japan	27.3				50.0	22.7	10.1
Philippines	39.0				17.5	43.5	

Notes: The sum of columns 1, 5 and 6 equals 100 per cent. Column 1 is the sum of columns 2, 3 and 4. Column 7 is part of column 6.
Source: Nadiri (1972).

The central role of capital accumulation in economic growth is borne out in each of the regions and for each of the three periods used. In the entire period 1960-87 this was most pronounced in the less developed regions (Africa, Latin America and South Asia) and least pronounced in the more developed ones (East Asia and Europe, the Middle East and North Africa). On the other hand, the contribution of total factor productivity growth to output growth was lower in Africa, Latin America and South Asia than in East Asia and Europe, the Middle East and North Africa. Increasing returns to scale did not feature at all as the partial elasticities of output with respect to capital and labour do not add up to one (World Bank, 1991, p. 43).

The results obtained by Fry (1991) for ten developing Asian economies for four periods, 1961-67, 1968-74, 1975-81 and 1982-88, were less clear-cut (Table 4.4). They were far more variable than those obtained by the other studies, possibly because the periods chosen were too short. But they did lead to the conclusion that 'growth in the capital stock accounts for over 50 per cent of real GNP growth only in relatively slow-growing economies, such as Bangladesh, Indonesia, Malaysia, Philippines and Sri Lanka. In the fast-growing economies of the Republic of Korea and Taipei, China, over 50 per cent of their economic growth came from improved total factor productivity over the period 1982-88' (Fry, 1991, p. 17). In other words, capital accumulation was the most important contributor to output growth in the slower-growing and poorer economies, whereas this role was played by technical progress in the faster-growing and more efficient ones.

4.4 ECONOMIC ANALYSIS OF RESULTS

The empirical studies on the sources of output growth have produced a number of important findings. First, capital accumulation is by far the most important contributor to economic growth in developing countries, followed by additions to the labour input and, a long way behind, technical progress. Second, for developed countries the most important source is technical progress, with capital accumulation a distant second and additions to the labour input even further behind. Third, by implication, as development proceeds, technical progress becomes more significant and capital accumulation less so. Fourth, increasing returns to scale do not contribute to output growth in either group of countries.

The finding that capital accumulation matters so much more to economic growth in developing countries than in developed countries

Table 4.3   *Contributions of growth in factor inputs and total factor*
            productivity to output growth, 1960-87 (%)

Region and Period	Contributions of growth in:		
	Capital	Labour	Total factor productivity
1960-73			
Africa	59	22	17
East Asia	50	16	35
Europe, Middle East and North Africa	51	10	38
Latin America	55	20	25
South Asia	81	20	0
Total	56	18	26
1973-87			
Africa	92	37	-27
East Asia	62	17	20
Europe, Middle East and North Africa	68	19	14
Latin America	94	51	-48
South Asia	55	19	24
Total	76	28	-6
1960-87			
Africa	73	28	0
East Asia	57	16	28
Europe, Middle East and North Africa	58	14	28
Latin America	67	30	0
South Asia	67	20	14
Total	65	23	14

Note: The sums do not always add up to 100 because of the
          rounding up process.
Source: World Bank (1991, p. 45).

Table 4.4 Contributions of capital growth ($\dot{K}$), labour growth ($\dot{L}$) and total factor productivity growth ($\dot{TFP}$) to output growth in selected Asian economies, 1961-88 (%)

	1961-67			1968-74			1975-81			1982-88		
	$\dot{K}$	$\dot{L}$	$\dot{TFP}$	$\dot{K}$	$\dot{L}$	$\dot{TFP}$	$\dot{K}$	$\dot{L}$	$\dot{TFP}$	$\dot{K}$	$\dot{L}$	$\dot{TFP}$
Newly industrializing economies												
South Korea	8.8	23.8	67.4	43.9	19.1	37.0	67.2	26.3	6.5	35.5	11.9	52.6
Taiwan	18.1	24.6	57.3	46.8	22.1	31.1	48.9	20.8	30.3	27.3	11.7	61.0
Southeast Asia												
Indonesia				22.0	20.9	57.1	61.1	16.8	22.1	92.5	-29.0	36.5
Malaysia	27.1	24.8	48.1	37.8	23.3	38.9	47.5	25.9	26.6	65.5	51.9	17.7
Philippines	35.2	39.8	25.0	35.1	32.3	32.6	56.7	27.2	16.1	72.5	107.5	-80.0
Thailand	26.2	18.2	55.5	50.5	28.6	20.9	44.6	33.9	21.5	37.9	38.0	24.1
South Asia												
Bangladesh	7.7	27.7	64.6	32.6	65.2	2.2	13.4	21.4	65.2	57.7	33.6	8.7
India	35.7	34.2	30.1	43.9	41.3	14.8	40.8	39.4	19.8	31.5	36.5	32.0
Pakistan	37.8	22.8	39.4	33.3	34.9	31.8	26.4	28.0	45.6	35.6	28.4	36.0
Sri Lanka	2.8	39.2	58.0	29.5	34.4	36.1	62.3	27.3	10.4	61.5	26.7	11.8

Note: Partial elasticities of output with respect to capital and labour are assumed to be 0.4 and 0.6 respectively.
Source: Fry (1991, pp. 18-9).

and technical progress so much less is consistent with what is known about the pattern and process of economic development. It is also intuitively plausible. By and large, developing countries lack capital and are much less technologically advanced. The only resource in which they have an abundant supply of is unskilled labour. Indeed in the early days of the study of economic development, developing countries were defined as countries which are short of physical capital and technologically backward. The growth of such economies will be enhanced greatly by the injection of physical capital embodying a low level of technology. For capital-scarce and labour-abundant economies, providing each worker a little more capital to work with can increase productivity and output very significantly and rapidly. This is especially if 'social capital' such as transport and educational facilities are provided as these will increase a country's productive capacity and facilitate its directly productive activities. At the same time the use of capital will increase the division of labour and bring with it the gains from specialization, which can be very considerable.

In developed countries each worker has already a large quantity of capital to work with, the infrastructural system is well developed and specialization and the division of labour are already at a high level. Under these conditions capital-deepening will not do much to increase output. Economic growth is much more likely to be driven by technical progress where capital is accumulated but in the form of more productive equipment. This tendency will be strengthened by the relative shortage of labour and the power of the trade union movement.

There are therefore strong *a priori* reasons for capital accumulation being so crucial to the economic growth of developing countries. Certainly their governments lay great stress on it as can be seen in the development plans formulated and implemented by most. These normally begin by setting a target rate of growth for the per capita output, the target chosen being governed importantly by political and social factors. The next step is to estimate of the investment required to achieve the target. Once this is done, the ability of the economy to generate the savings needed for this investment is assessed. If the savings level appears inadequate, then policies and programmes will be introduced to increase domestic private and public savings and to make the country more attractive to direct foreign investment.

The model often used to work out the investment needed to produce a target output growth rate is the Harrod–Domar model, which was originally introduced to establish the conditions needed for equilibrium growth in developed countries (Harrod, 1939, 1948; Domar, 1947) but soon used widely for planning economic growth in developing countries. The model assumes that the output of the economy depends on the amount of capital invested and produces a growth equation given by $g = s/k$, where g is the growth rate of output, s the savings ratio and k the capital–output ratio, a measure of the productivity of capital. The model can be used for an open economy.

The central role played by capital in the use of the Harrod–Domar model can be seen from the fact that for the economy to grow, it must save and invest more out of its output (that is, increase s) and/or increase the productivity of its investment (that is, decrease k). For example, if five dollars of capital are needed to produce one dollar's stream of GNP (that is, k equals 5), then to achieve a target growth rate for the per capita GNP (g) of 3 per cent a year, an investment and a savings ratio of gk (15) per cent per year will be required. If the savings ratio comes to only 12 per cent, the target output growth rate can be achieved only by increasing the productivity of capital, that is, by reducing the value of k to 4. The capital-centred nature of the approach flows from the fact that policies recommended for achieving greater economic growth are aimed at increasing the savings ratio (from 12 per cent to 15 per cent for s) and the productivity of capital (by reducing the value of k from 5 to 4).

A good example of the adoption of a capital-centred approach to development planning can be seen in the early development plans of Malaysia (Lim, 1982-83). The first attempts, the Draft Development Plan 1950-55 and the First Malaya Plan 1956-60, were basically development programmes for the public sector. These were formulated without any check for internal consistency and no attempt was made to relate the capital requirements of the private and public sectors to target levels of such variables as income and employment. The next attempt, the Second Malaya Plan 1961-65, adopted the aggregate Harrod–Domar model. It began with a review of the progress made in the previous five years and followed this up with an analysis of the prevailing problems of the country and a statement of the objectives of the current plan. The financial resources needed to fulfil these objectives were then estimated using the Harrod–Domar growth equation and this was followed by an examination of the possible sources of these funds. The savings ratio required for the target output growth rate of 4.4 per cent per year worked out to be 17.6 per cent for a capital-output ratio of 4.

The Federation of Malaysia came into being in 1963 and the First Malaysia Plan 1966-70 was also based on the aggregate Harrod–Domar model. The real GDP was projected to grow at 4.9 per cent per annum and, with a capital–output ratio of 3.9, the savings and investment ratios were estimated to be 19.1 per cent each. The plan then allocated the funds between the private and public sectors and between the economic sectors. The First Malaysia Plan was the last plan in which the Harrod–Domar or capital-centred approach to planning was used explicitly but such an approach was adopted in the succeeding plans implicitly and in a more sophisticated way.

The widespread use of the Harrod–Domar model and other more sophisticated capital-based planning models shows that at least in the early days of planning decision-makers in developing countries saw the shortage of capital as the crucial constraint to economic growth. This was certainly the view taken by a number of influential scholars. Thus Arthur Lewis, who was awarded the Nobel Prize for Economics in 1979 for his contribution to development economics, claimed that 'the central problem in the theory of economic growth is to understand the process by which a community is converted from being a 5 per cent to a 12 per cent saver – with all the changes in attitudes, in institutions and in techniques which accompany this conversion' (1955, pp. 225-6). Interestingly, the higher savings ratio of 12 per cent was estimated using the Harrod–Domar growth equation for a target output growth rate of 3 per cent and a capital–output ratio of 4.

The need for savings and capital formation for economic growth was also the underlying theme of Arthur Lewis' most celebrated work, his model of economic development with unlimited supplies of labour (1954, 1958). The economy in the model has two sectors. One is the traditional rural subsistence sector where there is not enough work to employ the entire labour force full-time and people end up sharing whatever work there is. This sector has what is commonly known as disguised unemployment, with a marginal product of labour that is very low. The second sector is the modern urban industrial sector with high productivity and which absorbs the surplus labour from the subsistence sector.

The process of transforming such a dualistic economy into an integrated one with a higher overall level of productivity depends critically on the ability to tap the savings hidden in the disguised unemployment in the subsistence sector and using it to generate a surplus in the modern sector. The availability of disguised savings in the subsistence sector was recognized by Nurkse (1953). The high level of disguised unemployment means that some of the workers can be removed without causing a drop in output, provided those remaining now work full-time. If the workers who have been removed from the subsistence sector can find more productive work elsewhere, then this re-allocation of the surplus labour is a major source of savings and capital formation.

In the Lewis model productive work can be found in the modern urban industrial sector. Figure 4.2 shows that this sector's initial demand curve for labour is DL, which is the curve of the marginal product of labour. Labour is available at the fixed industrial wage OW in unlimited quantities. This wage is equal to the average real income in the subsistence sector plus a premium to compensate for the higher costs of living and the greater job uncertainty in the urban sector. It is fixed and can attract an unlimited supply of workers because of the large pool of disguised unemployed in the subsistence sector. It is in this sense that the Lewis model is said to be built on classical lines as it adopts the Ricardo–Marx position that labour is available in unlimited quantities at a fixed wage rate. The neo-classical position sees labour as a scarce factor of production which has to be paid higher wages if it is to be attracted away from other forms of employment.

The maximization of profit in the industrial sector will result in labour being employed to the point where its marginal product is equal to the wage rate, that is, employment will be OM. The total output produced is $ODEM$, of which $OWEM$ goes to workers in the form of wages and WDE to the owners of capital in the form of profits. If these profits are reinvested, this will lead to greater capital formation and increase the total product of labour, thereby causing the demand curve for labour to shift upwards to D_1L_1. As the industrial wage remains constant at OW because of an unlimited supply of labour, the industrial sector can afford to employ MM_1 more workers. The profits will increase from WDE to WD_1E_1. If these profits are reinvested again, this will increase the capital stock further and raise the level of employment, leading to another round of growth.

There are problems with the Lewis model. The ability to shift workers from the subsistence sector to the industrial sector may have been exaggerated, the use of labour-saving industrial equipment ignored and the constraints to capital accumulation (e.g. from rising food prices) neglected. If valid, these criticisms can limit the usefulness of the model in providing analytical and policy guidance for initiating the development process. However, the point in introducing the Lewis model is not to assess its usefulness in this light. It is to show that the most widely accepted general theory in the 1950s and 1960s of the development process in labour-surplus developing countries is a capital-centred one. The essence of its development process is the generation of surplus funds for greater capital accumulation, with the reallocation of surplus labour from the subsistence sector providing the initial source of savings and capital formation.

Figure 4.2   Lewis model of capital accumulation

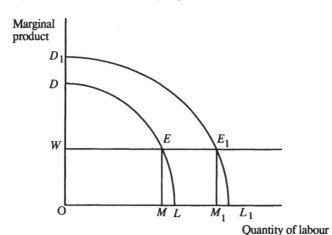

The crucial role played by capital accumulation in the growth process was also brought out by Rostow (1960) in his analysis of the economic transition of countries. According to this, there are five stages of economic growth through which all countries must proceed: traditional, pre-conditioning, take-off, drive to maturity and high mass consumption. Each stage has certain key characteristics and these must be present before a country can move on to the next stage.

The traditional country has a low productive capacity because of its low savings rate and lack of access to modern science.   The pre-conditioning stage is a transitional period during which traditional values are discarded and society moves toward the take-off stage. The important characteristics of this period are a recognition that through systematic examination and action society can manage the environment, a rise in investment, the appearance of entrepreneurs, the construction of infrastructural facilities and the building of an effective nation state. This is a long and slow period of change and can take up to a century. By contrast, the take-off is a short and decisive stage, taking only two or three decades. Its major characteristics are a rise in the investment ratio from around 5 per cent to around 10 per cent, the development of at least one manufacturing activity as a leading sector and the appearance of 'a political, social and institutional framework which exploits the impulses to expansion in the modern sector' (Rostow, 1960, p. 39). The drive to maturity stage is a period of sustained growth during which modern technology is extended to all parts of the system and economic growth becomes more or less routinized. The stage of mass high consumption is a stage of high living and gadgetry.

Rostow claims that his stages of economic growth are not just descriptions of the sequence of development of modern societies. They have an inner logic and continuity and constitute a theory of economic growth as well as a partial theory about modern history as a whole. For such claims to be valid each stage must be distinctive and the examination of the characteristics of each stage will enable its completion and the emergence of the next to be predicted. But as with all previous stage theories, the one by Rostow is no more successful. However, it did attract the attention of decision-makers in developing countries as it offered hope in its suggestion that the development process follows a well-ordered sequence. They were particularly interested in the conditions needed for taking off into self-sustaining growth for they believed that their economies had long escaped the limited confines of the pre-Newtonian world of the traditional stage and had been in the transitional stage long enough to enable them to pass on to the next one. A very important condition they had to fulfil is to increase their investment level substantially and to continue to do this in the take-off stage itself. Thus the message from Rostow is the same as that from Lewis as far as developing countries are concerned. Capital accumulation has an important role to play in the generation of sustained economic growth.

The result from the production function analysis that capital accumulation is a very important source of output growth in developing countries is therefore consistent with the views expressed by writers who have influenced thinking on the development process and with the position taken by the developing countries. It is also consistent with the results of the *a priori* analysis of economic growth for countries lacking capital and technological sophistication but have a surfeit of unskilled labour. For such countries output growth will depend much more on the availability of physical capital. As development proceeds increases in factor inputs *per se* become less important and growth is propelled more by technical progress. This will explain the other important finding of the production function studies, that technical progress is by far the most significant source of output growth in developed countries.

The finding that increasing returns to scale plays no part in the growth of output in developed and developing countries alike may appear strange at first as so much has been made, starting with Adam Smith, of the virtues of large-scale operation. However, the result is intuitively sensible. If there were increasing returns over the entire output range and 'if the entrepreneur could purchase labour and capital on the market at fixed prices and sell his output without changing the price, then it would be profitable always to expand output' (Walters, 1968, p. 279). Correspondingly, if decreasing returns were to exist over the whole range of output, it would always be possible for profits to be made simply by dividing the operation into smaller and smaller parts. The unit cost of production will fall as the size of the operation is reduced. In neither case does the result make any economic sense.

4.5   THE NEXT ANALYTICAL STEP

The first step in the stepwise and backtracking framework for analyzing the causes of economic growth, the identification of the sources of output growth, has been carried out in this chapter. This shows that the sources are capital accumulation, additions to labour and technical progress, with increasing returns to scale playing no part at all. For developing countries, by far the most important source of output growth is capital accumulation, followed by additions to the labour input and, a long way behind, technical progress.

The second step in the analysis is to identify the factors behind capital accumulation, increases to the labour input and technical progress, and the third, the identification of the economic policies needed to produce the factors themselves and to use them efficiently. In the next chapter (Chapter 5), the second and the third steps will be used to deal with the issues related to capital accumulation. Chapters 6 and 7 will deal with the issues related to increases to the labour input and to technical progress respectively. This is a more effective method of presentation than the alternative of having one chapter on the second step dealing with the factors behind all three sources of output growth and another on the third step on the economic policies needed to increase the supply of the factors and to ensure their efficient use. Not only would the latter format produce two unduly long chapters, it would also diffuse the arguments. Chapter 8 will then deal with the social and political factors conducive for economic development.

NOTES

1. The elasticity of output with respect to capital, α, is $(dQ/Q)/(dK/K)$, which can be rewritten as (dQ/dK) (K/Q). Under perfect competition the price of capital, r, is its marginal product, which is (dQ/dK). Hence α becomes $r(K/Q)$, which is the share of capital in total output. Similarly β will measure the share of labour in total output.

2. The elasticity of substitution (b) is the proportional change in the ratio of factor inputs due to a proportional change in the marginal rate of substitution between capital and labour (MRS). Thus b is d log $(K/L)/d$ log (MRS), which can be shown to be equal to one. The MRS is $\delta K / \delta L$, which is $(\delta Q / \delta L) / (\delta Q / \delta K)$ which becomes $\alpha K/\beta L$. Taking the logarithm of $\alpha K/\beta L$ makes it equal to log (α/β) + log (K/L). Differentiating this with respect to log MRS then gives a value of 1 to b.

3. The Cobb-Douglas production function, with an elasticity of substitution of one, is a special case of the constant elasticity of substitution production function. So is the Leontief or input–output production function, where its fixed requirement of each input to produce one unit of output gives it an elasticity of substitution of zero.

4. If the rate of capital accumulation is rapid, the average age of the capital stock will fall. The variable ΔA becomes negative and the decrease in the average age of capital will then increase the productivity of capital by $\alpha \dot{P} \Delta A$.

5. Output is obviously generated by the amount of capital and labour used, not by the level of capital stock and the labour force available. The labour variable is usually measured by the number of person-hours worked so the problem of using the wrong estimate does not arise. But there is a problem on the capital side as the variable is usually measured by the level of capital stock. The partial elasticity of output with respect to capital will be understated as the response of output to changes in the actual level of capital services utilized will not be captured. What will be captured is the response to changes in the actual level of capital stock and as such changes are much smaller, the real extent of the response and therefore the value of the partial elasticity will be underestimated.

5. Economic Policies for Capital Accumulation

5.1 FACTORS BEHIND CAPITAL ACCUMULATION

With capital accumulation being the most important contributor to output growth in developing countries, the faster growing economies can be expected to be those with a higher investment ratio. The data for Asian economies certainly support this. Table 5.1 shows that in the 1950s and 1960s the gross domestic investment to GDP ratios of the faster growing newly industrializing economies (NIEs) were considerably higher than those of the slower growing economies of Southeast Asia and South Asia. By the 1980s the gap in the ratios between the NIEs and the Southeast Asian economies had, on average, narrowed but remained very large between the NIEs and South Asia. Throughout the 1971-90 period the rapidly growing Chinese economy had a very large investment ratio.

It is possible that countries with a lower investment ratio may end up growing faster because they use their capital stock more efficiently. But the little data there is on capital productivity suggests that there is no clear-cut relationship between the two. Table 5.2 shows the average gross domestic investment to GDP ratio and the average incremental capital-output ratio for the 1981-89 period for fourteen developing countries in Asia. The Spearman rank correlation coefficient is 0.40, which is statistically significant. However, a similar analysis for twelve of these countries for the 1963-73 period produced no such relationship. The data provided by Sato (1971) for the two variables for seven income-groups of countries for 1950-64 also does not show any relationship.

A high level of investment is only possible with a commensurate high level of domestic and foreign savings. The NIEs have been more successful than most of the other Asian countries in raising these two types of savings. The superior performance on the domestic front can be seen in Table 5.1. Not only have the gross domestic savings to GDP ratios for the 1960-90 period of the NIEs been higher than most, they have also, unlike most, increased consistently over each of the three sub-

Table 5.1   *Gross domestic investment and gross domestic savings as percentage shares of GDP, 1960-90 (%)*

Region	Gross domestic investment/GDP			Gross domestic savings/GDP		
	1960-70	1971-80	1981-90	1960-70	1971-80	1981-90
Newly industrializing economies						
Hong Kong	21.7	26.5	27.5	20.6	27.5	30.5
Singapore	24.0	41.1	42.0	14.9	30.0	42.3
South Korea	17.6	28.9	30.5	13.7	22.3	31.8
Taiwan	–	30.6	22.6	19.8	32.2	32.9
Southeast Asia						
Indonesia	9.4	24.8	30.2	4.9	22.6	31.8
Malaysia	17.7	20.5	30.8	20.6	30.4	33.2
Philippines	19.3	26.7	20.0	18.2	23.4	19.0
Thailand	20.7	25.9	26.6	19.9	21.5	24.5
South Asia						
Bangladesh	9.9	7.3	11.4	7.8	2.2	2.6
India	17.6	20.8	23.9	15.3	20.5	20.3
Myanmar	15.0	13.9	15.6	11.4	12.3	12.4
Nepal	6.0	16.2	19.9	2.9	5.7	10.4
Pakistan	16.3	16.4	18.7	8.9	10.1	10.3
Sri Lanka	14.9	19.4	24.8	11.8	13.8	13.3
China	–	34.2	34.6	–	32.5	33.7

Note: – not available.
Sources: World Bank (1983, pp. 504 and 553); Asian Development Bank (1991, pp. 284-5).

periods. This superior saving performance of the NIEs is also borne out in a study by Chandavarkar (1993).

The difference between the gross domestic investment to GDP ratio and the gross domestic savings to GDP ratio is the resource gap, which shows the dependence on foreign savings to finance investment programmes. Table 5.1 shows that in recent years the NIEs have relied more on foreign funds to cover their investment needs. This also reflects the greater attraction that the NIEs have for foreign investors, which is borne out directly by Table 5.3, which shows that they have been more

Explaining Economic Growth

successful than most of the other Asian countries in attracting Japanese
direct foreign investment. Only Japanese figures have been provided
because Japan has traditionally been the main source of such investment
in the developing economies of Asia. By far the largest share of this
investment over the 1951-88 period (30.6 per cent) had gone to
Indonesia to ensure a steady supply of raw materials to Japan. The next
three most important recipients were Hong Kong, Singapore and South
Korea. The NIEs as a group accounted for 46.8 per cent of the total
Japanese investment, followed by the Southeast Asian group whose share
was largely influenced by the amount going to Indonesia. By contrast,
between them the South Asian countries attracted less than one per cent
of the investment.

Table 5.2 *Average gross domestic investment to GDP ratios and*
incremental capital–output ratios, 1981-89

Region	Average gross domestic investment to GDP ratio	Average incremental capital–output ratio
Newly industrializing economies		
Hong Kong	27.5	4.2
Singapore	42.8	7.1
South Korea	29.4	3.3
Taiwan	23.7	3.0
Southeast Asia		
Indonesia	28.8	5.9
Malaysia	30.3	6.1
Philippines	20.2	11.9
Thailand	25.4	3.8
South Asia		
Bangladesh	11.7	2.8
India	22.3	3.8
Nepal	19.9	4.1
Pakistan	18.5	2.8
Sri Lanka	24.6	6.0
China	31.5	3.2

Source: Arndt (1993, p. 244).

Table 5.3   Japanese direct foreign investment in Asia, 1951-88

Region	Amount (US $m.)	Percentage distribution (%)
Newly industrializing economies	15,018	46.8
Hong Kong	6,167	19.2
Singapore	3,812	11.9
South Korea	3,248	10.1
Taiwan	1,791	5.6
Southeast Asia	14,750	46.0
Indonesia	9,804	30.6
Malaysia	1,834	5.7
Philippines	1,120	3.5
Thailand	1,992	6.2
South Asia	270	0.9
Bangladesh	11	0.04
India	148	0.5
Pakistan	18	0.1
Sri Lanka	93	0.3
China	2,036	6.3

Source: Riedel (1991, p. 140).

In Step 1 of the analytical framework proposed, capital accumulation was established as the major source of output growth. In Step 2, which has just been completed, the factors behind capital accumulation were identified as domestic savings and foreign savings in the form of direct foreign investment. In Step 3, the economic policies needed to produce a high level of domestic and foreign savings over a long period of time will be identified. This will involve establishing, first, the determinants of savings and, second, the economic policies behind the determinants. We will start with domestic savings.

5.2   ECONOMIC POLICIES FOR DOMESTIC SAVINGS

5.2.1   Sources of domestic savings

Domestic savings consists of private domestic savings and government savings. Private domestic savings itself is made up of household savings and corporate savings. Household savings is that part of the household's disposable income that is not consumed. It also includes the savings from those business enterprises which are not incorporated such as sole proprietorships and partnerships. Corporate savings is the retained earnings of incorporated enterprises, which is the corporate income after taxes and shareholder dividends have been deducted.

Government savings consists mainly of budgetary savings, the surplus of government revenue over its expenditure. Government revenue is made up of tax revenue (e.g. taxes on income, profits and capital gain, social security contributions, domestic taxes on goods and services and taxes on international trade and transactions) and non-tax revenue (e.g. fines, administrative fees and entrepreneurial income from government ownership of property). Government expenditure comprises the expenditure by all government offices, departments, establishments and other bodies that are agencies or instruments of the government. It includes both current (consumption) and capital (development) expenditure. Examples of current expenditure are the salaries of civil servants and the expenses incurred in maintaining school buildings. Capital expenditure on national defence and security is, by convention, treated as current expenditure. Examples of capital expenditure are the expenses incurred in building roads, bridges and industrial estates. In countries where the government is involved in directly productive activities, the profits made can form a part of government savings.

Table 5.4 shows the percentage contributions of private savings, general government savings, public corporations' savings and deficit on current account to the gross domestic investment of our sample of Asian economies for 1973. By far the most important source is private savings, though general government savings and foreign savings, as measured by the deficit on the current account, cannot be ignored. Savings by public corporations featured only in 3 countries (Singapore, Thailand and China). Table 5.4 also shows government savings and private and foreign savings as percentages of the GDP for 1988-90. With the exception of Singapore, private and foreign savings dominated government savings.

Table 5.4   *Percentage distribution of sources of domestic investment, 1973 and government savings and private and foreign savings as per cent of GDP, 1988-90 (%)*

Region	Per cent of gross domestic investment, 1973 (%)				Percent of GDP 1988-90 (%)	
	Private savings	General govern- ment savings	Public corpor- ation savings	Deficit on current account**	Govern- ment savings	Private and foreign savings
Newly industrializing economies						
Hong Kong	90.8	26.5	0	-17.3	4.0	31.5
Singapore	70.0*	38.7*	17.1*	-25.8*	30.0	12.5
South Korea	66.9	15.7	0	17.4	3.5	32.5
Taiwan	–	–	–	–	–	–
Southeast Asia						
Indonesia	–	–	–	–	2.5	33.5
Malaysia	82.0*	34.9*	0*	-16.9*	1.0	34.0
Philippines	96.5	17.5	0	-14.0	-0.5	17.5
Thailand	82.3	-4.6	15.4	6.9	5.0	26.5
South Asia						
Bangladesh	–	–	–	–	0	2.5
India	78.2	12.8	0	9.0	-3.0	23.5
Myanmar	88.0	-4.8	0	16.8	-2.0	13.0
Nepal	–	–	–	–	3.0	5.0
Pakistan	76.0	7.6	0	16.4	-0.5	13.0
Sri Lanka					-1.7	13.1
China	60.3*	11.8*	16.5*	11.4*	3.4	34.1

Notes: – not available.
           * for 1970.
           ** surplus indicated by negative (-) sign.
Sources: World Bank (1976, pp. 428-9); Asian Development Bank (1991, p. 33).

With the different sources of domestic savings, any attempt to identify the economic policies which will increase its overall level will need to examine theories on why households, corporations and governments save.

In most developing economies, private domestic savings are dominated by household savings. Corporate savings are low because the corporate sector is small. This is due in turn to the advantages of incorporation being not as great as they are in developed countries. Thus the limitation of the firm's liability to the amount invested may not be much of an incentive as the collection of commercial claims through the legal system may be difficult. Likewise, the right to raise funds by issuing shares may not amount to much if capital markets do not exist or are poorly developed. According to Gillis et al. (1992) in all but a few of the more affluent developing economies such as South Korea and Brazil, 'the great bulk of private-sector farming and commercial and manufacturing activity is conducted by unincorporated, typically family-owned enterprises ... and ... the chief source of household savings is probably household income from unincorporated enterprises' (p. 286). In view of this, the discussion on the determinants of private domestic savings will be only on household savings.

The relative importance of government savings in total savings varies significantly between developing countries. In the 1980s countries such as Chile and Mexico had public savings which were more than twice private savings, while in countries such as Indonesia, Malaysia and the Philippines it was just half of private savings (World Bank, 1993a, p. 210). For most countries government savings have been generated by running budgetary surpluses rather than savings from government enterprises. Because of the minor role of the latter, the discussion on the determinants of government savings will be confined to budgetary savings.

5.2.2   Determinants of household savings

As the concern is to sustain a high level of savings over a long period of time in order to make possible the capital accumulation needed for output growth, the search should be for the determinants of long-term household savings behaviour.

Income level
The literature suggests that the income level is a major determinant of household savings. The absolute income hypothesis of Keynes (1936) sees current consumption as being directly dependent on the current

disposable household income, with the average propensity to consume being greater than the marginal propensity to consume. Such a consumption function will look like CF_0 in Figure 5.1. By implication, savings will also depend on current income, with the average propensity to save (the savings ratio) rising with increases in the income level. When aggregate consumption expenditures are plotted for a cross-section of household income-groups at one point in time, the shape corresponds to those of CF_0, CF_1 and CF_2 in Figure 5.1. This shows that households with higher incomes have a higher savings ratio than those with lower incomes. However, when aggregate consumption expenditures are plotted against disposable income for the same country over different years, the consumption function appears as a line emanating from the origin with a slope that stays relatively constant at 0.9, such as C_L in the figure (Chenery and Eckstein, 1970; Mikesell and Zinser, 1973).

Figure 5.1   Long-run and short-run consumption functions

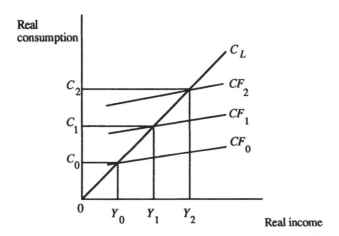

This suggests that the Keynesian absolute income hypothesis can explain household consumption and therefore savings behaviour in the short run but not in the long run. For long-run behaviour, the hypotheses which see relative income rather than absolute income as the determinant of savings seem to do much better. The most widely known of these relative income hypotheses is the one by Duesenberry (1949). This sees consumption and therefore savings as being determined not only by current disposable income but also by previous income, especially the previous peak income. As income falls, consumers reduce consumption as little as possible, thereby reducing savings substantially. When income rises towards its previous highest level, consumption moves up slowly, with most of the increase in income going to restore the savings rate. It is only when income moves on to a higher peak that consumption responds directly to current income. Thus consumers find it easier to increase consumption than to decrease it and an upward ratchet effect on consumption or a downward one on savings is created. In developing economies this effect is strengthened by the tendency of the wealthy to emulate the spending habits in developed countries.

In Figure 5.1 Duesenberry's hypothesis explains the secular upward drift of the consumption function from CF_0 to CF_1 to CF_2. Suppose society's income level is Y_0. A fall in this will not reduce consumption by much as consumers will defend their living standards by reducing their savings. In the figure the consumption level will stay as close as possible to C_0. In a subsequent recovery as income moves back towards Y_0, consumption rises by only a little as consumers attempt to recover the previous peak savings level. The movement is only along CF_0. But when Y_0 is reached, the previous consumption and savings peak levels are restored and further increases in income will cause a sharp rise in the marginal propensity to consume. This is akin to an upward shift in the consumption function from CF_0 to CF_1. Similarly if income exceeds Y_1 the consumption function will shift to CF_2. This upward drift in the short-run consumption function will trace out the long-run consumption function, shown as C_L in Figure 5.1.

The hypotheses which emphasize relative income as a determinant of long-term savings may be more realistic and acceptable than those which emphasize absolute income but they also do not go far enough. Consumption depends not only on current income, whether absolute or relative, but also on expectations of future income. An important attempt to take such expectations into account is the hypothesis of Ando and Modigliani (1963), which argues that consumption is based on the entire income expected over the life-cycle. In the early years, the household tends to save little or even borrows because it is trying to build up its stock of durable goods at a time when its income is low. In the middle period, its income is higher which enables it to save in order to pay off accumulated debts and to put aside funds for retirement. In the later years, dis-saving sets in as retirement reduces the income level. Thus the effect that an increase in income has on consumption or savings will depend on whether it is part of an increase in the life-time income or just a one-time change. This income hypothesis:life-cycle hypothesis has been able to explain adequately the savings behaviour of households with different life-time earning patterns but less so the behaviour of aggregate savings (Landsberger, 1970; Kelley and Williamson, 1968).

A closely related hypothesis is the income hypothesis:permanent income hypothesis of Friedman (1957). The actual, observable income of a household in any period has two components, permanent and transitory. Permanent income is the long-run income with a present value that is equal to the household's assets and expected future income. This can be seen as the 'normal' income which tends to be stable over time. Transitory income is unexpected income arising from changes in asset values and relative prices and from other unpredictable windfalls. According to Friedman, households have a good idea of what their permanent income is and will base their consumption on it. Savings will occur primarily out of transitory income. Thus families with actual incomes that are below their permanent levels will consume a higher proportion of their income. Those whose actual incomes exceed their permanent incomes will consume less. In general, the permanent income hypothesis has performed well in explaining savings behaviour. It is true that permanent income has been found to affect current savings but its impact is much less than that of transitory income (Williamson, 1968; Friend and Taubman, 1966).

In summary, long-run savings behaviour can be explained by the income hypothesis:relative income hypothesis of Duesenberry, the life-cycle hypothesis of Ando and Modigliani and the permanent income hypothesis of Friedman. However, the usefulness of this finding for the purpose of identifying economic policies to increase domestic private savings is rather limited. While it may be useful for short-run forecasting, it does not provide much insight into the development process as income is used as a blanket variable to capture the effects of the very factors being sought. Thus little policy-prescription can follow from the finding that savings depends on relative, life-long or permanent income. In any case, the use of income as a proxy variable has not been all that successful because a significant proportion of the variations in the savings ratio remains unexplained.

There is, therefore, a need to find other hypotheses of savings behaviour which produce determinants of the savings ratio that can be directly influenced by changes in policies. As for the relative, life-time and permanent hypotheses, they should be tested using non-income variables as determinants to produce operationally more useful results.

Age
A good example of recasting the testing framework is Kelley and Williamson (1968) where the age factor is used in the testing of the Ando–Modigliani life-cycle model for Indonesia. They regressed per capita household savings against per capita household income for five

household age-groups for 1959 and found that statistically significant results were obtained for all but the 40-49 age-group, with the marginal propensity to save rising from 0.46 for the youngest group (20-29 years) to 0.60 for the oldest group (60-69 years). The results support the life-cycle hypothesis well and have been obtained in a way which provides policy-makers with an easily identifiable policy instrument: household savings can be improved by having policies which reduce the proportion of the young in the population.

The same can be said of the results obtained by Leff (1969) in his test of the life-cycle theory. The savings performance, measured by the gross savings ratio and the per capital savings, was regressed against the per capita income, the growth rate in per capita income, the percentage of the population below 15 years (D_1) and the percentage of the population over 65 years (D_2). The last two variables are dependency ratios and refer to those members of the population who are either too young or too old to work. They have also been combined to produce the total dependency ratio (D_3) and used in the regression analysis. The relationship between these dependency ratios and savings performance is expected to be negative. Children and the old consume and do not produce and their presence in a household will directly reduce its ability to save. Their consumption burden will also reduce the public sector's savings. If taxation is levied out of discretionary expenditure, which is spending above that required for a minimum standard of living, then a high dependency ratio will reduce discretionary expenditure. This will, in turn, reduce tax revenue and the potential for the public sector to have a surplus of revenue over expenditure.

There was strong support for the life-cycle hypothesis when the analysis was conducted for 1964 for the total sample of seventy four countries: 47 developing countries, 20 Western developed countries and 7 Eastern European countries. The coefficients of D_1 (-1.3), D_2 (-0.4) and D_3 (-1.5) were negative, statistically significant and much larger than those of the income variables. The same results were obtained when the analysis was conducted separately for the developed and developing countries. Support for the hypothesis was further shown by the finding that the coefficient of D_1 for developing countries (-1.3) was over three times that for developed countries (-0.4), reflecting the fact that a much larger percentage of the population in the former is below the age of 15. On the other hand, developing countries have a smaller percentage of their population above 65, which accounts for their coefficient of D_2 (-0.4) being slightly smaller than that (-0.5) for developed countries.

Gupta (1971) divided Leff's sample of forty seven developing countries into three groups according to their per capita income level and repeated the regressions. The dependency ratios only came out as determinants of the gross savings ratio or the per capita savings in the highest income group. There was thus only partial support for Leff's findings that demographic conditions affect the savings performances of developing countries. The results obtained by Landsberger (1970) for Israel for 1957-58 and 1963-64 also did not provide very strong support for the life-cycle hypothesis.

Leff tested what is known in the life-cycle literature as the 'level effect'. This refers to the weakening of the positive relationship postulated by the income hypothesis:life-cycle hypothesis to exist between savings and the rate of economic growth. For two households with the same life-time income, the one with more children will consume more and therefore save less because child-raising typically occurs in the early years of the household's life-span. Hence the larger the percentage of the population below 15 years, the lower will be the rate-of-growth effect on savings. Thus the larger the youth dependency ratio (D_1), the smaller is the increase in the savings ratio brought about by the acceleration in the rate of economic growth. Household size affects the timing of consumption and therefore of the savings ratio.

Fry (1991) found that the level and the timing of savings were adversely affected by an increase in the dependency ratio in his study of ten Asian developing economies over the 1961-88 period. These findings confirm those obtained in an earlier study on seven Asian developing economies by Fry and Mason (1982). An increase in the annual population growth rate of one percentage point, with the accompanying increase in the dependency ratio, was found to decrease the national savings ratio by about five percentage points. Other things being equal, countries whose populations grew at two per cent ended up with savings ratios which were around five percentage points greater than those whose populations grew at three per cent. Thus there was a strong negative 'level effect'. There was also a significant negative 'timing effect'. An increase in the population growth rate would reduce the rate-of-growth effect on savings proportionately. For example, an increase of three per cent in aggregate income would decrease the savings ratio by about three per cent. The two effects would then combine to produce a very substantial adverse impact on savings. A one percentage point increase in the population growth rate would, with a three per cent growth in income, reduce the savings rate by around eight percentage points.

Thus the results obtained show that a high dependency ratio will reduce the savings rate. In fact, the adverse effect would have been larger if the studies examined had also looked at the indirect effect of the dependency rate on the savings rate. This will show that a high dependency rate will reduce the labour force participation rate and therefore output and the savings rate. The indirect effect works from the supply side, unlike the direct effect which operates from the demand side. Gupta (1975) used a simultaneous-equation model to estimate the impact of the direct and indirect effects of the dependency rate on the savings performance of forty developing countries in the 1960s. He found that the total impact was nearly 60 per cent greater than that of the direct effect.

The policy implication of these results is that efforts should be made or expanded to reduce the birthrate if the savings needed for capital accumulation for economic growth is to be available. In urban areas, where the motivation to have smaller families is already present, the emphasis should be on reducing the cost and the pain of birth-reducing techniques. In other areas, it should be on 'creating the conditions for new attitudes toward choice in family size and on reducing the technical rigidities which may inhibit national choice in this area' (Leff, 1969, p. 893). These should be complemented by policies which promote savings. For example, the introduction of reliable and attractive savings schemes which provide income for old age would increase the effectiveness of birth-control programmes. Fry has suggested that 'there might well be a case for government subsidy of especially attractive "sterilization accounts" available only to households that had taken the ultimate form of family planning measures' (1991, p. 23).

Export instability

A possible determinant of household savings that has evolved from the permanent income hypothesis of Friedman is export instability. Permanent consumption is based on permanent income, which is the income that consumers feel they can rely on, while savings comes out of transitory or windfall income. The hypothesis is that households facing fluctuating and uncertain income will save more than those facing more stable income because higher reserves are needed to maintain permanent consumption levels during shortfalls in the income level (Knudsen and Parnes, 1975; Knudsen and Yotopoulos, 1976).

The counter-argument is that export instability creates uncertainty which increases, among other things, the costs of investment and so discourages it. Households, on seeing an important reason for abstaining from consumption becoming less attractive, will accordingly save less. There is another criticism. It may be true that savings would be high in good times to maintain consumption in bad times. But it may be equally true that this higher savings will be matched, on average, by lower savings or dis-savings when times are bad, so that there is no reason to believe that export or income instability *per se* would produce a higher average propensity to save over the cycle.

Unfortunately there has only been one empirical study (Lim, 1980a) on the relationship between export instability and savings. Previous studies on the impact of export instability on economic growth have estimated only the relationship between these two variables, on the assumption that the structural relationship between instability and savings exists. In Lim (1980a) the impact of export instability on the savings ratio was tested for 1968-73 for a sample of twelve developed and fifty two developing countries and for six sub-groups of countries: 12 developed; 52 developing; 52 developing less the 4 Middle East ones; 18 Western Hemisphere developing; 12 African developing and 13 Asian developing. Linear multiple regression analysis shows that the signs of the instability variable were positive and statistically significant for five of the seven groups of countries. In the other two (developed countries and Western Hemisphere developing countries) the signs were negative but statistically insignificant. There is therefore some support for the transitory approach to export instability, derived from Friedman's permanent income hypothesis, in most of the developing countries. The increase in savings in good times, when only the 'permanent-equivalent' level of consumption is maintained, is not matched equally by the decrease in savings when times are bad. An upward 'ratchet effect' had been operating. However, as the hypothesis that export instability increases the savings ratio is not supported in all of the results in this study and as there is only one study of this kind, the findings should not be used at this stage as the basis for policy prescription.

More studies are needed. If, contrary to Lim (1980a), these were to show that export instability hinders rather than promotes savings, then enough is known to show that policies need to deal with the fundamental causes of export instability and not just its symptoms. The fundamental causes of export instability are generally accepted to be the low price elasticities of supply of and demand for the exported items and the frequent shifts in their supply and demand (Lim, 1991). It is also widely accepted that the supply and demand conditions in the primary commodity sector approximate these conditions closely and that shifts in supply are more important than shifts in demand in de-stabilizing export earnings at the country level (UNCTAD, 1985). The price elasticities of supply of agricultural products, especially those of perennial crops, and of mineral products are considerably less than one. These low values reflect the inherent lags in supply responses found in the production of most primary commodities. At the same time, their price elasticities of demand are also low as the demand for them is a derived one, in which the cost of the primary commodity is only a very small percentage of the cost of the final product.

Changes in the supply of primary commodities are brought about by at least four categories of factors. The first includes changes in the availability and cost of inputs such as fertilizers, pesticides and water; the second diseases, plant exhaustion and production cycles. The third includes inadequate quality and supply control, poor warehouse and storage facilities and inadequate farm management practices, while the fourth consists of unexpected changes in government policies. Changes in demand can come about from changes in economic conditions in the major consumers (the developed countries) and in the world's strategic environment. Speculation and monopsonistic practices can also be important determinants.

Another plausible explanation of export instability is a high degree of commodity and geographical concentration. The dependence on a few commodities will reduce the chances of having fluctuations in one direction in some of exports being offset by movements in the opposite direction in the other exports. The same risk will be present if there is dependence on a few countries for the exports. There is empirical support for the concentration hypothesis but not to the extent popularly believed.

These findings on the causes of export instability suggest that to reduce it policies have to be targeted at the factors which cause supply instability at the sectoral level. This means that programmes such as the Compensatory and Contingency Financing Facility of the International Monetary Fund (IMF-CCFF) and the Stabex scheme of the European Union could not provide a long-term solution to the problem. They provided financial assistance only to deal with the adverse consequences of supply inelasticity and quite deliberately steered clear of any attempt to eliminate the root causes of export instability. In line with this, the assistance they gave was of the general 'fungible' type designed only to help with balance-of-payment difficulties. No attempt was made to ensure that the funds were used to tackle the causes rather than the effects of supply instability.

The same criticism can be made of the establishment of marketing boards and domestic loan schemes to stabilize the prices and incomes of primary producers at the national level. If there are government policies which increase price and income instability, the answer is to eliminate such policies. It is not to create yet more government bodies to deal with the effects of the original offending policies.

In any case, the empirical evidence shows that the IMF-CCFF had not been successful even in its limited aim of stabilizing export earnings because a number of its features acted against that. The Stabex scheme functioned basically as a vehicle for transferring foreign aid and did not pretend to be a stabilizing agency. Also, the experience of marketing boards suggests that they were used primarily to extract resources from the primary sector and not to stabilize prices and incomes.

Thus to reduce export instability on a long-term basis, supply instability at the sectoral level has to be decreased and this means ensuring greater reliability and lower costs in the supply of key production inputs, more efficient production and storage facilities and greater certainty in government policies. To a certain extent, it also means reducing the commodity and geographical concentration of the country concerned.

Income distribution

In the lifetime or permanent model of consumption, current consumption and therefore current savings depends on lifetime and not current income. Current income affects current savings only insofar as it affects lifetime income. If current income remains the same but future income changes, lifetime income will change and so will current savings.

If the savings behaviour of individuals is affected by their lifetime income and individuals have different lifetime access to income, then the distribution of income will determine the level of aggregate savings. This can be shown by referring to the simple model of saving by Gersovitz (1988). In this, the individual lives, earns and consumes over a number of periods; borrows or lends in any period whenever income differs from consumption; and does not receive or leave bequests. The aim is to maximize the sum of the discounted utility of consumption in each period, subject to the constraint that the present value of lifetime consumption does not exceed the present value of lifetime income. By assuming further that the number of savers with a given level of lifetime resources is greater than the number of dis-savers with the same lifetime resources, the savings of all the individuals with the same lifetime resources is positive. Under these conditions, if the marginal propensity to save in the first period rises with lifetime resources, then any equalization of the distribution of lifetime incomes will reduce aggregate savings.

The Cambridge school of economic growth sees the impact of income distribution on savings in a different way (Sen, 1970, p. 16). In a well-known version of this, Kaldor (1955-56) has the savings ratio depending essentially on the distribution of income between workers and capitalists. It will be higher the larger is the share of total income going to the capitalists because they have a higher average propensity to save than workers. Capitalists or entrepreneurs save more because they need to maintain their depreciating capital stock, prefer internal to external sources of funds for investment and have better information about investment opportunities (Kelley and Williamson, 1968). A sociological explanation may be that entrepreneurs simply have 'what it takes' to abstain more from current consumption.

Houthakker (1961) used international data to test this hypothesis. By regressing personal savings against property income and labour income, he found that the former explained considerably more of the variation in savings than the latter. This result was confirmed in a later study by Houthakker (1965), which used better data and a more suitable system of weights. This functional income distribution model was applied to panel data for a number of Asian countries by Williamson (1968) and produced results which again showed that the distribution of income is an important determinant of Asian savings.

Kelley and Williamson (1968) examined the role of income distribution in savings performance by estimating the average and the marginal propensities to save of entrepreneurs and all other persons from a sample of 490 families in the Jogjakarta area of Indonesia in 1959. They found that the marginal propensities to save of entrepreneurs, as represented by the occupational groups of owners of business, and traders and craftsmen, ranged between 0.31 and 0.43, which were considerably higher than those for farmers (0.11), government employees (0.05) and other wage-earners (0.11). The entrepreneurial average propensity to save was around 0.6, compared to the non-entrepreneurial average of -0.005. There is thus strong support for the argument that the distribution of income is a determinant of savings in Indonesia. The saving propensities differ significantly between different occupational classes and aggregate savings will vary depending on the distribution of income between these occupational classes. This finding appears to be supported by a study on India (Ramanathan, 1969) but not by one on West Africa (Snyder, 1974).

It is not possible to repeat the exercise for a large group of developing countries as data on the distribution of income by occupation is not available. What is available is data on the percentage share of household income by percentile group of households for a large group of countries. While these shares cannot be rearranged to correspond to entrepreneurial and non-entrepreneurial incomes, they can be used to test the general hypothesis that an uneven income distribution has a greater savings potential than an even one.

Della Valle and Oguchi (1976) made use of such data for thirty seven countries to test the general hypothesis. They found no support for it, except when the analysis was limited to time-series data pooled over ten developed countries, which they attributed to these countries' greater homogeneity and better data. The same conclusions were reached by Musgrove (1980) in a study which made use of income distribution data from surveys conducted in over thirty countries.

Lim (1980a) regressed the savings ratio separately against the share of the national income going to the poorest 20 per cent and to the richest 5 per cent of the households for sixty four countries as a group and with them broken down into six sub-groups for the 1968-73 period. There was support for the hypothesis for only the group of 18 developing economies in the Western Hemisphere and the group of 13 developing economies in Asia. Nothing showed up for the total sample, the 12 developed countries, the 52 developing countries, the developing countries without the 4 Middle East ones and the 12 African developing countries. This finding that income inequality does not lead to greater savings is consistent with those reported elsewhere (World Bank, 1991, p. 137), which suggest, if anything, that inequality is associated with slower economic growth.

Thus there is no support for the contention that income inequality *per se* produces more savings. However, if the distribution were in favour of the entrepreneurial group, then the support is very strong. The policy implication depends on the reasons for the higher propensity to save of entrepreneurs. If it were due to their puritan ethic, then policies should not discriminate against the development of the entrepreneurial class. If entrepreneurs save more than others because the latter have limited profitable outlets for saving, then other policies may have to be introduced. For example, a grossly imperfect capital market will produce a low rate of return on investment in land and encourage landlords to consume more. Wage and salary earners will also not be encouraged to save to improve their skills. The solution then lies in improving the capital market.

If the empirical evidence suggests that greater income equality per se enhances rather than retards economic growth, then policies which promote greater equity should be introduced. This means reducing industrial protection and the dependence on indirect taxes as the main source of government revenue. The former provides capital subsidies which lead to more capital-intensive methods of production and worsen distribution. The latter is much more regressive than income taxes. It also means making the labour market less fragmented so that people with similar attributes are able to obtain similar rewards or employment. Land reform also helps as does well designed and implemented public programmes in education, health and nutrition. On the other hand, market-distorting interventions and direct income transfers do not and often end up worsening the distribution of income (World Bank, 1991, pp. 137-9).

Capital inflows

In the Harrod–Domar growth model, the role of all kinds of foreign savings is to augment domestic savings and thereby increase investment and economic growth. In the dual-gap model, this role has been extended. Domestic savings may be perfectly adequate for domestic investment but the absence of a savings–investment gap does not mean that foreign savings is not needed. Many of the goods necessary for growth cannot be produced locally and foreign exchange is needed to obtain them. If the country does not possess enough foreign exchange and a foreign exchange gap exists, then economic growth will be retarded and part of the domestic savings remain unused. Thus in the dual-gap model foreign savings not only supplements domestic savings, if that is in short supply, but also provides the foreign exchange to pay for the imported inputs essential for growth.

It can be argued that foreign savings does not supplement domestic savings but reduces it (Haavelmo, 1965). An increase in foreign funds will psychologically cause the country to relax its saving effort. If foreigners are willing to save on its behalf, there is less need for it to abstain from current consumption. Policies which encourage both the private and public sectors to save will simply be deferred or not be introduced at all.

This psychological hypothesis can be illustrated with the help of Figure 5.2. Before the inflow of foreign savings, the developing country can produce investment and consumption goods along the production possibilities curve, PP. If there is no international trade, the country's welfare is maximized at A, the point of tangency between PP and the country's indifference curve IC_1, with investment at OI_1 consumption OC_1, and domestic savings equal to $(Y-C_1)$, where Y is total output.

With the production possibilities frontier PP, the country can increase its investment from, say, OI_1 to OI_2 only by reducing its consumption from OC_1 to OC_2, that is, by increasing its savings. If the increase in the level of investment, I_1I_2, is funded by foreign savings, then there is no need for the country's consumption to be reduced and its savings increased. Investment will rise to OI_2 but consumption and savings remain at the pre-foreign savings level of OC_1 and $(Y-C_1)$ respectively.

For developing countries, foreign savings consists mainly of direct foreign investment and foreign aid. While the full amount of the first will be invested, the same cannot be said of the second, as the various

Figure 5.2   Impact of foreign savings on investment and consumption

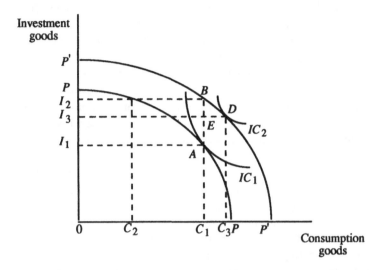

forms in which foreign aid is given enable the recipient country to use it for either investment or consumption purposes. Some forms of aid such as budget support and programme aid are deliberately designed to give the recipient country flexibility in the use of the funds. The reason is that a development plan is more than just a list of discrete projects and the recipient country should be able to substitute the resources between investment projects. But it also enables the resources to be spent on consumption. Even if aid were given in the form of project aid to prevent it from being used for consumption purposes, substitution is still possible. The government or the private sector of the recipient country could have earlier identified certain projects for investment or expansion with its own funds. If foreign aid is then successfully sought for these projects, the domestic resources earmarked for them can be released for other purposes, including consumption (Mosley, 1980). There are, of course, examples of aid designed for consumption being used for investment purposes but these are far fewer in number. A good example is food aid which is clearly given to countries when they do not produce enough food for their own population and when they do not have the foreign exchange to import the amount required. It is thus meant for consumption but used in food-for-work programmes does have investment elements.

These examples show that foreign aid is malleable or fungible, more often in terms of it being converted from investment to consumption purposes. Thus if a donor country gives AB amount of financial assistance with the sole intention of increasing the investment level from OI_1 to OI_2, the effect will be to move the production possibilities frontier in Figure 5.2 outward from PP to $P'P'$. The recipient country will maximize its welfare by producing at D, where the levels of investment and consumption goods are OI_3 and OC_3 respectively. Of the amount of aid given, only AE has been invested. BE's worth of investment goods has been consumed, that is, used to increase the consumption level from OC_1 to OC_3. The inflow of foreign aid has thus increased investment and consumption by I_1I_3 and C_1C_3 respectively and has enabled this to happen with domestic savings remaining unchanged at $(Y-C_1)$. The availability of this foreign largesse can encourage the government of the recipient country to seek more aid, so that it can be relieved of some of the burden of funding OI_1 investment. If this request is granted, then it allows the recipient country to reduce its savings from $(Y-C_1)$ and foreign aid would have substituted for domestic savings.

There is a large empirical literature on the impact of foreign savings on domestic savings but unfortunately the results have not always been clear-cut. For example, when Rahman (1968) regressed the average propensities to save of thirty one developing countries against their capital inflow ratio (net capital imports/GNP), he found that the coefficient of the capital inflow ratio was negative, statistically significant and less than unity (-0.25). Thus foreign savings substituted but only partly for domestic savings. This conclusion was challenged by Gupta (1970a) who, on repeating Rahman's regression for a bigger sample of fifty countries, found the coefficient of the capital inflow ratio to be positive (0.03) but not statistically different from zero. When the sample of countries was divided into three groups according to their per capita income, the coefficient was negative (-0.02) for the middle group and positive for the other two (0.33 and 0.42) but none was statistically significant.

The results obtained by Landau (1971) in his testing of the psychological hypothesis are also mixed. The average tax rate was regressed against the per capita income and the capital inflow ratio, for ten Latin American countries. Support for the hypothesis would be shown by the appearance of a negative and statistically significant coefficient for the capital inflow ratio. The coefficients were negative in five of the countries but they were statistically insignificant. They were positive in the other five countries but only two of them were significant. The hypothesis was also tested by regressing government consumption, government investment and government saving separately against the same independent variables. Support for it would be shown by the appearance of a positive and significant coefficient between government consumption and the foreign capital inflow ratio, and negative and significant coefficients between the other two dependent variables and the foreign capital inflow ratio. Again the results were not conclusive.

The same can be said of the results obtained by Singh (1975). He found that the average propensity to save (APS) was negatively and significantly related to either the foreign capital inflow to GNP ratio or the foreign capital inflow to savings ratio. However, the degree that foreign savings substituted for domestic savings varied inversely with the APS. The higher the APS, the lower would be the degree of substitution and when the APS exceeded fifteen per cent, an increase in foreign savings would actually lead to an increase in domestic savings. In other words, the impact that foreign savings has on domestic savings is not a straightforward negative one. If the APS was greater than a minimum critical level, it could have a positive impact.

The same degree of ambiguity can be seen in the results obtained when only the effect of foreign aid was examined. Griffin (1970) and Griffin and Enos (1970) found that foreign aid and savings across countries were negatively and significantly related. This result supported what they called the 'revisionist' hypothesis that foreign aid discourages domestic savings by encouraging the recipient countries to, for example, increase their government consumption and reduce their efforts to collect taxes. Stewart (1971) challenged this conclusion and argued that it was a spurious one which resulted from the omission of important variables from the analysis. One such variable is the per capita income. Countries with higher per capita incomes tend to have higher savings ratios and smaller current account deficits and, by implication, smaller foreign aid receipts, than those with lower per capita incomes. If aid were distributed according to need and the per capita income were used by donors as an index of need, then foreign aid and savings would be negatively but spuriously correlated because countries with low per capita incomes would simultaneously have low savings rates and large aid inflows.

This point was also taken up by Papanek (1972). He disaggregated foreign savings into foreign aid, direct foreign investment and other financial flows (primarily short-term flows and errors and omissions) and found that all three had a negative and significant impact on the domestic savings of developing countries in the 1950s and 1960s.

However, he pointed out that the negative relationship between domestic savings and foreign aid could be due to wars, political disturbances, sudden changes in the terms of trade and national disasters being omitted from the analysis. Any of them could have lowered domestic savings and increased foreign aid at the same time.

In a study of fifty developing countries over the 1960-83 period, Snyder (1990) found no support for the 'revisionist' school. Aid had little impact on domestic savings and earlier findings of a strong adverse effect were due to the failure to control for omitted variables, especially per capita income, the unsuitable use of foreign capital inflows as a proxy for aid and the use of samples of developing countries which were too small and covered too short a period.

Other studies have also shown that foreign aid does not systematically affect domestic savings across countries. In a time-series study of seven Asian developing economies, over roughly the 1956-71 period, Chen (1977) found aid to have affected domestic savings in only India, Taiwan and South Korea. Moreover, while the impact was adverse in the first two, it was beneficial in the third. In his test for Granger-causality between foreign aid and domestic savings for twenty developing countries using time-series data, Bowles (1987) found that no causality of any type could be inferred in about half of the countries. For the others, aid sometimes helped domestic savings and sometimes deterred it.

It is also worth pointing out that in those studies which found foreign aid and other components of foreign savings to have deterred domestic savings, the impact is smaller after the indirect effects have been taken into account. The direct effect of foreign savings on domestic savings may be negative because of the substitution effect. However, as foreign savings helps to increase the income level and this in turn increases domestic savings, foreign savings may have an indirect positive effect on domestic savings. The net effect may turn out to be positive. If it remains negative, this will be smaller than that measured by only the direct effect. Gupta (1975) used a simultaneous-equation model to estimate the total impact of foreign aid, foreign private investment and other foreign inflows on domestic savings in a cross-section study of forty developing countries for the 1980s. For each component of foreign savings, he found that the total impact was negative but considerably smaller than the negative direct impact.

In all of these studies care must be taken in interpreting the results because of the way domestic savings is defined. In developing countries it is very difficult to measure domestic savings (S) so it is usually obtained as the difference between domestic investment (I) and foreign capital inflows (F); that is, $S = I - F$. Now if both F and I were to increase but F by more than I, with the difference being spent on consumption, then S must fall for the equality to hold. In other words, if a proportion of the foreign capital inflows is consumed, there will be, by definition, a negative relationship between domestic savings and foreign savings. Under these circumstances, the existence of a negative relationship does not mean that foreign savings has substituted for domestic savings. It simply reflects the fact that a proportion of foreign savings has been consumed.

In their survey of the literature up to the early 1970s, Mikesell and Zinser concluded that 'there was substantial agreement among the investigators that saving in developing countries is negatively related to net capital imports' (1973, p. 19). They might have been overstating the case but, on balance, they were probably justified in their conclusions. The results of subsequent studies have also not been unambiguously clear but, on balance, they also suggest that some switching may be going on, especially on the aid front.

The policy implication of this less than clear-cut finding is, however, clear. It is not to ban the inflow of foreign funds but to introduce policies which will turn its effect from one of substituting domestic savings to one of supplementing it. For example, private domestic savings can be increased by having attractive real interest rates. Firms can be encouraged to save and plough back their profits with an appropriate corporate tax and incentive system. Government savings can be increased by having more prudent spending and a more effective tax collection system. It is interesting to note that these are the very policies, together with political stability, which bring about greater economic growth. They are also the policies which attract direct foreign investment in the first place. Generous investment incentives do not matter as much and are sometimes seen by foreign investors as an attempt to compensate for a poor economic track record.

If a psychological argument can be invoked in presenting the substitution hypothesis, so can one be used in presenting the opposite case. If foreign savers can be attracted into investing in a developing country, local entrepreneurs can drawn confidence from this and increase their own investment level. If foreign governments can provide aid out of their citizens' forced savings and if the citizens themselves give aid of their own accord, then the governments of the recipient countries can do more to increase domestic savings and to make more of the aid received.

Foreign indebtedness

In the early stages of development the only foreign capital that a developing country will be able to attract is foreign aid. There will be very little direct foreign investment. With development and an increase in the size of the market, direct foreign investment will increase. Aid will continue and even increase relatively if it is tied to trade. In the later stages of development both the private and public sectors will be able to borrow from the international banking system. Aid will be reduced and direct foreign investment increased. At the final stage, governments of developing countries will be able to borrow money from the issue of bonds backed by large banks (Hughes, 1979).

Under such a stylized pattern of foreign borrowing, the servicing of it is not a problem as countries tend to borrow and are lent according to their ability to use these funds effectively and to repay them. Households will not expect higher future tax burdens in order to service the foreign debt and will therefore have no incentive to transfer assets abroad in order to avoid bearing this burden (Eaton, 1987).

The presence of petrodollars in the 1970s short-circuited this process. The large increases in the price of oil, orchestrated by OPEC, in 1973-74 and 1979-80 left the oil-producing states of the Middle East with huge dollar surpluses. Most of these were invested in bank deposits in the United States and Europe. The commercial banks, awash in petrodollars, were therefore keen to find profitable lending outlets and found these in middle-income developing countries, especially those in Latin America and East Asia. As a result of the availability of petrodollars from the wealthy oil exporters, many of the developing countries were able and allowed to borrow large sums of money, possibly before they were ready and earlier than prudential loan assessment would warrant.

For all developing countries, the weighted ratio of the total external debt to exports of goods and services, the most widely used debt indicator and commonly known as the debt to export ratio, rose from 127 per cent in 1980 to 171 per cent in 1990. For the sub-group of severely indebted ones, the ratio increased from 181 to 274 per cent. By regional grouping, the debt to export ratio over the same period rose from 97 to 324 per cent for sub-Saharan Africa, 89 to 91 per cent for East Asia and the Pacific, 163 to 282 per cent for South Asia, 91 to 126 per cent for Europe, 115 to 180 per cent for the Middle East and North Africa and 197 to 257 per cent for Latin America.

Countries which had borrowed heavily and had managed their economic affairs poorly soon began to have difficulties in servicing their foreign debts. In 1978 only three countries had to reschedule their debt payments. By 1985 this number had increased to fifteen. When difficulties in repaying foreign debts reach such proportions, households begin to fear that taxes will be raised to help pay them and respond by moving their assets overseas in order to avoid paying the increased taxes. As pointed out by Fry (1991), the possibility of such a reaction was recognized as long ago as 1817 by Ricardo, as the following paragraph, also reproduced by Fry (1991), shows:

> A country which has accumulated a large debt, is placed in a most artificial situation; and although the amount of taxes, and the increased price of labour, may not, and I believe does not, place it under any other disadvantage with respect to foreign countries, except the unavoidable one of paying those taxes, yet it becomes the interest of every contributor to withdraw his shoulder from the burthen, and to shift this payment from himself to another; and the temptation to remove himself and his capital to another country, where he will be exempted from such burthens, becomes at last irresistible, and overcomes the natural reluctance which every man feels to quit the place of his birth, and the scene of his early associations. A country which has involved itself in the difficulties attending this artificial system, would act wisely by ransoming itself from them, at the sacrifice of any portion of its property which might be necessary to redeem its debt. (Ricardo, 1951, pp. 247-8)

If the governments of highly indebted countries find it difficult to raise this tax, they may resort to inflationary financing which further destabilizes their economies and exacerbates the capital flight. As the foreign debt has to be repaid in hard foreign currencies, debtor governments may also resort to devaluing their currencies in order to stimulate exports. Domestic savers will thus have another reason for sending their assets abroad as the gross real returns from such assets could be higher than those from assets held domestically.

In order to prevent capital flight debtor governments pass laws prohibiting it. All that this does is to produce capital flight through the over-invoicing of imports and the under-invoicing of exports. In the former, the importer simply submits an invoice for an amount which exceeds the true cost of the imports, with the difference then placed in the foreign bank account. In the latter, when surrendering foreign exchange to the central banks, the exporter presents an invoice for an amount that is smaller than that actually received for the exports, with the difference having been placed in the exporter's foreign bank account.

There is empirical support for the hypothesis that a high level of foreign indebtedness will reduce a country's ability to save. For example, in a study of eleven Asian developing economies over the 1961-88 period, Fry (1991) found that the national savings ratios and the level of foreign indebtedness, measured by the stock of government and government-guaranteed foreign debt at the start of the year divided by the previous year's GNP, were negatively related in a statistically significant way.

The policy implication of this funding is that countries should borrow and spend judiciously if their ability to save is not to be adversely affected. While there are no hard and fast rules on the level of foreign indebtedness which will produce this adverse impact, certain general guidelines can be laid down. For example, if the bulk of a country's exports of goods and services has to be spent servicing the repayment of the principal and the payment of interest, then the country will have reached the upper limit. There would be little left for financing new investment and ordinary imports. If it has to borrow in order to service the debt, then it will have truly overstepped the mark.

Two common rules of thumb have been used to show when countries have reached this critical level. The first is when the debt to export ratio has reached 200 per cent, the second when the debt to GNP ratio has reached 40 per cent. These rules amount to the same thing for a country with an export to GNP ratio of 20 per cent (Williamson, 1991).

It should be noted though that two countries can have the same 'unsafe' level of foreign indebtedness but one has no problem in servicing it while the other has to ask for its debt payments to be rescheduled. The former has clearly used its foreign borrowing and other funds effectively, especially in export-oriented projects, while the latter has either squandered the funds or used them mainly in providing infrastructural facilities which have a long gestation period and do not contribute immediately to directly productive activities. This shows that what is important is not only how much has been borrowed but what has been done with the loan.

Inflation

The idea that demand inflation, as opposed to cost or structural inflation, may increase the savings rate goes back a long way. The argument is easy to see for countries where deficient aggregate demand has resulted in underutilized resources. The use of inflationary financing, brought about by governments running budget deficits financed by printing money or issuing government bonds, will increase output and therefore savings. If savings and income are not related proportionately, the savings ratio will also rise. The ability of the Keynesian multiplier to operate effectively in developing countries and, by implication, the ability of inflationary finance to increase savings, can be questioned. However, there is empirical evidence that properly implemented deficit-financed projects to eliminate production bottlenecks can do much to increase output and savings.

When resources are fully utilized, inflationary financing will redistribute income from the personal to the corporate sector because wage increases tend to lag behind price increases in the short and long run. It will also shift income from the private to the government sector. This redistribution will increase the overall savings rate if the sum of the propensities to save of the personal and private sectors is greater than the sum of the propensities to save of the corporate and government sectors.

Another way of looking at the impact of inflation on savings is through its ability to bring about 'forced savings'. Generally people are willing to hold some money balances even as the value of those balances declines, because it is very convenient to have money as a means of exchange and a unit of account. Under these conditions, inflation acts as a tax on holdings of money. The tax consists of the reduction in the real purchasing power of money and the real resources that holders of money must forgo to restore the value of their money holdings. The base of the inflation tax is the level of real cash balances and the tax rate is the rate of inflation. The real yield from the tax is the product of the two and will be maximized when the elasticity of the tax base with respect to the tax rate is -1. If the inflation rate is too high, it will erode the tax base and eventually the size of the inflation tax. At the same time, it will reduce voluntary saving as people find no incentive to save and every incentive to consume.

Thus under full-employment conditions, inflationary financing can increase savings through its redistributional effect and 'forced savings'. However, if the inflation rate is kept too high for too long the level of forced and voluntary savings will decline. In a study of sixty one countries (18 developed and 43 developing) with inflation rates of less than 10 per cent, Thirlwall (1974) found that inflation did not affect the savings ratio independently of other variables, whether the analysis was conducted for the total sample, separately for the developed and developing countries or separately for the richer and poorer developing countries. The only analysis (Landau, 1971) where the savings ratio and the inflation rate were related in a statistically significant way was for the Latin American countries. The impact in these countries was a negative one, a result which could be explained by the structural inflation and the high inflation rates experienced by Latin American countries.

The absence of a positive and statistically significant relationship between the savings rate and inflation for most countries could be explained by the weakness of the redistributional effect. The available empirical studies clearly show that the average propensity to save of the personal sector is lower than that of the corporate sector (Houthakker, 1961, 1965; Williamson, 1968). However, the results on the average propensities to save of the private and government sectors are less clear-cut. On the one hand, researchers such as Houthakker (1965) found that the propensity to save of the government sector was higher. This direct evidence is supported by indirect evidence from the studies by Morss (1968) and Singh (1975) which showed that the savings ratio was positively related to the tax ratio across countries. On the other hand, Please (1967, 1970) found that the marginal propensity to consume by governments out of increased tax revenues is very high and in several cases increased taxation could have led to reduced national saving. The so-called 'Please effect' was also found by Landau (1971) in his study of nineteen Latin American countries. It is possible that the positive relationship noted between the savings ratio and the tax ratio held only for an earlier period. In more recent times the propensity to consume of governments has grown more rapidly than the GDP, with the result that the ratio of general government consumption to the GDP for all developing countries increased from 10 per cent in 1965 to 13 per cent in 1990, without a concomitant increase in the tax ratio.

These results suggest that the higher propensity to save of the corporate sector *vis à vis* the personal sector may be offset by the lower propensity to save of the government sector *vis à vis* the private sector. The end result may well be a weak or neutral redistributional effect. In seeking explanations for the observed weak relation between inflation and savings, Thirlwall (1974) suggested that the countries in his sample could have adjusted much more quickly to the effects of inflation than traditionally envisaged and therefore neutralized these efficiently. Another explanation is that the cross-country approach adopted could not capture the different responses that countries had to inflation or the different effects that different types of inflation had on them.

The results thus show that demand inflation does not lead to higher savings. If anything, the impact is negative, suggesting strongly that policies should be introduced to control inflation. Even if a positive relationship had been found, the policy recommendation may not be to raise savings by deliberately creating demand inflation. The economic costs may be too high. The inflating country will lose its competitive edge and worsen its balance of payments, necessitating controls on imports and foreign exchange, measures which will lead to the misallocation of resources. Investment will be in speculative areas such as property and inventories rather than in plant and equipment. Voluntary saving will be discouraged as will the use of money as a medium of exchange, with the attendant losses in resources and welfare. At the same time the social consequences of the redistributional effect may not be acceptable as the strong gain relative to the weak.

It may be argued that a mild dose of demand inflation can increase savings without the accompanying adverse economic and social effects. The problem with this argument is that it is easy to create demand inflation but difficult to control its level and duration. Once it is introduced, its use becomes addictive and prolonged, if not permanent. The truth of the matter is that countries whose collection of conventional taxes does not lag far behind the growth in their income have no need for the inflation tax.

Budget deficits

If the government incurs a high domestic debt by running large budget deficits persistently, it can reduce savings. The fear that assets may be taxed more heavily in the future to pay for the debt can lead to capital flight and therefore lower savings. Budget deficits lead to inflation (Harberger, 1981) and as the inflation tax penalizes savers severely they will be discouraged from saving. Thus the direct effect of an increased government deficit is to lower the measured national saving.

This adverse impact on saving will be reinforced by the measures introduced by governments to facilitate and minimize the cost of borrowing from the private sector. Examples of such measures include the sale of low-yielding government bonds to captive buyers (e.g. in South Korea, Nepal and Sri Lanka) and the imposition of ceilings on the interest rate payable on private financial claims (e.g. in India). These policies result in what has been called financial restriction, which reduces the total level of financial savings.

Budget deficits tend to raise interest rates, unless the central bank engages in substantial monetization of the deficit by buying a significant number of the government bonds. The increase in the interest rate will reduce private investment, producing a crowding-out effect. If the government uses the borrowing ineffectively and if the budget deficits are severe and increase the interest rate significantly, this crowding-out effect will dominate any increase in the GNP, and reduce the productive and saving capacity of the economy in the long run. This long-term effect will swamp any short-term increase in savings brought about by the rise in the interest rate.

If the central monetary authority decides to avoid the rise in the interest rate by monetizing the deficit, this can increase the inflationary pressure. Having monetized deficits is more inflationary than having non-monetized ones because using expansionary monetary and fiscal policies together is more inflationary than just using expansionary fiscal ones. As shown previously, inflation can reduce savings.

In a study of eleven Asian developing economies over the 1961-88 period, Fry (1991) found that deficit financing by the government, measured by the ratio of public or government credit to total domestic credit, was negatively and significantly related to the national saving ratio. This led him to conclude that the most direct and effective way to improve domestic resource mobilization is to reduce government deficits.

The policy implication is to avoid running sustained government deficits when full employment exists and to avoid depressing the financial sector in trying to finance the deficit more cheaply. The two reinforce each other in reducing the supply of private savings. It should be noted though that any programme to increase private savings by reducing the budget deficit will be more effective if the deficit were to be decreased by lowering expenditure and not by increasing taxes. In a study of thirteen developing countries, Corbo and Schmidt-Heppel (1991) show that while a dollar's increase in public savings obtained by decreasing expenditure reduces private savings by between 16 and 50 cents, the same increase in public savings obtained by raising taxes will decrease private savings by between 48 and 65 cents.

Real interest rate

A household may choose to save its present income in order to enjoy a higher consumption level later. Or it may choose to borrow from its future income in order to increase its present consumption. As the interest rate is the price at which present and future income can be exchanged any change in it will influence savings. For example, an increase will shift consumption now to consumption later because every dollar given up now will buy more dollars next year. Thus the substitution effect of a higher interest rate is to increase savings. However, there is also an income effect which will lower savings because the higher interest rate will enable the household to provide the same addition to next year's consumption by saving less. The net effect may therefore be either an increase or a decrease in savings and cannot be determined *a priori*.

In a study of six Asian developing economies, Williamson (1968) found that the real interest rate was negatively and significantly correlated with the national saving in half of the countries. The interdependence of saving and investment decisions in Asian households was given as a possible explanation. Asian households often were headed by subsistence farmers or small independent entrepreneurs. The capital markets they faced were so imperfect that there was no safe outlet for their savings other than investing in their own farms or businesses.   Under such conditions, a higher interest rate would discourage investment and therefore savings. The same data were used later by Williamson (1969) to test for the effect of interest rates on savings using distributed lag and wealth-consumption models. No effect was found and no attempt was made to reconcile this with the earlier result.

Williamson's findings, especially the one where no relationship was found between the interest rate and savings in India, were criticized by Gupta (1970b) for being based on unreliable data and the use of a single rate of interest. When he regressed the Indian household disposable income, in aggregate and per capita terms, against five measures of the real rate of interest, he found that while at the aggregate level the coefficients of the interest rate variables were positive but not statistically significant, at the per capita level they were both positive and significant. In a later study examining rural–urban differences in Indian household savings, Gupta (1970c) found that the permanent interest rate, defined as the three-year moving average of nominal interest rates, also had a positive and significant impact on saving. It would thus appear that, contrary to Williamson's findings, higher real interest rates had increased household savings in India.

A similar conclusion was reached by Brown (1971) in a study on South Korean monetary reform in the 1960s. He found that the real rate of interest on long-term and savings deposits had a positive and statistically significant relationship with various measures of the aggregate and average private, household and domestic savings levels. Emery (1970, 1971) and Chandavarkar (1971) also found that increases in bank deposit rates were accompanied by large rises in savings deposits, but without any adverse effect on investment, in South Korea, Taiwan and Indonesia. On its own, this finding may only show that total savings has been redirected with no increase in the national saving propensity. However, savings has now been channelled into a form which allows for productive investment and this finding, together with Brown's finding, suggests strongly that the national savings rate would have been raised as well.

In a study of eleven Asian developing economies over the 1961-88 period, Fry (1991) found that the real deposit rate of interest, defined as the 12-month deposit rate of interest less the rate of change in the GNP implicit deflator, both continuously compounded, was positively and significantly related to the national savings ratio. The impact of interest rates on savings was direct and indirect. The latter works through the positive effect that the availability of real positive interest rates has on the development of financial intermediaries, which produces more efficient investment and therefore greater economic growth, which results, in turn, in higher savings.

Thus while economic theory indicates that savings may be increased or decreased by a rise in the real interest rate, the empirical studies show very strongly that the impact is a positive one. The policy implication is that the real interest rate must be positive and high if private savings is to be encouraged. This can be achieved by keeping inflation and budget deficits under control. High inflation rates do not lead to high savings. Their volatility also tends to make real interest rates often negative and unpredictable and increases the risks associated with building financial assets. As the running of budget deficits can reinforce the inflationary process, avoiding them and restraining inflation will keep the real interest rate positive and predictable and give people the confidence and the incentive to save (World Bank, 1993a, p. 205).

Summary
The survey of the theoretical and empirical literature on household savings shows that it is determined by:

- the household's relative, life-time or permanent income: the higher this is, the higher will be the level of household savings;
- the youth dependency ratio: the larger the percentage of the population below the working age, the greater the consumption and the lower the savings;
- the inflation rate: a high rate can produce 'forced savings' and redistribute income toward the higher saving sectors of the economy but this will be more than offset by the drop in voluntary savings;
- the real interest rate: the positive substitution effect on saving of a rise in the real interest rate is stronger than the negative income effect so that the level of savings rises;
- the level of foreign indebtedness: the higher this is, the greater the incentive to move assets overseas in order to avoid paying higher future taxes and to earn higher real returns, which will lead to a decline in savings;
- the budget deficit: a large and sustained deficit will lead to inflation, an outflow of funds and the crowding-out of private investment, factors which reduce the saving capacity; and
- the degree of income inequality: a reduction in this by redistributing income from entrepreneurs will decrease savings.

The finding that the household's income, in whatever form, is an important determinant of its savings has rather limited value. The income variable acts as a proxy for all the factors which produce income and these would include the factors which promote savings. As the aim is to identify the determinants of savings, the finding by itself has little use for policy-makers. They would be more interested in the findings on the non-income determinants of household savings.

These suggest that household savings will be raised by policies which decrease the birthrate, inflation, foreign indebtedness and the budget deficit and increase the share of income going to entrepreneurs. Some of these policies reinforce each other. For example, greater prudence in government spending will reduce the size of the budget deficit and the level of foreign indebtedness as well as reduce the inflationary tendency, reinforcing each other in raising the level of savings.

5.2.3 Determinants of government savings

Government savings
This is the difference between government revenue and government expenditure. The savings of government can therefore be increased by raising its revenue and/or reducing its expenditure. As noted earlier, the analysis will be limited to government revenue and expenditure not generated by the operation of government enterprises. For revenue this refers to tax revenue and for expenditure it refers to government spending on public and merit goods and services and on income redistributional programmes.

Tax revenue
In order to increase tax revenue it is necessary to identify, first, the basic determinants of the amount of tax that a government collects and, second, the policies needed to influence these determinants.

There are three such determinants. The first is the surplus of production over consumption, the so-called potential taxable surplus which constitutes the necessary condition for any tax to be collected. The second is the ability of the government to extract this potential taxable surplus. This depends on the presence of so-called 'tax handles'. For example, if exports and imports are an important part of the GDP, then this ability will be high because the movements of internationally traded goods are relatively easy to monitor as these pass through only a few points. It will be a different story altogether if the economy were dominated by small-scale family agricultural activities. The third determinant is the determination of the government to collect taxes, which depends on its political will. A weak or corrupt government may not collect much tax, even though the potential taxable surplus may be large and there is no shortage of 'tax handles'.

The general functional relationship can be written as:

$$T/Y = f(\overset{+}{S}, \overset{+}{H}, \overset{+}{W}) \tag{5.1}$$

where T/Y is the tax revenue to GDP ratio, S the surplus of production over consumption, H the presence of 'tax handles' and W political will. Each of the determinants is expected to be positively related to the tax ratio.

There are no successful direct studies of these three determinants taken together, probably because of the difficulty of measuring government determination or its political will to collect taxes. The importance of the first two determinants, the potential taxable surplus and the presence of 'tax handles', has been tested in the international tax comparison method of measuring a country's tax effort (Tait, Gratz and Eichengreen, 1979). This method, pioneered by the International Monetary Fund, has two steps in measuring this tax effort. The first is to obtain the country's taxable capacity, by estimating the tax ratio that it could achieve, given its economic conditions and characteristics, if it had made use of the tax bases to the same average extent as a sample of countries. The second is to compare the country's actual tax ratio to this estimated taxable capacity ratio. The higher the resulting ratio, the greater the tax effort.

The estimation of a country's taxable capacity itself has two steps. The first is to estimate the determinants of the tax ratios for a group of countries. In this the potential taxable surplus and the presence of 'tax handles' often appear as determinants. An early example of this is the work by Lotz and Morss (1967), on 72 developed and developing countries for the early 1960s. The potential taxable surplus, measured by the per capita income (Y_p), and the presence of 'tax handles', measured by the share of exports and imports in the GDP (F/Y), came out as statistically significant determinants. The equation obtained was:

$$T/Y = 10.47 + 0.0081Y_p + 0.0790\ F/Y \tag{5.2}$$
$$\qquad\quad (10.8900) \qquad (2.7400)$$

$$\bar{R}^2 = 0.639$$

with the regression coefficients being statistically different from zero at the 95 per cent of confidence, as shown by the values of the t statistic in the parentheses.

The second step, again using the Lotz and Morss results as an example, is to fit the average per capita income and the average share of exports and imports in the GDP of the country concerned into the estimating equation obtained. This will produce the tax ratio that would have resulted if the country had made use of its tax bases to the same extent as the 72 countries in the sample, its so-called taxable capacity ratio. For example, if the country analyzed was Malaysia, this ratio would have been 18.8 per cent.

The ratio of the actual tax ratio to the taxable capacity ratio will give the country's tax effort. If it is significantly less than one, then its tax performance is well below its potential, possibly because of an inefficient tax system and the lack of political will to improve on it. In the case of Malaysia, its tax effort, using the Lotz and Morss results, would have been 1.08.

In this roundabout way, the international tax comparison method tests for the importance of the three determinants of government tax collection. It has been used widely, with the potential taxable surplus and 'tax handles' measured differently but with results which largely confirm those of Lotz and Morss. Examples of such studies are Chelliah (1971), Chelliah, Baas and Kelly (1975), Tait, Gratz and Eichengreen (1979) and Cao and Lim (1984).

The other method of measuring a country's tax effort, the tax buoyancy and elasticity method, does not directly test the importance of any of the determinants. However, their role is implicit in the framework adopted. The tax effort is the difference between the tax buoyancy and the tax elasticity of the country. The elasticity is the automatic response of the tax system to changes in the national income. The buoyancy is the total response of the tax system, including tax increases due to discretionary fiscal policies, to changes in the national income. If discretionary policies had been introduced, then the tax buoyancy will exceed the tax elasticity. The larger the difference between the two, the greater would have been the effort made to increase tax revenue through the use of discretionary fiscal measures.

The elasticity and the buoyancy of the tax system can be obtained by fitting the following equation to time-series data, in real terms, on the tax revenue (T) and the national income (Y):

$$\log T = \log a + b \log Y \tag{5.3}$$

If the actual tax revenue collected is used, b will be the estimated buoyancy of the tax system. If the tax collection is adjusted to exclude increases due to discretionary changes in tax policies, then b will be the estimated tax elasticity.

The Sahota–Prest method is usually used to estimate the tax collected without the help of discretionary tax measures (Sahota, 1961; Prest, 1962). This involves deducting from the actual tax collected each year an amount attributable to discretionary fiscal policies. The adjusted tax revenue is then divided by the actual tax collected to give, for each year, the proportion of the tax revenue that would accrue automatically to the government, to obtain an adjusting factor. As each discretionary change has a continuing effect on the tax revenues of subsequent years, it is necessary to multiply each year's adjusted tax collection by the adjusting factor in each of the previous years, in order to find the amount of tax that would have been collected if the tax system had remained the same as in the base year.

The influence of the potential taxable surplus and 'tax handles' in the tax collected is implicitly covered in the estimation of the elasticity and buoyancy. There must be a taxable surplus for taxes to be collected while the presence of 'tax handles' will make this collection easier. Thus the size of the elasticity and the buoyancy will be influenced by the presence of these two variables. The size of the tax buoyancy will also be influenced by the government's determination or political will to collect more taxes by introducing discretionary fiscal measures.

The tax elasticity and buoyancy method has been extended to identity the underlying factors behind changes in the revenue collected for a given tax. This is done by decomposing the tax's elasticity into the tax-to-base elasticity and the base-to-total income elasticity by estimating the following equations for the period concerned:

$$\log \text{tax} = \log c + d \log \text{tax base} \tag{5.4}$$

$$\log \text{tax base} = \log e + f \log \text{national income} \tag{5.5}$$

The coefficients d and f will be the required tax-to-base elasticity and the base-to-total income elasticity respectively. As complete information on the legal bases on which taxes are assessed are not usually available, proxy bases are used instead. For example, the final private consumption expenditure is used as the proxy base for excise duties, the compensation of employees for personal income tax and imports for custom duties.

As with the use of the tax buoyancy and elasticity method, the influences of the taxable surplus, 'tax handles' and government political will have been incorporated implicitly in the use of the extended method.

The international tax comparison method and the tax buoyancy and elasticity method have been used, sometimes jointly, to assess the tax performances of countries. In the process, they show that the presence of a taxable surplus, 'tax handles' and political will is important in raising the level of tax collected. The finding that taxable surplus is a determinant has no particular operational significance on its own. It simply confirms the truism that only in countries where everything is not consumed to sustain life is there any surplus left to be saved or taxed. To advise countries with no surplus of the need to generate this surplus is of no direct use as far as increasing government savings is concerned. The policies needed would be those for increasing the rate of economic growth, not government savings *per se*.

The policy implication of the finding that 'tax bundles' are important is that taxes should be designed to be administratively efficient. Taxes have to be collected and there is little point in having those where a high percentage of the revenue collected is dissipated in administrative costs. It should be obvious that the appearance of, for example, the international trade sector as a 'tax handle' should not be interpreted literally. The policy implication for tax collection is not, for example, to increase the relative importance of the trade sector in the economy, though this may be advisable for general economic reasons. It is to choose taxes, if new ones are to be introduced, which are administratively easy to collect. The policy implication of the finding that political will is needed to collect more taxes is self-evident and need not be elaborated here. The political systems that might generate such determination will be discussed in Chapter 8.

Government expenditure

It is not easy to provide a common conceptual framework for analyzing ways in which governments of developing countries can reduce their expenditures. The ideological positions of countries differ so that a level of expenditure considered to be the absolute minimum in a country with socialist tendencies may be unacceptably high in a country favouring *laissez faire* principles. The scope for reducing government spending in the two will be quite different as will the method for doing so.

The situation is not clearcut even if the analysis were limited to market economies. While the market is efficient for the production, distribution and exchange of most goods and services, there are some, called public goods, which cannot be provided by the market at all. These are goods and services where use by one person does not reduce the benefits available to others and where once available are impossible or prohibitively expensive to prevent others from using them. Accepted examples of public goods are defence and lighthouses.

While there is universal agreement that the government should come in where the market fails totally, it is not possible to use the framework which produces this conclusion to predict accurately the actual level of spending on all public goods. This is particularly true of spending on defence. Leaders of countries interested in subjugating their populations or populations in neighbouring countries will expand the size of their defence forces beyond the level implicit in the treatment of defence as a public good—that needed for self-defence purposes. Even if the whims of tyrants and expansionists can be ignored and self-defence assumed to be the sole aim of defence spending, the level, as shown, for example, by Smith (1980), will still depend crucially on the strategic environment the government finds or feels itself to be in. As this varies according to the regions countries are in and to the perceptions of their leaders, the appropriate level of defence spending cannot be a technical issue, decided by analysis on the provision of public goods.

In market economies there are also diverse views on the extent to which government should provide so-called merit goods. These refer to goods and services whose conferment of external benefits to society will not be recognized in the private estimation of benefits. The market will therefore under-supply them. There is general agreement that services such as primary education, vaccination against contagious diseases and mosquito abatement are best supplied by the state but no such agreement exists on the provision of higher levels of education and other forms of medical services. Views also differ on the extent to which housing and community services should be provided and income maintenance services supplied to protect the incomes of the sick, unemployed and elderly.

The diversity of views on the size of the public sector will be even greater when mixed economies are included in the analysis. Typically, the governments of these economies try to improve the functioning of the private sector by spending on transport and communications, industry assistance schemes, and labour market and employment programmes. The extent of such expenditures also differs markedly from one mixed economy to another.

The situation is worsened when countries with socialist leanings are included. As a matter of course, the governments of such economies have extended the size of the public sector to include, in varying degrees, the ownership and operation of airlines, shipping, banks, utilities and manufacturing.

Given the diversity in the ideological stances adopted by governments, it is not possible to devise policies to reduce government expenditure which are applicable to all countries. This is why the existing theories on the size of government spending and, by implication, on ways of reducing it are not particularly useful for our purpose.

One of these is the 'displacement effect' theory of Peacock and Wiseman (1961). This sees government spending evolving in a step-like pattern, with each peak coinciding with social upheavals, especially wars. During peacetime the public's tolerance for taxation is low which prevents government expenditure from rising or rising rapidly. In times of crisis this tolerance rises and will remain at the higher level even after the crisis is over. This permanent displacing of the tax burden upward will enable the government to implement desirable but previously unaffordable programmes.

Another explanation of government expenditure over the long term is that of Wagner (1883). This sees government spending rising in absolute or relative terms with social progress because administrative and law and order services have to be expanded to carry out the greater protective, regulatory and distributional duties that accompany such progress. Other writers, in particular Musgrave (1969), have made use of Wagner's central idea to derive more detailed hypotheses of government expenditure patterns. These have the per capita income or its composition, the size or age structure of the population and the 'stage' of a country's development as important determinants of government spending.

Then there is the public choice explanation which has government expenditure being determined by the interaction between politically mediated supply and demand (Downs, 1957; Black, 1958). The bureaucratic element in this analysis sees bureaucrats, when allowed to wield undue influence on the budget, as being keen to increase the size of government spending because with size comes greater pay, prestige, power and promotion prospects (Niskanen, 1968).

These explanations of government spending may not provide much help to the policy-makers of developing countries in their search for ways of reducing such expenditure. First, the results obtained for some of them have not been consistent. This is particularly true of the 'displacement effect' theory (Henrekson, 1993) and of the version of Wagner's theory which sees the ratio of government spending to national income rising with the per capita income (Gemmell, 1993). Second, their underlying assumptions may be unrealistic in developing countries. Those behind the median voter model may be especially so. In this the government, in trying to maximize its chances of being re-elected under a simple majority voting system, will respond to the demand of the median voter for public expenditure. As the governments of most developing countries do not cater to this need in the manner assumed, the explanatory power of the theory will be limited.

Third, the variables identified theoretically or empirically as important determinants of the growth in government spending are either operationally inappropriate or irrelevant for reducing the growth of this spending. For example, the per capita income has often been found to be an important determinant of government spending, as predicted by Wagner (1883) and Musgrave (1969), but reducing it cannot be the answer to decreasing government spending.

Ultimately, the answer for each country has to be found by carrying out a case-study for that country. Such an approach will enable the country's special ideological and economic characteristics to be taken into account and produce policies for reducing its public spending which are consistent with these circumstances. However, it is still possible to provide some general guidelines. The first is to eliminate or reduce spending in areas which are not consistent with the ideology adopted. The second is to ensure that the remaining expenditure programmes are administered efficiently. The third is to make sure that in the cost-cutting exercise a correct balance is maintained between capital and current expenditures. The governments of many developing countries tend to regard capital expenditure as investment and current expenditure as consumption (Heller, 1979). As economic growth depends crucially on investment, government current expenditure tends to be reduced to generate 'public savings' for investment. This can lead to the inefficient use of government funds (Lim, 1983a). For example, new schools are built and opened without there being sufficient numbers of qualified teachers to work in them. There are also strong political reasons for such behaviour, at least in the short run. Governments are more likely to obtain greater political benefits by having more, but may be less efficient, projects than by having fewer, but maybe more efficient, ones. The former are more visible and therefore more politically rewarding. If government expenditure is to be reduced in order to increase government savings, it is therefore tempting to reduce the current part of it. An indiscriminate reduction in this can reduce the overall productivity of government projects, especially those which have a high degree of complementarity between their current and capital components.

The fourth guideline that can be followed by all countries is to keep defence spending under control because its purported benefits are smaller and its opportunity costs higher than expected. The claim that it will increase domestic demand significantly is unwarranted because of its high import content. The greater emphasis on weaponry will also limit the number of jobs provided, while the skills and organizational ability that such jobs generate may not be easily transferable to the civilian sector. The basic infrastructure created to meet the needs of the military is not necessarily the same as that required by the public and private sectors.

On the other hand, the opportunity costs of military spending are high. It diverts scarce funds from investment in education and health, which is needed for long-term economic growth. Because of the trend towards arms import, some of these funds will be scarce foreign exchange needed for consolidating or expanding the country's export capacity. If such funds are from foreign borrowings, it will increase the level of foreign indebtedness and bring with it additional problems.

Then there are the less obvious opportunity costs. The overall employment level can drop. The decrease in employment in the civilian sector, resulting from the diversion of investment funds, will not be compensated by the increase in employment in the military sector because of the greater use of weaponry. The increasingly technical and sophisticated military activities may also divert scarce technicians, engineers and other skilled workers from the civilian sector and affect its growth adversely.

The *a priori* case against defence spending thus appears to be stronger than the one in its favour. This appears also to be borne out by the weight of the empirical evidence. The early finding of Benoit (1978), that a positive link exists between defence spending and economic growth, has been supported (e.g. Kennedy 1984). However, the majority of the studies have contradicted it (e.g. Lim, 1983c; Faine, Annez and Taylor, 1984; Maizels and Nissanke, 1986). The level of defence spending may indeed be needed for security reasons but there is not a strong case for saying that it will increase economic growth at the same time. If government expenditure has to be reduced in order to increase government savings, defence spending can be targetted once the security situation improves.

5.3 ECONOMIC POLICIES FOR FOREIGN SAVINGS

5.3.1 Sources of foreign savings

Foreign savings in developing countries are simply the funds made available from the savings of foreign governments, firms and individuals. The savings from foreign governments come as grants, soft loans and commercial loans. Table 5.5 shows the first two, technically known as official development assistance and popularly as foreign aid, are far more important than the third. They are channelled to developing countries bilaterally (i.e. directly from one government to another) and multilaterally (i.e. through an international agency such as the World Bank), with the former being greatly preferred.

The savings of foreign firms and individuals find their way into developing countries in a number of ways. Table 5.5 shows that a very important way is as direct foreign investment, where typically multinational corporations set up enterprises in the host country as either wholly owned subsidiaries with full control or joint ventures with partial control. Then there is portfolio investment, the purchase of the host country's bonds or stocks by foreigners, which has become more significant recently. At the start of the 1980s lending by international commercial banks to the governments and enterprises of developing countries was by far the most important form of foreign private or public savings. The debt crisis has reduced this importance though in 1992 international bank lending ranked only behind official development assistance as the most important source of foreign savings. Another form of foreign savings is export credits, given by exporting firms and their commercial banks and by official banks (e.g. the EX-IM Bank of the USA) to promote sales. Such credits enable the payment for the imports to be delayed and are usually given at commercial interest rates. They were used very widely in the 1970s and the 1980s but seemed to be out of favour by the start of the 1990s, lagging even behind the contribution of grants from non-governmental organizations as a source of foreign funds.

Only the economic policies which attract foreign private savings will be examined because political factors feature prominently in the granting of bilaterial foreign aid to developing countries. Of the components of foreign private savings, only direct foreign investment is analyzed. The other major component, international bank lending, is not examined because under normal circumstances its determinants will be similar to those for direct foreign investment as both aim to maximize their investment returns.

5.3.2   Determinants of direct foreign investment: host government's views

Almost all governments of developing countries believe that the availability of fiscal incentives is a very important determinant of direct foreign investment, the principal form of foreign savings in developing economies. A corollary of this is the belief that the greater the generosity

Table 5.5   *Sources of foreign savings in developing countries, 1970, 1980 and 1992*

		1970	1980	1992[a]
I.	Government savings	44.7	29.6	42.2
	1. Official development assistance (ODA)[a]	39.7	23.6	34.8
	• bilateral[a]	34.2	16.8	24.2
	• multilateral	5.5	6.8	10.6
	2. Non-concessional development finance	5.0	6.0	7.5
	• bilateral	1.5	1.9	4.8
	• multilateral	3.5	4.1	2.7
II.	Private savings	55.3	70.4	57.8
	1. Direct foreign investment	18.6	9.7	14.9
	2. Portfolio investment	1.5	0.9	8.4
	3. International bank lending[b]	15.1	42.3	23.7
	4. Export credits	13.6	13.9	0.9
	5. Grants by non-governmental organizations	4.5	2.1	3.3
	6. Other private	2.0	1.5	6.6
III.	Total net resource flows			
	1. Per cent	100.0	100.0	100.0
	2. Current, $billion	19.9	115.9	168.8
	3. At 1991 prices and exchange rates, $billion	91.4	191.4	159.1

Notes: [a] Excluding forgiveness of non-ODA debt for the years 1990 to 1992.
   [b] Excluding guaranteed financial credits.
Source: OECD (1993).

of the incentive programme, the greater will be the level of direct foreign investment attracted. Thus if F measures the level of direct foreign investment and IG the generosity of the incentive package, then

$$F = f_1 \; (\overset{+}{IG}) \tag{5.6}$$

where F and IG are expected to be positively related.

Other important determinants are the presence of natural resources and a proven record of economic performance. Thus if ME measures the availability of natural resources and EP the proven economic track record respectively, equation (5.6) can be expanded to

$$F = f_2 \overset{+ \quad + \quad +}{(IG, ME, EP)} \tag{5.7}$$

where F is expected to be also positively related to ME and EP.

The position taken by the governments of most developing countries is, of course, usually not stated as explicitly as this. However, equation (5.7) does represent fairly the stand implicitly taken by most of these governments. Differences may arise over the relative importance of the various determinants but all assume the provision of fiscal incentives to be a necessary, though not sufficient, condition for attracting direct foreign investment.

This belief is supported by the widespread use of such incentives to produce the funds for the investment programme needed to achieve a target output growth rate. If the ability of the economy to generate the savings is found wanting, policies will be introduced to increase both domestic and foreign savings. The major policy instrument used to attract the latter is the fiscal incentive, which can be a tax holiday exempting firms from the prevailing corporate tax and/or any of a number of cost-lowering incentives such as the accelerated capital allowance, the investment allowance and the investment subsidy.

5.3.3 Methodology for testing effectiveness of incentives

A number of methods have been used to assess the effectiveness of incentive programmes (Lim, 1980b). The first is the rate-of-return method where the post-tax rate of return of a project is calculated and then compared with the world rate of interest. When the former is greater than the latter, there is no need for incentives as they would be redundant. If the reverse applies, the firm would not be interested in the project because it can earn a higher return in other countries. The provision of incentives to raise the post-tax rate of return so that it exceeds the world rate of interest is then necessary to induce the firm to invest. This method is useful in assessing the effectiveness of fiscal incentives in attracting direct foreign investment only if meaningful estimates of the world rate of interest can be obtained. Moreover, it is not much good in assessing the net impact on direct foreign investment. It is concerned only with firms covered by the incentive programme and does not take into account the possibility that the subsidized firms may have displaced other potential new firms, the investment planned by existing firms or have driven some existing firms out of business.

In the accounting cost–benefit method, the cost of offering incentives is the revenue forgone while the benefit is the value to the host country of the employment opportunities created by the firms established under the scheme. If the ratio is less than one, then the incentive programme is seen to be effective in attracting direct foreign investment. This method is fundamentally flawed as it ignores the basic issue. If incentives play no part at all in attracting the investment, the jobs created do not represent any net gain, while the revenue sacrificed constitutes a real loss. If the incentives are absolutely necessary, the benefit is real as the jobs would not have been created without them, while no cost is involved as there would have been no revenue to collect. As this approach does not deal with this fundamental issue, the cost–benefit ratios obtained are not very useful.

Another method is the investment function approach. This establishes the determinants of investment and then assesses the effect that the incentives have on these determinants. By knowing the impact that incentives have on the determinants of investment, it would be possible to assess the impact that incentives have on the investment decision itself. Profit maximizing can be incorporated into the model, and different production functions adopted to obtain the investment function used.

The procedure for using this method begins with estimating the investment function adopted by the firms before they were given the incentives. The next step is to limit the analysis to the incentive period and to substitute for the determinants the values obtained when the subsidy element of the incentives has been incorporated. The investment level obtained is therefore that which results when the influence of the incentives is taken into account. The third step is a repetition of the second step, but incorporates the values for the determinants without the subsidy element of the incentives. The investment level obtained is that which would have resulted if the incentives had not been provided. The difference in the two levels of investment is therefore the investment that has been induced by the provision of the incentives.

There are two problems with the investment function approach. First, it is essentially concerned with the pre-incentive and the post-incentive profitability of firms that have received tax incentives. The impact of these incentives on the investment plans of firms not covered by the programme is not considered. Second, the data required is unlikely to be available. A large number of firms currently enjoying incentives may have been established only after the incentives were given, allowing no comparison between pre-incentive and post-incentive positions. Even if this problem does not exist, it is highly unlikely that the firms would provide the data required.

A popular method is the survey method, where firms now enjoying tax incentives are asked whether the granting of incentives was instrumental in their decision to invest. The weaknesses of such a method are obvious. First, there may be no correspondence between what the respondents say and what they do. Second, the sample of respondents is not likely to be random and will probably consist mostly of the most favoured and adversely affected firms.

It would thus appear that while some of the methods may be satisfactory in testing the effectiveness of incentives in attracting new direct foreign investment, none is satisfactory in testing their effectiveness in increasing the net level of such investment. This is because they ignore the fact that the subsidized firms could have discouraged potential new investment or driven out existing investment. A method which goes some way to remedying this weakness has been suggested by Lim (1983b). This is to estimate equation (5.7), presented earlier in this chapter, with data for a sample of developing countries which offer fiscal incentives.

The dependent variable F is to be measured by the average annual per capita real total direct foreign investment in US dollars for the period studied. As the total investment level is measured, the adverse effect on the existing investment level would have been incorporated. However, it does not take care of the investment that might have been discouraged by the granting of incentives to the beneficiaries.

Data on the total level of direct foreign investment for developing countries is readily available. However, the same cannot be said of data to measure IG, the generosity of the incentive package. IG has to be presented as a dummy variable, with its construction based on the *a priori* analysis of the generosity and effectiveness of the different categories of incentives. The incentives can be divided conveniently into three categories. The first is the pure tax holiday, which exempts firms from the existing corporate tax for a certain period. The second is a modified tax holiday, whose duration and therefore value depends on the investment level and occasionally on the employment level. The third category consists of cost-lowering incentives, of which the most popular are the accelerated depreciation allowance, the investment allowance and the investment subsidy.

It has been argued that if the provision of fiscal incentives does stimulate direct foreign investment, then the granting of cost-lowering incentives will have a greater stimulative effect than the granting of the pure or modified tax holiday (Fromm, 1971; Bird and Oldman, 1975). First, tax holidays provide a 'perverse' subsidy, giving no assistance when it is needed – by firms which make no profits – and a great deal of assistance when it is not needed – by firms which make a great deal of profits. Second, their time-perspective is too limited. When tax holidays are granted the implicit assumption, whether or not understood by the host government, is that the firms being courted maximize profits in the short run, with their profit expectations formulated clearly enough for the effects of the tax holiday to be considered meaningfully. Thus for firms which extend their investment plans over a long period, tax holidays over the normal period of two to five years may not provide any incentive to invest. If the exemption period is extended over a time-span over which these firms become profitable, then for such firms the tax holiday becomes meaningless because they will no longer be needed. For such firms cost-lowering incentives will be more attractive. These are given with a much longer and a much less precise profit-perspective in mind as they are meant primarily to lower the costs of production in the often difficult early years of production. The third reason for arguing that the tax holiday has a smaller stimulative effect is that, unlike cost-lowering incentives, it offers little incentive to risky investment projects because the subsidy it provides only materializes when profits are made.

These considerations of time-perspectives and risks may have special relevance for attracting private foreign investment. The implicit assumption behind granting tax incentives to private foreign firms is that these maximize profits in the short run and see exemption from the normal incidence of corporate taxation as the best way of enabling them to achieve this. This assumption may be justified for those small firms which are neither subsidiaries nor associates of large international companies but may be inconsistent with the objective of the majority of investing firms, which are large and have international interests.

These considerations suggest measuring *IG* by giving it a value of 1 for each of the developing countries which provide tax holidays in the pure or modified form and a value of 2 to each of those which provide cost-lowering incentives. Some countries offer both categories of incentives, in which case a value of 3 is given to each of them. Other things being equal, the more categories of incentives given, the larger the range of investment objectives satisfied, and the greater the number of investors and investment level attracted. Thus developing countries which give the most generous package of incentives will be assigned a value of 3 in the measurement of *IG*, those with the second most generous package the value of 2 and those with the least generous package the value of 1. The variables *F* and *IG* are expected *a priori* to be positively related.

The measurement of *ME*, the availability of natural resources, should not present any problem. The average annual percentage share of minerals in the country's total merchandise exports over the period analyzed can be used to test for the influence that the presence of non-human resources has in attracting direct foreign investment. F and ME are expected to be positively related.

Two variables can be used to capture the influence of proven economic performance, EP, in attracting direct foreign investment. The first is EPY, the level of economic development in the period prior to the investment being made. Other things being equal, the higher the level of economic development, the greater the domestic market and the better the infrastructural facilities and therefore the greater the opportunities for making profits and the incentive to invest. EPY can be measured by the average annual per capita real GDP in US dollars and is expected to be positively related to F. The second is EPG, the rate of economic growth. Other things being equal, a more rapidly growing economy provides greater profit opportunities than an economy that is growing slowly or not at all. Foreign investors may find it financially attractive to invest in a country with a low per capita income that has experienced rapid economic growth recently. The recent favourable economic performance may reflect the adoption of more rational economic policies by the government, which may offset the adverse effect that a low per capita income, the result of past neglect and inefficiency, has on investment. Of course, a country with a high and a rapidly growing per capita income will be preferred to one that enjoys only one of these two attributes. EPG and F are expected to be positively related.

If equation (5.7) is estimated for a group of developing countries which offer fiscal incentives and the variable IG appears with a positive and statistically significant coefficient, then the granting of such incentives would have increased direct foreign investment. Provided the period of analysis is long enough, the results will show that the investment attracted exceeds that driven out, to produce a net increase in the investment level.

5.3.4   Empirical verification

Equation (5.7) was estimated for a group of twenty-seven developing countries for the 1965-73 period by Lim (1983b). The dependent variable F and the independent variable ME were measured for the 1965-73 period as described earlier. The data for constructing the independent variable IG came from a detailed description of the incentives offered over the period by Shah and Toye (1978), which made possible a meaningful classification of the developing countries by the category of incentives granted.

The independent variable *EPY* was measured by the average of the annual per capita real GDP over the 1960-65 period. A five-year lag period was thus allowed. The independent variable *EPG*, the rate of economic growth, was measured in two ways. The first was as the average annual growth rate of the real per capita GDP over the 1965-65 period (EPG_1), the second as the average annual growth rate of the real GDP over the same period (EPG_2). The second is a much less demanding measure of economic growth but may still be useful as it indicates the direction that the economy must go before there can be improvements in the average standard of living. Again a five-year lag period was allowed.

The results, given in Table 5.6, were obtained by ordinary least squares analysis using the logarithmic formulation of the equation. The coefficients of *ME* are positive as expected and statistically significant. This confirms the view that the presence of natural resources is an important reason for the presence of direct foreign investment in developing countries. The coefficients of *EPY* and *EPG* came out with the expected positive sign but only those for *EPY* are significant. This suggests that, in deciding whether or not to invest, foreign investors were more concerned with proven economic performance over a long period of time, which produces a high per capita income, than with recent economic performance, which produces a high growth rate only over the period concerned.

The coefficients of *IG*, the variable measuring the generosity of the incentive package, appeared with the totally unexpected negative sign and, equally important, were statistically significant. These results, together with those for *ME* and *EPY* suggest that, for those developing countries which offered generous tax incentives, the level of direct foreign investment was discouraged beyond the level determined by the lack of natural resources and general economic growth. In other words, fiscal hyper-generosity was seen by foreign investors as a danger signal (a disincentive) and not as an attraction (an incentive). The offering of incentives is not only unnecessary but also counter-productive.

This interpretation may be rather extreme. A more reasonable one is that non-tax factors such as the availability of natural resources and proven economic performances are what impress foreign investors. The governments of developing countries which cannot demonstrate the presence of such resources or economic success know this and will compensate for such deficiencies by offering incentives, with competition between them over time resulting in ever more generous incentives being given. As this happens, even those developing countries with natural resources and good economic track records will be

Table 5.6 Logarithmic regressions explaining direct foreign investment,
      1965-73

Independent variables	Dependent variable F	
Constant	-9.001	-9.127
	(-2.435)**	(-2.225)**
IG	-0.356	-0.369
	(-3.628)*	(-3.849)*
ME	0.353	0.355
	(15.646)*	(16.030)*
EPY	1.875	1.882
	(13.280)*	(13.217)*
EPG_1	0.003	
	(0.160)	
EPG_2		0.083
		(0.370)
$\bar{R}^2$	0.555	0.556
F-ratio	9.112	9.132

Notes: Figures in parentheses are t values and statistical significance
      at the 0.005 and 0.01 confidence levels are indicated by * and
      ** respectively.
Source: Lim (1983b).

dragged into the act and offer incentives, for fear that they will lose out
in any future battle for foreign funds. In the process foreign investors
end up with the best possible world as they 'decide where and how much
to invest in accordance with non-tax criteria, knowing that they will pay
precious little to the exchequer wherever they go' (Shah and Toye, 1978,
p. 285). The compensating effect of incentives is only an illusory one.

   In the symbols used, this explanation can be represented by two
hypotheses. The first is that F is positively related to ME and EP
because direct foreign investment is determined by factors other than
incentives. The second is that IG is negatively related to ME and EP
because the absence of natural resources and economic growth
encourages developing countries to be extra generous in the incentives
provided. The negative and statistically significant relationship
obtained between F and IG in Table 5.6 can be derived as a logical
implication of the two hypotheses. Thus, if F is positively related to ME
and EP, and IG is negatively related to ME and EP, then F and IG will be
negatively related. Presented in this way, the inverse relationship
between F and IG is purely a statistical one and has no behavioural

significance in its own right. However, it does show indirectly that fiscal hyper-generosity cannot compensate for the absence of natural resources and economic growth. While such generosity is not seen by foreign investors as a sign of economic desperation on the part of the host countries, thereby encouraging them to stay away from countries which offer the most generous incentives, it is seen as being not instrumental in any decision to invest.

The finding that the provision of incentives *per se* does not encourage a higher level of direct foreign investment is consistent with that obtained by Shah and Toye (1978). After a comprehensive survey of the theoretical and empirical literature, they concluded that the effectiveness of fiscal incentives in increasing such investment in developing countries was either slight or unknown, with the continued provision of generous incentives under such conditions an apparent paradox. The World Bank (1993a) was less damning of the relevance of incentives but did conclude that the results from using them in such economies as Malaysia, Thailand and South Korea were disappointing. The advice was that 'while incentives are probably necessary to attract investment to an economy with high corporate taxes, the Hong Kong alternative – few incentives and a low, universal corporate tax – would appear to be a simpler and more dependable way to achieve the same results' (World Bank, 1993a, p. 231).

5.4 POLICY PERFORMANCES OF ASIAN DEVELOPING ECONOMIES

5.4.1 Summary of economic policies for capital accumulation

In this section we will examine the record of Asian developing economies in introducing the economic policies which produce greater household, government and foreign savings. Have the newly industrializing economies (NIEs) been more successful in introducing these policies, which then gave them the rapid and sustained capital accumulation that was crucial for their spectacular economic development? Before we attempt to answer this, it will be useful to present a summary in one place of the economic policies which will increase all three forms of savings.

Household savings will be raised by policies which decrease the budget deficit, foreign indebtedness, inflation and the population growth rate, increase the real interest rate and facilitate the operations of entrepreneurs. Government savings will be increased by improving the tax effort, reducing waste in all forms of expenditure and curtailing defence spending. Foreign savings in the form of direct foreign investment will be increased by pursuing policies which promote economic growth. These are the same policies which lead to greater domestic savings. Fiscal incentives are not the fundamental determinant of direct foreign investment. They play only a secondary role, though once given are difficult to withdraw.

In the following discussion, most attention will be focussed on household savings because it is the most important source of savings and because its determinants are also those which determine ultimately the level of direct foreign investment.

5.4.2   Policy performances in increasing household savings

Table 5.7 shows that the NIEs have been, on the whole, more successful than other Asian developing economies in pursuing policies which have kept the budget deficit, inflation, foreign debt and the youth dependency ratio under control and the real interest rate high.

The better budgeting performance of the NIEs is shown by the fact that over the period 1985-9 Hong Kong, Singapore and Taiwan had budget surpluses, in the cases of the first two amounting to 2.5 and 1.3 per cent respectively of their GDP. Only South Korea ran a budget deficit but this came to only 0.3 per cent of its GDP, which is very small compared to those recorded by the developing economies in Southeast Asia and South Asia and by China. By keeping a tighter rein over the government budget, the NIEs have been able to reduce inflationary pressures, capital flight and the crowding out of private investment and therefore encourage and enable the household sector to save more.

Their greater success in keeping inflation under control is shown by the generally lower average annual changes in consumer prices over the 1981-90 period. Singapore (2.3 per cent) and Taiwan (3.1 per cent) had the lowest rates of increase among the sample of countries. The performance of South Korea (6.5 per cent) was significantly worse but even then it was bettered only by those of Malaysia (3.3 per cent) and Thailand (4.4 per cent). The rate recorded by Hong Kong (8.2 per cent) was on the high side but it was still lower than those registered by most of the other countries.

The monetary policies pursued by the NIEs have not only kept their inflation rates relatively low but also produced real interest rates over the 1982-8 period which compared favourably with those in most of the Asian developing economies, especially those in South Asia. The

Table 5.7   *Government budget, real interest rate, inflation rate,*
external debt and dependency ratio of Asian developing
countries (%)

Region	Government surplus or deficit/GDP 1985-9	Real deposit rate of interest 1982-8	Average annual changes in consumer prices 1981-90	Total debt service/ exports of goods and services 1990	Population between 0-14 years/ total population 1989
Newly industrializing economies					
Hong Kong	2.5	–	8.2	–	21.6
Singapore	1.3	–	2.3	1.4	23.7
South Korea	-0.3	5.1	6.5	11.0	18.0
Taiwan	0.1	5.5	3.1	0.9	–
Southeast Asia					
Indonesia	-5.7	7.6	8.8	30.7	36.8
Malaysia	-7.8	5.4	3.3	11.4	37.8
Philippines	-2.7	-0.3	14.6	30.3	40.1
Thailand	-1.1	7.7	4.4	15.4	33.4
South Asia					
Bangladesh	-6.2	2.3	10.7	19.0	44.6
India	-5.3	1.1	9.1	26.4	37.1
Myanmar	–	–	11.7	26.0	37.5
Nepal	-9.5	–	10.5	19.1	43.0
Pakistan	-7.0	3.0	7.5	21.8	45.3
Sri Lanka	-11.4	4.1	12.3	19.6	32.5
China	-1.8	–	7.7	9.2	27.2

Note: – not available.

Sources: Asian Development Bank (1991, pp. 286, 301 and 306);
Fry (1991, pp. 18-9); World Bank (1991, pp. 254-6).

performances of the NIEs in these two areas have given their household
sectors a strong incentive to save.

The same incentive has been provided by their judicious foreign
borrowing. Table 5.7 shows that in 1990 the debt–service ratios (the

ratio of interest and principal payments to export receipts) of Taiwan and Singapore were only 0.9 per cent and 1.4 per cent respectively, which were by far the lowest among Asian developing economies. South Korea had a ratio of 11 per cent, higher than that of China (9.2 per cent), but certainly well below those of most of the other countries. Having a low debt–service ratio by itself is no guarantee of economic efficiency. What matters is what is done with the foreign borrowing. However, when taken with the performances in the other economic indicators, it does show that the NIEs have not only borrowed sensibly from overseas but have also used the funds wisely.

Thus the NIEs, much more than the other developing economies of Asia, have pursued budgetary, monetary, fiscal and foreign borrowing policies which encourage household savings. They have also performed better in keeping their population growth rates under control. This resulted in the share of their population under the age of 15, the youth dependency ratio, being significantly below those of the other countries. Thus in 1989 the average ratio for Hong Kong, Singapore and South Korea was only 21.1 per cent, compared to the 27.2 per cent for China and the average of 37 per cent and 40 per cent for Southeast Asia and South Asia respectively. While children in developing countries often begin full-time work before they reach 15 years, with this practice becoming less common the more developed the countries become, the difference between the ratios is sufficiently large to conclude that households in the NIEs end up having a significantly greater potential to save. But the decline in population growth and the lowering of the youth dependency ratio did not come about by chance. Effective family planning programmes had to be introduced and implemented. Economic growth and increases in the standard of living had also helped to reduce the population growth rate. Thus the economic policies which produced economic growth in the NIEs were also important. It is a case of demographic and economic policies complementing and reinforcing each other. The former reduces population growth directly, thereby making it easier for the latter to generate economic growth. As growth proceeds it changes the values of society and makes demographic policies easier to implement. The net result is a sustained drop in the population growth rate and the youth dependency ratio and an increase in the savings potential.

The NIE's pursuit of market-friendly policies and educational excellence has also facilitated the activities of entrepreneurs. As entrepreneurs save more than other groups of society, these policies would have been partly responsible for the higher savings ratios of the NIEs.

The governments of the NIEs intervene in the market but largely to make it function more efficiently and not to supplant it. Such an approach provides the appropriate market incentives and creates the climate which allows large and small businesses to respond to them. It fosters entrepreneurship because it allows the more productive businesses to prosper. This is not to deny that the potential supply of entrepreneurs may depend crucially on the cultural values of the society. It is to argue, at the very least, that the actual supply of entrepreneurs depends importantly on incentives being provided to embark on productive and profitable activities. Without such incentives the entrepreneurship will remain dormant. With them it will be activated. It may even be the case that the potential supply will be increased by the presence of such incentives.

It is certainly the case that the potential and actual supply of entrepreneurs will be increased if the educational system provides the general and technical skills required to choose the most appropriate technology and inputs available, the best credit facilities on offer and the most profitable outlets for their products. The role of education in the economic development of the NIEs will be discussed in Chapter 6. All that needs to be said here is that it has given the entrepreneurs in these economies the skills to make the most of the economic opportunities presented.

Thus the market-friendly economic policies adopted and the educational support services provided by the NIEs have a favourable impact on the activities of entrepreneurs. They reinforce the monetary, fiscal, budgetary and demographic policies pursued to produce the higher domestic household savings of the NIEs.

5.4.3 Policy performances in increasing government savings

Government savings will be increased by improving its tax effort, eliminating or reducing expenditure in areas not required for ideological or technical reasons and reducing waste in all the remaining programmes. The data needed to show the effectiveness of programmes to reduce expenditures is unfortunately not available. However, data on the tax effort is available to show that the larger budgetary savings of the NIEs shown in Table 5.7 is not due to their greater tax effort. It is due, by implication, more to the greater control they exert over their spending.

Table 5.8 shows the tax ratio (the tax revenue as a percentage of the GNP) and the tax effort (the tax ratio as a percentage of the taxable capacity estimated by the international tax comparison method) for Asian developing economies over two periods, 1969-71 and 1972-6. For

1990, only data for the tax ratio is given. The absence of data on the tax effort in 1990 does not matter much because the rankings of countries by the two measures do not differ significantly for the sample of countries. The Spearman rank correlation coefficient for the 1969-91 period was 0.90 while that for the 1972-6 period was 0.73, both statistically different from zero. The use of the tax ratio to assess the tax performance of countries also avoids the many problems associated with the use of the international tax comparison method. For example, there is no longer a need to accept the dangerous assumption that cross-country results will be applicable to changes in a country over time, that the average obtained will show what is possible in any particular country (Bird, 1978). Nor is there a need to assume that the explanatory variables used in the estimating equation for a country's taxable capacity will always reflect that country's capacity to pay tax. Some of the variables may also measure the country's demand for public expenditure, in which case the equation obtained would not help to produce a meaningful measure of the country's tax effort (Bolnick, 1978).

Table 5.8 shows that the tax performances of the two NIEs for which data is available (Singapore and South Korea) have not been better than those of the other countries in the sample. Over the 1969-71 period, they were ranked sixth and fourth respectively in the sample of eleven economies on the tax ratio and seventh and fourth respectively on the tax effort. Over the 1972-6 period, when there were thirteen observations, their rankings for the tax ratio were fifth and eighth respectively and for the tax effort tenth and seventh respectively. In 1990 when data was available only for the tax ratio, they were ranked fourth and sixth respectively among the eleven economies in the sample.

This finding suggests that the greater budgetary savings of the NIEs does not originate from their greater tax collection. It must therefore originate more from the control they have over their spending, but unfortunately the data available does not allow this to be shown directly. To show that the governments of the NIEs have been able to save more by reducing their expenditures more effectively, data is required on the expenditures incurred in carrying out the consolidated government operations with the rest of the economy and the world. This requires data on the operations of the central, state and local governments and of the supranational authorities but excluding all the transactions between the different levels of government. The data would also have to include current and capital expenditures.

Unfortunately such data are not easily available. Cross-country data on central government expenditure can be obtained quite easily from the

Table 5.8   Tax ratios and tax efforts of Asian developing economies, 1969-90

Region	1969-71 Tax ratio	1969-71 Tax effort	1972-6 Tax ratio	1972-6 Tax effort	1990 Tax ratio
Newly industrializing economies					
Hong Kong	–	–	–	–	–
Singapore	13.2	0.80	15.7	0.78	17.1
South Korea	15.4	1.18	13.6	0.86	13.9
Taiwan	–	–	–	–	–
Southeast Asia					
Indonesia	10.0	0.66	16.3	0.80	16.8
Malaysia	19.3	1.19	22.5	1.19	21.6
Philippines	9.1	0.68	10.1	0.72	14.2
Thailand	12.4	0.92	13.9	0.97	18.2
South Asia					
Bangladesh	–	–	5.8	0.68	8.8
India	13.4	1.09	13.9	1.25	11.8
Myanmar	–	–	7.6	0.84	–
Nepal	4.4	0.34	5.4	0.49	8.3
Pakistan	8.8	0.73	11.4	0.91	13.9
Sri Lanka	17.7	1.37	17.9	0.98	19.1
China	17.8	1.30	19.9	1.12	–

Note: – not available.
Sources: Chelliah, Baas and Kelly (1975) for 1969-71; Tait, Gratz and Eichengreen (1979) for 1972-6 and World Bank (1992) for 1990.

International Monetary Fund. They cover both current and capital expenditures but only those by the central government so they would understate the level of government spending, especially in countries where lower levels of government are responsible for providing many economic and social services. Cross-country data on general government consumption can be obtained from the World Bank. They cover expenditure by all levels of government but only the current side of it. The use of such data to measure the size of government spending will also undertake it, especially in countries and periods where there is a preponderance of capital-intensive projects. Such data deficiency thus precludes a direct testing of the hypothesis that the NIEs have kept a tighter rein over their spending. The hypothesis has support but this has only been indirectly arrived at by a process of elimination. This is unsatisfactory but cannot be avoided for the time being.

5.4.4   Policy performances in increasing direct foreign investment

It was found earlier that direct foreign investment was attracted to developing countries more because of the presence of natural resources and a proven economic track record than the provision of fiscal incentives.

Incentives are probably necessary in economies where corporate taxes are already high. They will probably be introduced as a defensive measure by those economies with abundant natural resources and good economic performances, for fear that their hard-won gains may be lost to latecomers offering generous incentives.

The NIEs have been able to attract more direct foreign investment than most of the other Asian developing countries. According to the above finding, this will have been because of their better economic performances as they possess no natural resources. The NIEs do offer generous incentives but these have played only a secondary or supporting role.

The superior economic performances of the NIEs have been due partly to the pursuit of those economic policies which have led to high domestic household savings and partly to the pursuit of export-oriented policies. As we have seen, the NIEs have introduced more of the fiscal, monetary, budgetary and demographic policies which produce higher household savings, enough to compensate for their lack of natural resources and the generous fiscal incentives offered elsewhere, to become attractive destinations for direct foreign investment.

There are very strong theoretical reasons for believing that the pursuit of export-oriented policies, by which is meant policies which do not discriminate between production for the domestic market and production for export, will lead to greater economic growth. Such policies promote allocative and dynamic efficiency and also self-correcting mechanisms for efficient macroeconomic management. Recent theoretical work has argued the contrary, that where significant market power, economies of scale and externalities exist, deviation from such policies can improve economic growth (Krugman, 1979,1980). However, there is very little empirical support for this position, compared to that for the export-oriented position.

The greater export-orientation of the NIEs is brought out very clearly by Table 5.9. Two indices are used, the country's merchandise exports to GDP ratio and its share of world exports. The usefulness of these indices can be weakened by the fact that the importance of international trade is inversely related to the size of the country. However, there is no such relationship for the sample of countries used. The NIEs are therefore considerably more open to trade than most other developing economies and have grown much faster as a result because exporting promotes and demands economic efficiency.

Table 5.9   *Merchandise exports/GDP and share of world exports, 1981 and 1990 (%)*

Region	Merchandise exports/GDP		Share of world exports	
	1981	1990	1981	1990
Newly industrializing economies				
Hong Kong	73.9	116.3	1.18	2.47
Singapore	141.6	144.4	1.13	1.52
South Korea	29.6	27.3	1.15	1.92
Taiwan	46.5	41.9	1.21	1.97
Southeast Asia				
Indonesia	27.3	22.9	1.28	0.73
Malaysia	46.7	67.6	0.63	0.86
Philippines	14.8	17.6	0.31	0.24
Thailand	19.8	28.6	0.38	0.70
South Asia				
Bangladesh	6.1	6.6	0.04	0.04
India	4.6	6.6	0.04	0.55
Myanmar	9.6	4.1	0.02	0.01
Nepal	6.5	6.0	0	0.01
Pakistan	9.2	12.2	0.15	0.15
Sri Lanka	24.2	24.0	0.05	0.05
China	8.1	10.3	1.16	1.78

Source: Asian Development Bank (1990, pp. 235-6 and 1991, pp. 291-2).

5.4.5   Summary of Asian policy performances

Economic policies which promote greater household savings are those which reduce the budget deficit, foreign indebtedness, inflation and the youth dependency ratio, produce positive real interest rates and encourage entrepreneurial activities. The ability of Asian developing countries to introduce and implement the monetary, fiscal, budgetary and demographic policies required varies markedly. The NIEs have been more successful and consequently have been able to achieve much higher household savings.

Direct foreign investment is attracted more by the presence of abundant natural resources and a proven economic record than by the provision of fiscal incentives. The NIEs have been more successful than most in attracting this form of foreign savings, in spite of not having any natural resources. What enticed foreign firms is their impressive economic performance, itself the result of pursuing the economic policies which lead to high household savings, and an export-oriented development strategy.

Budgetary savings will be increased by a greater tax effort and less waste in government spending. The NIEs have larger budgetary savings and the analysis shows that this is not due to their greater tax effort. Unfortunately no data is available to show directly that more frugal spending is responsible. Such a conclusion has to be deduced. This is unsatisfactory but made more acceptable by the fact that government savings is the least important of the three types of savings analysed.

In summary, the NIEs have been more successful in introducing policies which encourage household savings, government savings and direct foreign investment. This has provided them with a high level of capital accumulation and therefore a crucial platform for rapid economic growth as capital accommodation is by far the most important source of output growth.

6. Economic Policies for Human Resource Development

6.1 CONTRIBUTION OF LABOUR TO OUTPUT GROWTH

Production function analyses for developing economies show that the contribution of labour accumulation to output growth cannot be ignored. The World Bank (1991) estimate of this at 23 per cent is at the lower end of the range of values obtained. In some studies labour's contribution is as high as 40 per cent. It is, therefore, also important that economic policies be in place to encourage increases to the labour input.

In this respect, in trying to explain the better economic performances of the NIEs, it is not simply a matter of accounting for their greater ability to increase the number of person-hours worked, the index of labour-time usually used to measure the labour input. If it were, the NIEs would have a distinct disadvantage as their populations have grown more slowly than those of most other Asian economies. Over the 1960-90 period the average annual population growth rate for the NIEs was 1.9 per cent, compared to the 2.6 per cent for Southeast Asia, 2.4 per cent for South Asia and 1.8 for China.

The index of labour-time has to be adjusted in two ways to produce a meaningful analysis of the contribution of labour to output growth. The first is to incorporate improvements in the skills of the labour force, arising from more formal and informal training and greater work experience. This was done after the early studies of the sources of output growth found the size of the residual factor to be unexpectedly high. The result of the adjustment is to increase the importance of labour in the growth process.

The second adjustment is to incorporate the health of the labour force and improvements in it into the index of labour-time. Other things being equal, an hour contributed by a healthy worker will be more productive than one contributed by a sick worker. The positive impact of better health on economic performance is shown by the finding that countries with higher initial health levels tend to grow faster in subsequent periods than countries with lower initial health levels (Asian Development Bank, 1989, p. 165).

It is therefore surprising that the need to adjust labour for the state of its health has been ignored in the literature on the sources of output growth. A possible reason is the implicit assumption that adjustments made for improvements in skills will automatically take care of the health issue. While this assumption is justified for the more highly educated and skilled workers, because these have the knowledge and funds to ensure that education and health go together, it is much less so for the other workers. The omission is a pity for two reasons. First, data for measuring improvements in the health of a country's labour force is available. For example, it is possible to obtain data on the percentage of the population with access to health services, safe water and sanitation as well as data on the population per doctor or nurse and the percentage of the GNP on public health expenditure. Second, there is an established literature on the impact of health and nutrition on economic growth (Behrman and Deolalikar, 1988).

There are, therefore, three factors behind labour's contribution to output growth. The first is simply the increase in the labour force, through a natural increase in the population and net international migration. The second is the improvement in the skills of the labour force, through greater education and work experience. The third is the improvement in the health of the labour force, through greater expenditures on health and nutrition programmes.

The next three sections will deal with the economic policies needed to increase the supply of these three factors. This will be followed by an examination of the record of Asian developing economies in introducing these policies, with the specific aim of seeing whether the NIEs have done better than other economies and have grown faster as a result.

6.2 ECONOMIC POLICIES FOR CHANGING LABOUR SUPPLY

6.2.1 Determinants of labour force

The size of a country's labour force depends on the size and the age distribution of its population as well as on the size of the net international migration. While net international migration was an extremely important determinant of the increase in the labour force of North America, Australia and New Zealand in the nineteenth and early twentieth centuries, it is of negligible importance today.

Other things being equal, the larger the population, the larger is the labour force. If the population increase is brought about by a high birth rate (fertility) and a low death rate (mortality), a large percentage of the population will be under the age of 15 because the dying is not limited to the young. The presence of a large dependent age-group will produce a rapidly expanding labour force in the future, even if the birth rate were to decline substantially now. This is because when the current generation of dependants reaches adulthood, the number of potential parents will far exceed the number of parents today. Even if the new parents have only enough children to replace themselves (two per couple compared to the larger number for their own parents), their far greater numbers will cause the population to increase significantly before levelling off. This is the so-called hidden momentum of population growth.

6.2.2   Population size and economic growth

Production function analysis can be used at a naive level to show that increasing the population and the associated delayed increase in the labour force produce greater output growth in developing countries. After all, a larger labour force means more pairs of hands available for work at low wages and a larger potential domestic market capable of generating economies of scale and lower production costs.

The analysis can also be conducted at a sophisticated level to show the same result. Take, for example, the following basic production function:

$$Q = f(K, L, R, T) \tag{6.1}$$

where output (Q) is a function of capital (K), labour (L), resources (R) and technology (T). If the resource base (R) is held constant, then the following result can be derived:

$$\dot{Q} - \dot{L} = \alpha\left(\dot{K} - \dot{L}\right) + \dot{T} \tag{6.2}$$

where $\dot{Q}$ is the rate of growth of output, $\dot{L}$ the rate of growth of the labour force, $\dot{K}$ the rate of growth of the capital stock, α the partial elasticity of output with respect to capital, and $\dot{T}$ the effect of technological change.

If constant returns to scale is assumed, then equation (6.2) shows that the rate of growth of per capita output ($\dot{Q} - \dot{L}$) is directly proportional to the rate of growth of the capital–labour ratio ($\dot{K} - \dot{L}$), to which is added the effect of technological progress. If there is no technical change, the higher the population growth rate ($\dot{L}$), the higher must be the rate of growth in the capital stock simply to maintain the same per capita output level. But the savings needed to generate this higher investment may not be available because a rapid population increase pushes up the youth dependency ratio and decreases the savings rate. This causes the per capita output to fall and with it a fall in savings and the start of a vicious circle. If the fall in income induces or forces poor families to have more children as a source of cheap labour and old-age security, it will exacerbate the situation. The youth dependency ratio will rise further, savings fall even more, reducing economic growth further. Another vicious circle will be in operation, with population growth both a cause and a consequence of poverty.

However, this depressing result is obtained only when no technological progress is assumed. Equation (6.2) shows that when this assumption is relaxed, the negative impact can be neutralized. If population pressure produces technological improvements and results in a significant value for $\dot{T}$, then this can offset the adverse effect that population growth has on capital accumulation. Technical progress could be so strong that it more than compensates for the drop in investment and produces a net positive effect, in which case population growth benefits economic growth.

There are certainly arguments and findings which show that population pressure leads to technological progress. Thus Easterlin (1967) suggested that it could increase individual motivation and produce better production techniques. In a study of agricultural development, Boserup (1965) found that population growth stimulated agricultural intensification and technological improvements. Ram and Schultz (1979) also noted that longer lifespans encouraged investment in human capital. In a cross-section study of twenty three developing countries, Thirlwall (1972) found that countries with a population growth rate of one percentage point above the average appeared to experience, on average, a rate of total productivity growth of 0.7 percentage points above the average.

The tendency to innovate and increase productivity would be helped by other arguments mounted in favour of rapid population growth. For example, Simon (1981, 1986) suggested that more entrepreneurs and other creators would become available and human ingenuity, the 'ultimate resource', would solve the problems created by population pressure. Easterlin (1967) also made the point that a young age structure would make a country more responsive to change and more willing to shift resources from low-productivity to high-productivity activities.

The positive effect that population growth has on productivity must have been far greater than the negative effect it has on capital accumulation in studies by Clark (1969, 1970), where it was found that countries with the highest population growth rates have the highest growth rates in per capita output, and that, historically, periods of economic growth were preceded by periods of population growth.

The implication of these arguments and findings is that economic policies should be introduced to increase the birth rate and decrease the death rate to produce a rapidly growing population and labour force. At the very least, it is to recommend that nothing should be done to curb the current rate of population increase. However, many analysts believe that neither advice would be appropriate in the circumstances facing nearly all developing countries. The rate of capital accumulation will be adversely affected by rapid population growth. Even if it were not, the existing limited capital has to be spread among more workers. This process, called capital widening, will prevent another process, called capital deepening, where more capital is made available per worker, from taking place. In countries where workers have very little capital to work with, capital deepening can increase productivity and output dramatically. At the same time funds will be diverted from programmes to improve the skills and health of the existing workers, preventing yet another opportunity to increase productivity. All these adverse effects will be more pronounced in overpopulated countries, where diminishing returns may have set in. Then there are the detrimental effects of population growth on the environment (Ehrlich, P.R. and Ehrlich, A.H., 1990). Against these disadvantages, the only argument that can be mounted in favour of population growth is the technical progress it may encourage out of necessity.

There is ample empirical evidence to show that rapid population growth is harmful to economic growth. Take, for example, the results from the pioneering dynamic modelling of the impact of population growth on Indian economic development by Coale and Hoover (1958). They found that a reduction in the birthrate would increase the growth in per capita income because of two reasons. First, the youth dependency ratio would fall, thereby decreasing consumption and increasing savings for any given income level. Second, when the hidden momentum of population growth was spent and the rate of growth of the labour force slowed down, capital-deepening would take place.

More or less the same conclusion has been reached by other studies. Typical of these is the one by the World Bank (1984). This acknowledged that the history of Europe, Japan and North America shows that population growth had benefited economic growth by stimulating demand, encouraging technological innovation, reducing investment risks and allowing the upgrading of the labour force. However, the population increase had been moderate, seldom exceeding 1.5 per cent a year. When population growth was much faster, such as the 2 to 4 per cent experienced by most developing countries, the story is quite different. Private savings was depressed, capital widening enforced and capital deepening discouraged, all of which reduced economic growth.

This brief review of the theoretical and empirical literature on the impact of population growth on economic growth shows that the debate is by no means settled (Birdsall, 1988; Cassen, 1976). There is also the argument that even if population growth were detrimental to economic growth, it is only one of many causes of poverty. Others, which may be more important, are the unequal international distribution of wealth and the failure of the governments of many developing countries to provide jobs and incomes to the poor and to women. However, the weight of the evidence suggests that, under the circumstances prevailing in most developing countries, rapid population growth and the accompanying rapid growth in the labour force, will harm economic growth. At the very least, rapid population growth intensifies the problems of underdevelopment and makes economic growth that much more difficult.

The most sensible strategy would thus be to reduce the rate of growth of the population and labour force of most developing countries. In the production function analytical framework, reducing the labour force growth rate will release funds for improving the skills and health of the labour force and increase the contribution of labour to output growth, more through an increase in its productivity than through an increase in the sheer number of hours worked. The next section will discuss the policies needed to slow the rate of growth of the population and labour force.

6.2.3   Policies for slowing population growth

Having a high death rate will most certainly reduce the rate of population growth. But deliberately increasing the death rate or having a slower decline in it than is possible cannot be a policy prescription. Programmes must be directed at reducing the fertility rate and these can be divided into those which reduce the incentive to have children and those which enable the desired smaller family size to be realized.

The programmes needed to reduce the desired numbers of children are best identified by using the microeconomic theory of fertility

(Leibenstein, 1974; Nerlove, 1974; Cochrane, 1975), where children are seen as 'investment' goods by their parents, conferring benefits and imposing costs at the same time. In order to reduce the desired size of the family it will be necessary to increase the cost–benefit ratio.

The economic benefits of having children are the income they earn and their provision of old-age security in societies which do not provide institutional programmes to help the elderly. The economic costs are the explicit costs of providing them with food, shelter, clothing and education and the implicit cost of income foregone from looking after them when they were young. The number of children as 'investment' goods will be decided after a careful consideration of their costs and benefits. If the first two or three children are treated as 'consumption' goods because of their intrinsic psychological and cultural value, then the model can be used to decide on the additional number of children.

The use of the microeconomic approach to fertility produces the general prediction that the demand for additional children as 'investment' goods falls when the cost or price of them increases. The specific predictions are that the fertility rate falls when: (1) children cannot contribute to household income; (2) the infant mortality rate falls, because fewer births are needed to produce a given desired number of surviving children; (3) an institutionalized social security system is established, because parents no longer need to depend on their children for support in their old age; (4) job opportunities outside the home for women increase; (5) the education and status of women improve; and (6) income is lowered, because the explicit costs of having children are difficult to accommodate.

There is empirical support for the first five hypotheses. The corresponding policy implications are that population growth will be reduced by: (1) increasing the compulsory school age or the minimum age for child labour; (2) improving health and nutritional programmes for both parent and child; (3) introducing old-age and other social security systems outside the extended family system; (4) expanding female employment opportunities outside the home; and (5) improving the educational opportunities for females, especially at the primary and early secondary levels.

The prediction that fertility rises with an increase in income is not borne out. The empirical evidence from time-series and cross-section studies shows that the opposite is true. The explanation is that with higher incomes parents substitute quality for quantity by investing in fewer better educated children, whose future earning capacity will be greater (Becker, 1981). Also, children may be treated as 'inferior goods' whose demand, relative to that for material goods, declines when income increases.

Programmes to reduce fertility by decreasing the attractiveness of children as 'investment' goods have more chances of success when they are supported by family planning programmes to provide health and contraceptive services because these reinforce the desire for a smaller family and enable this desire to be realised. Programmes which provide better health services decrease the infant mortality rate and reduce the need to have more births than needed. The improvement in the general health of society also reduces to a certain extent the need to treat children as providers of old-age security. The programmes can highlight the fact that breastfeeding suppresses fecundity, thereby reducing fertility, and avoids the health risks of bottle-feeding, thereby decreasing the infant mortality rate. The period of breastfeeding is lengthened, which further delays the return of regular ovulation.

Programmes which provide information on, and access to, modern methods of contraception are even more helpful. They clearly make it easier for parents to have the desired number of children. They also provide information on the private and social benefits of having smaller families, which reinforces the earlier decision to have smaller families.

There is strong empirical evidence that family planning programmes help to reduce fertility. The World Bank (1984) reported that research in the late 1970s shows that declines in the birthrate over the 1965-75 period were most pronounced (29 to 40 per cent) in countries where family planning programmes were strong and the level of socio-economic development relatively high. The strength of family planning programmes was measured by a family planning index which is based on a country's performance in such areas as the availability of many contraceptive methods, inclusion of fertility reduction in official policy, adequacy of the family planning administrative system, and the use of the mass media and field workers. The level of socio-economic development was measured by such indicators as the literacy rate, life expectancy and the per capita GNP in a given year and over time. In countries where the family planning index was low but the level of socio-economic development high, the declines in the birthrate were only modest (10 to 16 per cent).

The results of the cross-country studies are supported by those obtained in case studies of countries over time. Where concerted efforts were made to introduce family planning services to the people, there had been significant increases in the use of contraceptives and fertility rates had declined rapidly, even when the women had little or no education. These results were obtained across widely different communities.

6.3 ECONOMIC POLICIES FOR INCREASING SKILLS

6.3.1 Determinants of skills

The skills of the labour force are increased by three types of education. First is formal education provided in schools and tertiary institutions, usually for those who have not joined the labour force. At the primary school level a general academic education is provided. At the secondary school level there is a choice between continuing the general academic thrust and starting on technical or vocational studies. At the tertiary level the choice is even wider.

The second type of education is non-formal education. This consists of organized programmes of learning that take place outside the formal educational sector. They are shorter, more narrowly focussed and more applied and are taken mostly by adults. They can be run by the public or private sector or jointly by them. The third is informal education which occurs outside any institutional or organized programmes. The most important source of this type of education is learning on the job.

There are clearly different approaches to learning. We are not concerned about this and assume that the skills have been taught and learned in the most efficient way in each type of education. Our concern is with the effect that such upgrading of the skills of the labour force has on economic growth.

6.3.2 Education and economic growth

Education contributes to economic growth in several ways. First, it improves generally the quality of the labour force by imparting skills and work knowledge. Second, it increases labour mobility and therefore promotes the division of labour. Third, it enables new information to be absorbed faster and unfamiliar inputs and new processes applied more effectively. Fourth, it improves management skills which leads to a more efficient allocation of resources. Fifth, it removes many of the social and institutional barriers to economic growth. Sixth, it encourages entrepreneurship by promoting individual responsibility, organizational ability, risk-taking in moderation, and planning over the long term.

The positive impact that education has on economic growth has been demonstrated many times over. Schultz (1961) showed that between 30 and 50 per cent of that part of American output growth between 1929 and 1956 not explained by conventional factor inputs were due to the increase in the quality of labour through education. Bowman (1964) and Denison (1962) reached roughly the same conclusion. The implied rate of return to investment in education is at least as high as, if not higher than, that on non-human capital. The same conclusion can be reached for developing countries from the social and private rates of return obtained from investing in primary, secondary and tertiary education in a number of developing countries (Psacharopoulos, 1985). In most instances, these exceeded the corresponding rates of return on alternative forms of investment.

Other approaches to assessing the impact of education on economic growth have produced the same results. In comparing the average number of years of schooling in the early 1980s with the average annual change in the per capita GNP over the 1965-86 period for thirteen Asian developing economies, the Asian Development Bank (1989) found a strong positive relationship. The countries fell into two distinct groups, the first consisting of countries with high educational attainment and high rates of economic growth, the other of countries with low educational attainment and low rates of economic growth. Only two countries, the Philippines and Sri Lanka, did not fit this pattern. Without them the regression line obtained was $Y = 1.16 + 0.93X$, where Y is the average annual change in the per capita GNP and X the average number of years of schooling. Variations in X 'explained' 71 per cent of the variations in Y and the regression coefficient of X was statistically significant. Even if the Philippines and Sri Lanka were included in the analysis, the relationship obtained is still positive and statistically significant.

Such an attempt to capture the impact of education on economic growth can be faulted in two areas. First, the relationship obtained may be spurious because it could have been generated by factors such as income and physical investment that influence one or more of them. The effect of these other factors has to be disentangled, which can be done by the use of multivariate analysis. Second, the direction of causation is not clear because there are good reasons for believing that it goes from growth to education (e.g. the wealthier the country the more it can afford or appreciate education) or that the causation flows in both directions. The easiest way of dealing with this is to use the 'simultaneous equations' technique to estimate the relations in both directions at the same time, as this identifies the strength and characteristics of each relationship while allowing for the existence of the other. Studies carried out by the World Bank (1980), which took into account the above problems, show that increases in literacy led to increases in investment and, given the level of investment, to increases in output per worker.

These results are supported by those obtained by microeconomic studies. For example, numerous studies have shown that more schooling leads to higher earnings for employees (Psacharopoulos, 1985). For studies on the self-employed in agriculture, where the complementary inputs required for improved farming techniques were available, the annual output of a farmer with four years of primary education was, on average, over 13 per cent higher than that of a farmer who had not been to school (World Bank, 1980). When the complementary inputs were not available, the difference was, as expected, smaller but still substantial.

There is also ample historical evidence that education contributes significantly to economic growth. For example, the rapid growth of the Japanese and South Korean economies probably owed much to the mass literacy and numeracy achieved early in the process. This produced a labour force that adapted rapidly to changes in technology and the economic environment. Together with good economic management, this enabled agricultural and industrial productivity to be increased.

6.3.3 Policies to increase educational attainment

The almost universal finding that education increases the output of a country, the productivity of its economic sectors and the earnings of its workers suggests that policies should be introduced to ensure a high level of educational expenditure by both the public and private sectors. If the total level of government spending cannot be raised, then more educational facilities can be provided only by increasing the efficiency of government spending in all sectors. Within education this can be achieved in many ways, including ensuring that current and capital expenditures are co-ordinated so that there are, for example, enough qualified teachers to teach in schools, and maximizing the use of resources by, for example, running two shifts a day. If this is not enough, then some savings from other sectors can be diverted to the educational sector. Given the findings of the theoretical and empirical analyses that a reduction in defence spending has no adverse effect on economic growth, the defence sector is a possible source of extra funding for the education sector.

However, it is important that this increase is not carried out blindly because the dynamics of the employment supply and demand process in developing countries tends to expand educational spending beyond the socially optimum level. In most developing countries wages in the modern sector are much higher than those in the traditional sector, which creates a very strong demand for jobs in the former. Entry into the modern sector depends initially on the level of completed education, creating, in turn, an equally strong demand for education. At the same time rapid population growth over a long period produces more workers than can be absorbed by the economy. Under such conditions employers tend to select by educational level, with, for example, workers who have completed primary education filling jobs that can be performed satisfactorily by those with no primary schooling. Individual workers safeguard their positions by acquiring a higher level of education, which increases the demand for each level of education. According to Todaro, the 'irony is that the more unprofitable a given level of education becomes as a terminal point, the more demand for it increases as an intermediate stage or precondition to the next level of education! This puts great pressure on governments to expand educational facilities at *all* levels to meet the growing demand' (1994, p. 374). Over time and with political pressure from the educated, the wage for a job becomes tied to the educational attainment of the job-holder and not the minimum educational requirements for the job.

The result of these developments is to produce social benefits to education which are far smaller than the private benefits and lead to a socially sub-optimal level of educational expenditure. This can be seen from the finding of numerous studies that the social rate of return to investment in education falls far below the private rate of return. For example, in the study by Psacharopoulos (1988), the social and private rates of return in African countries were 26 per cent and 45 per cent for primary education, 17 per cent and 26 per cent for secondary education and 13 per cent and 32 per cent for tertiary education.

In order to prevent overspending on education it is necessary to break the vicious circle in which overstated job specifications render over-education necessary for employment. This requires that realistic job qualifications be set by both public and private employers. The lead should be taken by the public sector as it usually sets the pattern for the private sector. In this respect, educational certification, the practice of requiring specified educational levels for specified jobs, should be eliminated for many of the low-skilled manual jobs, starting with the public sector.

A socially optimum educational programme also requires that attention be paid to the types of education provided. This need can be seen from the different rates of return to investment in primary, secondary and tertiary education. For example, Psacharopoulos (1988) presented data to show that in the 1970s and 1980s in the developing countries of Africa, Asia and Latin America, the social rates of return to investment in primary education were by far the highest, followed by those to investment in secondary and then tertiary education. Investment in primary education also provided the highest private rate of return, though there was a reversal in the rankings for investment in secondary and tertiary education. These results suggest that there was relative over-investment in secondary and tertiary education from the country and individual viewpoints.

At another level, this imbalance is reflected in the excess demand for vocational and technical skills and the high level of graduate unemployment. Many industrialization programmes have been hindered by the lack of workers with the appropriate manual skills. At the same time university graduates cannot find work and become increasingly frustrated. It is common to find in employment exchanges employers seeking unsuccessfully for electricians, plumbers or car mechanics, and graduates in history, mathematics and physics seeking unsuccessfully for jobs requiring their particular skills and education and ending up doing work that does not require these skills and certainly not a university degree. Thus stories abound of graduates becoming taxi-drivers. While there might be externalities in having educated taxi-drivers, it does show a poor fit between supply and demand and a need to be concerned with more than just increases in educational spending.

The analysis so far shows that an increase in the level of educational spending on its own is not enough to produce greater economic growth. The level and the type of educational expenditure must be consistent with the demands of society and the economy. The chances of this being achieved are increased significantly if a number of complementary methods are used to assess the human resource requirements.

The traditional method is the so-called manpower requirements method, which is based on a number of steps. Total reliance on it is likely to produce mistakes because progression along some of the steps is based on quite unrealistic assumptions. The first step is to estimate the output levels that have to be generated in the major sectors of the economy in order to achieve the target growth rate for the GDP over the planning period. The second is to work out the labour requirements for each forecasted sectoral output. This is done by extrapolating past trends or by using the analogy technique, where data from developed countries are used (Hollister, 1964). Neither technique is very reliable. The third step is to convert each sector's labour requirements into a number of mutually exclusive occupational groups. The analogy technique is also used for this. Sometimes a variant of it is preferred, where the occupation coefficient of the most advanced sector of the economy is used for the rest of the economy in the hope that this coefficient, and the implied production technique, will prevail in the future. Again neither technique is particularly reliable. The fourth step is to convert the occupational structure into an educational structure. The usual technique for doing this, by applying the mean number of years of schooling currently observed for each occupation, is difficult to justify as the skills required for the tasks associated with any particular occupation are obtained at a number of educational levels. The fifth step is to adjust the forecasts for deaths, retirements and emigration, which should not present any problem.

The manpower requirements method is attractive to administrators and policy-makers because of its operational simplicity (Psacharopoulos, 1984). However, its weaknesses have meant that using it has led to large prediction errors. The size of these errors will be reduced if other methods were used; for example, if the social rates of return to investment in different educational levels and occupations were estimated and employers asked for their views on their requirements (Richter, 1984; Amjad, 1987).

The impact of the right amount and mixture of educational spending on economic growth is weakened if the quality of the teaching is poor. In the standard method of estimating the rate of return to educational investment (Mincer, 1974), only the quantity of education, measured by the years or grades of schooling, is incorporated. The quality of the education (i.e. the quality of teaching, facilities and curricula) is not and Behrman and Birdsall (1983) have shown that this leads to an upward bias in the estimated rate of return to schooling. In their study of young Brazilian males they found that the upward bias in the private rate of return was very substantial and that the social rate of return to quality was also very substantially greater than that to quantity. The policy implication is that governments should spend more to upgrade existing educational facilities and less to increase the number of educational places. In other words, 'deepening' schooling by increasing quality is socially preferable to 'broadening' it by increasing quantity.

This finding is supported by casual observation that poorly trained teachers, lack of textbooks and inadequate school facilities lead to poor educational results and lower social and private returns to educational investment. The results reported by the World Bank (1980) of the international evaluation of educational achievement of students from fifteen developed and five developing countries also support the finding that the quality of teaching cannot be ignored. This quality is much higher in developed countries which explains why the mean score of students from developing countries, was typically only equal to the scores of the bottom 5 to 10 per cent of students from developed countries.

6.4 ECONOMIC POLICIES FOR IMPROVING HEALTH

6.4.1 Determinants of health

To most people the definition of health by the World Health Organization (WHO) as a state of complete physical, mental and social well-being is clearly far too idealistic and operationally meaningless. The absence of disease and hospitalization will do but even this is not without problems.   What would be considered diseases needing hospitalization in countries with high health standards may not be in countries with much lower health standards.

For our purpose, it is not necessary to pin down this elusive concept. It is enough to know that the health of a country will be improved the higher is the percentage of its population with access to health services, safe water and sanitation and does not suffer from malnutrition. One could add that its health will be improved by lowering the percentage of its population who smoke and drink but these are minor influences.

While there are conceptual and practical problems in defining health, there are no problems in measuring the consequences of ill health. The ultimate consequence is death. This is usually measured by the crude death rate, which is the number of deaths, regardless of age, per thousand of the population. The most sensitive measure is the infant mortality rate, the number of infants who die before reaching the age of one per thousand live births, because newly born infants are most susceptible to poor health conditions. This is followed by the under-five mortality rate and the maternal mortality rate, which is the number of women who die from pregnancy-related causes per hundred thousand live births.

One intermediate consequence of ill health is for children to be underweight. The usual measure of this is the percentage of children, under the age of five, below minus two standard deviations from the median weight-for-age of the reference population (UNDP, 1992). Another intermediate consequence is for children to be wasted, which can be measured by the percentage of children, between 12 and 23 months, below minus two standard deviations from the median weight-for-height of the reference population. Yet another consequence is for children to be stunted, which can be measured by the percentage of children, between 24 and 59 months, below minus two standard deviations from the median height-for-age of the reference population. Being underweight, wasted or stunted is a manifestation of severe malnutrition.

6.4.2   Health and economic growth

A reduction in any of the mortality rates or any of the malnutrition measures will show an improvement in the health of the nation. This is an end in itself but it can also contribute significantly to economic growth.

First, it increases output by reducing the number of work days lost to illness, increasing labour productivity, providing more opportunities to obtain better-paying jobs and prolonging working lives. The World Bank (1993b) reported that the elimination of deformity in India's 645,000 lepers would have increased the number of days worked by them and added $130m to the country's GNP in 1985. This increase is significant as it was equal to 10 per cent of the foreign aid received by India in that year. In a study of 250 Sudanese households, 68 per cent of the time lost from contracting malaria was made up by uninfected workers putting in more hours. If malaria had not struck, the extra time worked would have increased output. At the very least, it would not have increased the workload of some workers and increased their chances of becoming sick from over-work. Similar studies in Paraguay and Colombia show the same thing.

Behrman and Deolalikar (1988) found, in properly formulated studies, support for the idea that health and nutrition have a positive impact on labour productivity. Thus Strauss (1986) discovered that there was a significant positive link between agricultural labour productivity and nutrition, measured by the calorie intake per consumer equivalent, in Sierre Leone. Deolalikar (1988) found a positive significant impact of health, measured by weight-for height, on the farm output of agricultural households in semi-arid south India. Other micro-studies such as Immink and Viteri (1981) on sugarcane production in Guatemala, Wolgemuth et al. (1982) on road construction in Kenya, and Baldwin and Weisbrod (1974) on sugarcane production in St. Lucia showed weaker relationships but this could be explained by misspecification of the relationships. The latest micro-studies reported by the World Bank (1993b) show that healthier workers in Bangladesh and Côte d'Ivorie earn more because they are more productive and can get better-paying jobs.

What is probably more important is the finding that in the long run better health improves the way in which work is organized. Thus employers no longer have to build slack into their production schedules and are more willing to train their workers and to encourage specialization. Farmers no longer have to be risk-adverse, to behave like those in malarious areas in Paraguay, who respond to the threat of the disease by only growing crops of lower value but which can be cultivated outside the malaria season (World Bank, 1993b).

The second way in which better health can increase economic growth is by increasing the schooling productivity of children and therefore the productivity of the next generation of workers. It is almost trite to say that children who have better health and nutrition are more ready to go to school, with the effect on girls particularly noticeable as they suffer more from iodine or iron deficiency. Healthier and better nourished children learn faster because iron-deficiency anaemia decreases their cognitive ability, iodine deficiency retards their mental prowess permanently and vitamin A deficiency is the primary cause of blindness among children.

In a study of 350 children from the plains of Nepal, Moock and Leslie (1986) found that badly nourished children, as measured by low height-for-age figures, not only have a lower enrolment level but also performed less well. In a study of over 3000 children from urban and rural areas in China, Jamison (1986) also found that height-for-age had a strong effect on performance. These results are supported by the findings of studies reported by the World Bank (1993b). Thus children in northeast Brazil who are inadequately nourished and who have bad eyesight have below-average promotion rates and above-average dropout rates in their schooling. In Jamaica children with moderate whipworm infection did 15 per cent less well than uninfected children but the gap almost disappeared when they were treated.

These studies could have exaggerated the impact of improved health and nutrition on schooling productivity. The samples would not include those who have left school and as these are likely to be the poor performers the impact would have been biased upwards. The results could also have been spurious if the samples contain naturally better endowed children. These might do better in school and be healthier, without better health leading to better schooling performance, so that a positive relationship between health and academic performance is only a statistical artefact, with no economic significance. However, the statistical weaknesses of the studies are not such as to invalidate totally the results, especially since these are consistent with casual observation.

The third way in which improvements in health can contribute to economic growth is by reducing infant and child mortality, which decreases fertility and population growth, leading in turn to more rapid economic growth. Using data from 1964 urban household surveys from Rio de Janeiro, San Jose and Mexico City and a 1970 rural household survey from India, Schultz (1978) found that the level of fertility was positively related to the level of child mortality. Rosenzweig and

Schultz (1982) came to the same conclusion in their study of Colombia, as did Olsen (1983) in his study of Malaysia. These results thus show that the demographic transition, where falls in the birth rate follow falls in the death rate, first noticed in Europe in the eighteenth and nineteenth centuries, is also operating in today's developing countries. Given our earlier finding that a decline in the population growth rate increases economic growth, an improvement in health therefore promotes economic growth.

Fourth, it contributes to growth by making available natural resources that had been made inaccessible by diseases. For example, the malaria eradication programme in Sri Lanka over the 1947-77 period released areas previously blighted by mosquitoes for cultivation. The programme increased national income by $7.6 billion, with an implied benefit–cost ratio of 140. The fight against river blindness in eleven sub-Saharan countries under the Onchocerciasis Control Programme has already freed 25 million hectares of previously inaccessible land for agricultural cultivation. It is also a very cost-effective programme, with an estimated internal rate of return of between 16 and 28 per cent (World Bank, 1993b).

There is a fifth way in which improved health can contribute to economic growth. Some diseases lead to heavy or even disproportionately high treatment costs later on. If health conditions are improved now and the incidence of the diseases reduced, there will be huge savings in future treatment costs. These savings can then be used for alternative projects to produce greater economic growth.

A good example is AIDS. It is found mostly in adults in their most sexually active years so that the spread effect is very large (Lim, 1993b). Together with the expensive health care involved, this can lead to large treatment costs. Thus the World Bank (1993b) reported, from research in nine developing and seven developed countries, that the prevention of one AIDS case saves, on average, an amount equal to twice the per capita GNP in discounted lifetime costs of medical care. In urban areas the savings could be much higher. Such savings can be used for productive investment elsewhere. It should also be mentioned that AIDS affects mainly adults in their most productive years so that the direct and indirect costs of this loss will be very substantial. Thus if health conditions are improved and the incidence of AIDS reduced as a result, there will be large savings in treatment costs and a sharp decline in output loss in the future. In this sense, improved health can contribute to economic growth.

Thus the theoretical and empirical literature shows that improved health and nutrition increases labour productivity, reduces the number of work days lost to illness, improves work practices, raises schooling productivity, reduces population growth, makes available previously inaccessible natural resources and prevents large future treatment costs. The sum effect should be an increase in the rate of economic growth, a result which is obtained in a number of cross-country studies. Thus Malenbaum (1970) found changes in agricultural output after the Second World War to be affected by infant mortality and the availability of doctors for a sample of twenty two developing countries, after holding constant the share of labour in agriculture, the use of commercial fertilizer and the illiteracy rate. In a study of fifty four developing countries, Wheeler (1980) discovered that life expectancy and calorie availability had a positive and very significant impact on the GDP, with the elasticities of output for the two variables being very high at 1.7 and 2.7 respectively. A recent World Bank study (1993b) on the impact of the initial national income level, the initial educational level, and the initial health level (measured by the child mortality rate) on the growth of the per capita income of seventy countries over the 1960-90 period found the health variable to be a very significant factor. Behrman and Deolalikar (1988) urged caution in the interpretation of these results because of the problem of simultaneity. However, to the extent that they are consistent with those obtained by the more carefully formulated of the micro-studies, we can be more confident of the finding that better health and nutrition in a country increases significantly the growth of its GDP.

6.4.3 Policies to improve health

Much has already been done to improve health in developing countries, as can be seen in the dramatic increase in life expectancy from forty years in 1950 to sixty three years in 1990. However, much remains to be done. The child mortality rate is still ten times higher than that in developed countries, and the improvement is very unevenly spread across developing countries and across regions and groups within each country.

There is thus no question that health in developing countries has to be improved further, both because it is an end in itself and because it will contribute significantly to economic growth. For this to take place, we need to identify, first, the diseases which kill or lead to severe disability and, second, the policies which reduce the incidence of such diseases. The two steps should be taken in sequence, otherwise programmes to improve health conditions will not be focussed enough.

Data on the relative importance of the diseases which led to loss of life and disability in developed and developing countries in 1990 is provided by the World Health Organization and the World Bank. The number of life-years lost from death is measured by the difference between actual age at death and life expectancy at that age in a low-mortality population. The number of life-years lost from disability is measured by adjusting the expected duration of the condition for the severity of the disability compared to loss of life. The data for this is obtained from community surveys and expert opinions. The numbers of life-years lost from death and disability are then combined, with allowances for a discount rate of 3 per cent so that future years of healthy life are valued less, and for age weights so that years lost at different years are valued differently. This produces the number of disability-adjusted life-years (DALYs) lost. When this number is presented per thousand of the population it measures the burden of disease. The larger the number, the greater is the burden of disease.

This is not a complete measure because the social costs of disfigurement and dysfunction are not included. It also does not include the effects of the age-structure of the population. However, it does give a far better picture of the burden of disease than previous measures.

Table 6.1 shows that in 1990 1.36 billion DALYs were lost, which was equivalent to 42 million deaths of newborn children or 80 million deaths at the age of 50. The vast majority (65.6 per cent) of these was from premature deaths. Of such deaths, communicable diseases were responsible for 56.3 per cent, non-communicable diseases 32.1 per cent and injuries 11.6 per cent. Of the disabilities, the main cause was non-communicable diseases (61.5 per cent), followed a long way behind by communicable diseases (25.9 per cent) and injuries (12.6 per cent). The same patterns were observed for males and females.

Table 6.2 gives the percentage distribution of DALY losses by detailed cause and region. Sub-Saharan Africa has the highest burden of disease (575 DALYs per thousand population), more than twice the global average (259). India (344) is also significantly above this average, while countries in the Middle Eastern crescent (286) are not too far above it. Other Asia and islands are on the average (260) and Latin America and the Caribbean (233) and China (178) below it. As expected, the lowest burden of disease is recorded by the established market economies (117). The former socialist economies of Europe were some distance behind at 168.

For the world as a whole, communicable and non-communicable diseases were responsible for about the same number of cases (46 per cent and 42 per cent) but there were very significant differences in their importance among developing countries. Thus while in sub-Saharan

Table 6.1   Burden of disease by cause, type of loss and sex, 1990 (%)

	% distribution of DALYs by cause				DALYs	
	Communicable diseases	Non-communicable diseases	Injuries	Total %	No. (m.)	% distribution by loss type
Total					*1361*	*100.0*
• premature death	56.3	32.1	11.6	100.0	893	65.6
• disability	25.9	61.5	12.6	100.0	468	34.4
Male					*713*	*100.0*
• premature death	53.8	31.6	14.6	100.0	481	67.5
• disability	20.3	62.9	16.8	100.0	232	32.5
Female					*648*	*100.0*
• premature death	59.2	32.8	8.0	100.0	412	63.6
• disability	31.3	60.2	8.5	100.0	236	36.4

Source: World Bank (1993b, p. 25).

Table 6.2   Distribution of DALY loss by cause and region, 1990 (%)

Cause	World	Sub-Saharan Africa	India	China	Other Asia and islands	L. America and the Caribbean	Middle Eastern crescent	European ex-socialist economies	Established market economies
Population (millions)	5,267	510	850	1,134	683	444	503	346	798
Communicable diseases	*45.8*	*71.3*	*50.5*	*25.3*	*48.5*	*42.2*	*51.0*	*8.6*	*9.7*
Tuberculosis	3.4	4.7	3.7	2.9	5.1	2.5	2.8	0.6	0.2
STDs and HIV	3.8	8.8	2.7	1.7	1.5	6.6	0.7	1.2	3.4
Diarrhoea	7.3	10.4	9.6	2.1	8.3	5.7	10.7	0.4	0.3
Vaccine-preventable childhood infections	5.0	9.6	6.7	0.9	4.5	1.6	6.0	0.1	0.1
Malaria	2.6	10.8	0.3	*	1.4	0.4	0.2	*	*
Worm infections	1.8	1.8	0.9	3.4	3.4	2.5	0.4	*	*
Respiratory infections	9.0	10.8	10.9	6.4	11.1	6.2	11.5	2.6	2.6
Maternal causes	2.2	2.7	2.7	1.2	2.5	1.7	2.9	0.8	0.6
Paternal causes	7.3	7.1	9.1	5.2	7.4	9.1	10.9	2.4	2.2
Other	3.5	4.6	4.0	1.4	3.3	5.8	4.9	0.6	0.5
Non-communicable diseases	*42.2*	*19.4*	*40.4*	*58.0*	*40.1*	*42.8*	*36.0*	*74.8*	*78.4*
Cancer	5.8	1.5	4.1	9.2	4.4	5.2	3.4	14.8	19.1
Nutritional deficiencies	3.9	2.8	6.2	3.3	4.6	4.6	3.7	1.4	1.7
Neuropsychiatric disease	6.8	3.3	6.1	8.0	7.0	8.0	5.6	11.1	15.0
Cerebrovascular disease	3.2	1.5	2.1	6.3	2.1	2.6	2.4	8.9	5.3
Ischaemic heart disease	3.1	0.4	2.8	2.1	3.5	2.7	1.8	13.7	10.0
Pulmonary obstruction	1.3	0.2	0.6	5.5	0.5	0.7	0.5	1.6	1.7
Other	18.0	9.7	18.5	23.6	17.9	19.1	18.7	23.4	25.6
Injuries	*11.9*	*9.3*	*9.1*	*16.7*	*11.3*	*15.0*	*13.0*	*16.6*	*11.9*
Motor vehicle	2.3	1.3	1.1	2.3	2.3	5.7	3.3	3.7	3.5
Intentional	3.7	4.2	1.2	5.1	3.2	4.3	5.2	4.8	4.0
Other	5.9	3.9	6.8	9.3	5.8	5.0	4.6	8.1	4.3
Millions of DALYs	1,362	293	292	201	177	103	144	58	94
Equivalent infant deaths (millions)	42.0	9.0	9.0	6.2	5.5	3.2	4.4	1.8	2.9
DALYs per 1,000 population	259	575	344	178	260	233	286	168	117

Notes: DALY, disability-adjusted life-year; STD, sexually transmitted disease; HIV, human immune deficiency virus; * less than 0.05 per cent.

Source: World Bank (1993b, p. 25).

Africa communicable diseases accounted for over 71 per cent of the losses, in China the share was only 25 per cent. These two areas were also at opposite ends as far as the impact of non-communicable diseases is concerned. For sub-Saharan Africa such diseases were responsible for just over 19 per cent of DALY losses, whereas for China the share was 58 per cent. There were also differences in the impact of these two types of diseases on the other areas (India, Other Asia and islands, Latin America and the Caribbean and the Middle Eastern crescent) but these were much smaller. For DALY losses due to injuries, the highest incidence was registered by China (16.7 per cent) and the lowest by India (9.1 per cent), with an average of 11.9 per cent for the world. Thus the health requirements of regions and countries in the developing world differ and these differences preclude the adoption of a universal approach to the improvement of health in these areas. However, there is a pattern. A higher income level reduces the burden of disease. It also shifts the source of this burden, with communicable diseases becoming much less important and non-communicable ones much more so.

The table also shows that communicable but largely preventable or inexpensively curable diseases such as diarrhoea, measles, respiratory infections, worm infections and malaria, long thought to have been under control, still accounted for nearly 26 per cent of the DALYs lost for the world as a whole. By far the highest incidence of these infectious and parasitic diseases was in sub-Saharan Africa (43 per cent), though the incidence in Other Asia and islands (29 per cent), the Middle Eastern crescent (29 per cent) and India (28 per cent) was also substantial. These diseases are mostly childhood ones as Table 6.3 shows, for example, that 84 per cent of the DALYs lost because of diarrhoea were concentrated in the 0-4 age-group, with another 9.5 per cent in the 5-14 age-group. For the loss due to worm infection, nearly 74 per cent were felt by people below the age of 15.

After an exhaustive examination of the current and future pattern of diseases in developing countries, as reflected by the DALY and other data, the World Bank (1993b) recommended a three-pronged approach to improve the health of these countries. The first is to create an environment which enables households to improve the health of their members. The second is to improve the cost effectiveness of government spending on health. The third is to promote diversity and competition in the health sector.

The most effective environment for improving health is one where economic growth is rapid and benefits the poor significantly, where basic schooling, especially for girls, is adequate and where the rights and

Table 6.3   Distribution of DALY loss of four diseases by age-group, 1990 (%)

Disease	0-4	5-14	15-44	45-59	60+	%	No. (m.)
			Age-group (years)			Total	
Diarrhoea	83.6	9.5	5.6	0.8	0.5	100	99.1
Worm infection	1.2	82.5	10.4	4.1	0.8	100	24.0
Tuberculosis	5.4	14.8	52.3	19.3	8.2	100	46.5
Ischaemic heart disease	0.3	0.4	11.3	26.6	61.4	100	42.5

Source: World Bank (1993b, p. 28).

status of women are promoted. The poor tend to spend additional income on improving their diet, obtaining safe water, and upgrading sanitation and housing, expenditures which are very effective in improving health (World Bank, 1993b, p. 7). Better educational facilities also help because they enable households to seek and utilize health information more effectively. The impact will be greater if they do not discriminate against girls because 'it is largely women who buy and prepare food, maintain a clean house, care for children and the elderly, and initiate contacts with the health system' (World Bank, 1993b, p. 8). Promoting the rights and status of women will ensure that girls do not miss out on any expansion in educational and economic opportunities.

The economic policies recommended by the World Bank for promoting economic growth are the market-friendly ones described earlier in Chapter 2 and will not be repeated here. The introduction of the policies, described in Chapter 5, to increase domestic and foreign savings will also help, as will the policies described earlier in this chapter to reduce the rate of population growth and increase the skills of the labour force.

Government expenditure on health in many developing countries is often not cost-effective. First, there is misallocation. Too much is spent on advanced facilities and treatment which benefit only a relatively small and rich section of the population. Not enough is spent on basic public health programmes on immunization, AIDS prevention and the supply of essential clinical services, which are inexpensive and can effectively reduce the spread of communicable diseases to large numbers of people. Second, there is inefficiency. The decision-making process is too centralized. This results in the purchase of expensive brand-name pharmaceutical products, when the use of cheaper generic drugs will do just as well, and in the under-utilization of hospital beds. The morale of health workers is subsequently low and is probably worsened by the uncertainty created by wide fluctuations in the budgetary allocations to health.

The World Bank argued that the introduction of a number of highly cost-effective public health programmes and essential clinical services would do much to reduce the misallocation and inefficiency of existing government health expenses. For public health programmes, it was particularly keen to: (i) expand immunization programmes; (ii) improve school-based treatment of schistosomiasis, intestinal worm infections and micro-nutrient deficiencies; (iii) increase the supply of information on the benefits of family planning and good nutrition; (iv) introduce stronger measures to control the use of tobacco, alcohol and other addictive sustances; (v) provide a regulatory and administrative framework to ensure a healthier environment; and (vi) begin a massive early programme on AIDS prevention because late intervention in an AIDS epidemic is very expensive and ineffective.

A minimum of five groups of clinical services is recommended, each of which deals with important causes of DALY losses. These groups are: (i) services to provide pregnancy-related care, which could prevent most of the annual half a million maternal deaths; (ii) family planning services, which could save up to 850,000 children from dying and up to 100,000 maternal deaths every year; (iii) tuberculosis control, which could reduce significantly the 2 million deaths per year; (iv) control of sexually transmitted diseases, which could markedly decrease the 250 million new cases reported each year; and (v) care for the common serious illnesses of children (diarrhoea, acute respiratory infection, measles, malaria and acute malnutrition), which would reduce significantly the 7 million children who die from such diseases annually.

Table 6.4 shows the estimated costs and health benefits of the public health programmes and minimum clinical services recommended. Expenditure on the latter are more cost-effective. While their provision costs nearly twice that of public health programmes, their impact on reducing the burden of disease was 3 times as high. Together the two types of programmes would decrease the burden of disease by 32 per cent in low-income countries and 15 per cent in middle-income countries, which is equivalent to saving the lives of more than 9 million infants each year. In summary, what is recommended is adequate spending on health but with the expenditure favouring basic health and clinical programmes rather than expensive and sophisticated tertiary services.

*Table 6.4   Estimated costs and health benefits of public health and
            essential clinical services, 1990*

Group of developing countries	Cost		Approximate reduction in burden of disease (%)
	Dollars per capita per year	% of per capita income	
Low-income countries (per capita income = $350)			
• public health	4.2	1.2	8
• essential clinical services	7.8	2.2	24
• total	12.0	3.4	32
Middle-income countries (per capita income = $2,500)			
• public health	6.8	0.3	4
• essential clinical services	14.7	0.6	11
• total	21.5	0.9	15

Source: World Bank (1993b, p. 10).

The third prong is the introduction of more competition in the supply
of health services and inputs. This can reduce cost and increase quality,
provided there is strong government regulation in the private sector to
ensure safety and quality, universal access to insurance coverage, and
minimal overuse of services and escalation of medical costs.   The
competition will force the public health sector to be more efficient by
decentralizing its operations and introducing more efficient management
systems.

There are elements of the World Bank's package for improving the
health of developing countries that can be faulted. For example, it is
difficult to imagine a country with a badly run public health sector being
able to keep the private health sector under effective control. It is likely
that the programme to let the private sector play a greater role in the
supply of health services and inputs will lead to abuses and ultimately
unnecessary and high medical costs. A certain level of economic and
political maturity is required before the programme can work. However,
the other major thrusts of the package are sensible. The provision of
greater educational opportunities to girls, the empowerment of women,
and the redirecting of health expenditure from expensive sophisticated
programmes to basic public health and clinical programmes are sound
recommendations.   The first two increase the knowledge and
commitment of that section of the population which has traditionally

been responsible for the health of the family, the third produces a health programme which is more cost-effective.

6.5 POLICY PERFORMANCES OF ASIAN DEVELOPING COUNTRIES

6.5.1 Summary of economic policies for human resource development

In this section we examine the record of Asian developing countries in introducing the economic policies which increase the contribution of labour to output growth. Have the newly industrializing economies (NIEs) been more successful in introducing these policies, which then gave them the sound human resource base from which to launch their successful development programmes? We precede this discussion by summarizing what these economic policies are.

Labour contributes to output growth in three inter-related ways. The first is simply through an increase in its supply, the second and third through improvements in the skills and health of the labour force. Under the conditions prevailing in most developing countries, a judicious increase in the supply of labour is needed. This can best be achieved by making children less attractive as earners of income and providers of old-age security, thereby reducing the need to have a high fertility rate. This approach is made more effective if it is supported by family planning programmes to provide health and contraceptive services because these strengthen the desire to have fewer children and enable this to be realized more effectively.

If programmes to slow down the rate of growth in the population and the labour force are successful, they will release funds for programmes to improve the skills of the labour force. For such programmes to contribute significantly to output growth they must provide the socially optimum level and mixture of high-quality educational skills.

Improvements in the health of the labour force can also contribute significantly to output growth. Such improvements can best be obtained by providing greater educational opportunities to girls, promoting the rights and status of women, de-emphasizing the provision of sophisticated public tertiary care services in favour of the supply of basic public health and clinical services, and introducing more competition into the health sector. All these are to be conducted within a framework which promotes growth with equity.

What we have identified are three sets of policies which promote the efficient development of a country's human resources. These should be pursued together as they reinforce each other.

6.5.2 Policy performances in curbing population growth

The value of children as investment goods is reduced by increasing the compulsory school age or the minimum age for child labour; improving health and nutritional programmes for parent and child; introducing old-age and other forms of social security; and expanding educational and employment opportunities for females.

Available data suggests that the NIEs have, on balance, performed better than most other developing economies in introducing these programmes. Evidence of their greater success in increasing the compulsory school age or the minimum age for child labour is provided indirectly by Behrman and Schneider (1992), a result reported by the World Bank (1993a). Primary and secondary enrolment rates were regressed on per capita national income for over ninety developing economies for 1965 and 1987. The regressions show very clearly that the higher the per capita income, the higher the enrolment rates. However, the enrolment rates for the NIEs were higher than predicted for their income level. This was particularly evident at the primary level in 1965, and shows that from very early on the NIEs were well ahead of most other Asian developing economies in achieving universal primary education and, by implication, in successfully increasing the compulsory school age or the minimum age for child labour.

Arriving at this result this way is preferable to one obtained by examining the data on the compulsory school age or the minimum age for child labour. Such data are not accurate as the enforcement of government regulations on these matters is weak in most developing countries. The true state of the situation is better revealed by examining the actual school enrolment rates, especially at the primary level where the final year coincides with the minimum age for child labour, than by looking at intentions.

Table 6.5 shows the performances of Asian developing economies on the health and nutritional fronts. The better performances of the NIEs are also evident here. Their better health is shown by the higher life expectancy at birth. Figures on the daily calorie supply on a per capita basis and as a percentage of requirements, and on the percentage of children who are underweight, wasted and stunted, as defined earlier in Section 6.4.1, also show that the NIEs have better nutritional standards.

Table 6.5 Health and nutritional performances and social security benefits expenditure/GDP ratios, 1980-90

Region	% children suffering from malnutrition 1989-90			Daily calorie supply 1988		Life expectancy at birth (years) 1990	Social security benefits expenditure/ GDP (%) 1980
	Underweight (under 5years)	Wasting (12-23 months)	Stunting (24-59 months)	Per capita	% of requirements		
Newly industrializing economies[a]							
Hong Kong	–	–	–	2,899	123	78	–
Singapore	14	4	11	2,892	126	74	2.6
South Korea	–	–	–	2,878	121	71	–
Southeast Asia							
Indonesia	51	–	–	2,670	120	62	–
Malaysia	–	–	–	2,686	119	70	0.5
Philippines	34	14	45	2,255	99	64	0.2
Thailand	26	10	28	2,287	103	66	–
South Asia							
Bangladesh	66	28	66	1,925	83	52	–
India	61	–	–	2,104	94	59	0.5
Myanmar	38	17	75	2,572	117	61	–
Nepal	70	14	69	2,078	94	52	–
Pakistan	52	17	42	2,200	92	56	–
Sri Lanka	38	19	34	2,319	106	71	0.3
China	21	8	41	2,632	111	70	–

Note: – not available. [a] No data for Taiwan.
Sources: UNDP (1992, pp. 148-9, 152-3 and 158-9); World Bank (1992, pp. 218-9).

Data on the government provision of old-age and other forms of social security is not easily available. Table 6.5 has only 1980 data on the social security benefits expenditure to GDP ratio for just five economies: one NIE (Singapore), two Southeast Asian economies (Malaysia and the Philippines) and two South Asian economies (India and Sri Lanka). Though the sample is far too small for any final conclusion to be made, it is nevertheless worth pointing out that the ratio for Singapore (2.6 per cent) is more than five times larger than the next highest, which is 0.5 per cent for Malaysia and India.

Table 6.6 provides data on educational and employment opportunities for females. On education, the NIEs have done better than most. In 1990 their adult illiteracy for females was very much lower, bettering by a considerable margin even the rates registered by the Philippines and Sri Lanka, long considered to be exemplars of educational excellence. Figures on the percentage of the female age-group enrolled in secondary education in 1965 and 1989 also show that females in the NIEs have long been given greater employment opportunities than elsewhere, with the exception of those in the Philippines and Sri Lanka. The same picture emerges from the limited data on the percentage of the female cohort persisting to grade 4 in their education.

The average female to male ratio in the labour force for the NIEs is lower than the ratios for Indonesia, the Philippines, Thailand, Myanmar, Sri Lanka and China. Measured in this way, the provision of employment opportunities to females in the NIEs is no better than those in the majority of the other Asian developing economies in the sample. However, it is quite clear from the evidence available that, on balance, the NIEs have in place more of those programmes which reduce the attractiveness of children as investment goods. As the NIEs had performed better in most of these programmes in the years before they embarked upon their spectacular economic growth, it can be argued that such performances helped to decrease the rate of population growth by reducing the dependence of families on children as current and future providers. Rapid economic growth does lead to slower population growth and makes possible programmes which make children less necessary as income earners. But this line of causation is unlikely, given the sequencing of events.

The effectiveness of the policies and programmes introduced by the NIEs to reduce the attractiveness of children as investment goods has been increased by the effort put into family planning programmes. Table 6.7 shows that while the NIEs did not begin their official family planning programmes any earlier than other Asian countries, the size and quality of their programmes, as measured by the World Bank's family planning

Table 6.6 Educational and employment opportunities for females, 1965-90

Region	% of female age-group enrolled in secondary education		% of female cohort persisting to grade 4		Adult illiteracy rate for females (%)	Female/male ratio in the labour force (%)
	1965	1989	1970	1985	1990	1988-90
Newly industrializing economies[a]						
Hong Kong	25	75	94	–	5	57
Singapore	41	71	99	100	5	64
South Korea	25	84	96	99	5	51
Southeast Asia						
Indonesia	7	43	67	83	32	66
Malaysia	22	59	–	–	30	45
Philippines	40	75	–	82	11	59
Thailand	11	–	71	–	10	88
South Asia						
Bangladesh	3	11	–	40	78	7
India	13	31	42	–	66	34
Myanmar	11	23	39	–	28	60
Nepal	2	17	–	–	87	51
Pakistan	5	12	56	–	79	13
Sri Lanka	35	76	94	97	17	59
China	–	38	–	76	38	76

Note: – not available. [a] No data for Taiwan.
Sources: World Bank (1993b, pp. 218-9, 274-5 and 280-1); UNDP (1992, pp. 144-5).

Table 6.7 *Various indicators of family planning performances, 1972-89*

Region	Year official family planning programme started	Family planning index[a] 1972	Family planning index[a] 1982	Contraceptive prevalence rate (%) 1985-9	Average annual population growth rate (%) 1970-82	% population of working age (15-64 years) 1982
Newly industrializing economies						
Hong Kong	1973	B	B	72	2.4	66
Singapore	1965	A	A	74	1.5	66
South Korea	1961	A	A	77	1.7	62
Taiwan	–	–	–	–	–	–
Southeast Asia						
Indonesia	1968	C	B	48	2.3	57
Malaysia	1966	C	B	51	2.5	56
Philippines	1970	C	C	45	2.7	53
Thailand	1970	D	C	66	2.4	56
South Asia						
Bangladesh	1971	E	C	25	2.6	55
India	1952	B	B	34	2.3	57
Myanmar	–	E	E	–	2.2	55
Nepal	1966	D	D	14	2.6	55
Pakistan	1960	D	C	11	3.0	51
Sri Lanka	1965	C	B	62	1.7	60
China	1962	A	A	74	1.4	63

Notes: – not available. [a] A=very strong; B=strong; C=moderate; D=weak; E=very weak or none.
Sources: World Bank (1984, pp. 149, 200-01 and 258-9); UNDP (1992, pp. 170-1).

index, appear to be superior. Factors such as official political commitment, availability and quality of family planning services (public and commercial), the mixture of contraceptive methods, outreach, use of mass media, local financial support, and record keeping and evaluation went into estimating a country's family planning index. The data shows that the NIEs' performances in 1972 and 1982 were better than those of most of the other countries in the sample. By 1980-90 this had produced a contraceptive prevalence rate (the percentage of married women of childbearing age who are using, or whose husbands are using, any form of contraception) which was matched only by that of China.

The net result of the introduction by the NIEs of policies to reduce the need to treat children as investment goods and of family planning programmes to reinforce the impact of those policies is a slower rate of population growth. This is shown in Table 6.7, which also shows the corollary of this: a larger percentage of their population in the working age-group of between 15 and 64 years.

6.5.3 Policy performances in increasing skills

Labour can contribute significantly to output growth if its level of educational attainment is high, but not overtly so from the country's viewpoint, the mixture of skills attuned to the requirements of modernization and industrialization, and the quality of the skills acquired high. Data on these attributes is not easily available but what is available shows that the NIEs possess more of them.

The level of educational attainment is measured by the percentages of the respective age-groups enrolled in primary, secondary and tertiary education. The higher the percentages, the higher the level of educational attainment. However, if the social rate of return to investment in any of these educational levels is significantly smaller than the private rate of return, then over-investment has taken place from the country's viewpoint. The level of educational attainment may be high but it is not socially optimum.

Table 6.8 shows the level of educational attainment in 1965 and 1989. In 1965 the NIEs' level of educational attainment was higher than those of the other countries, with the exception of that of the Philippines. As 1965 was a year in which the NIEs had not or had only begun their rapid economic growth process, their educational performances could not have been due to their higher levels of economic development. The figures for 1989 show that the NIEs had managed to maintain the superior performance over time.

Table 6.8 *Level of educational attainment and social rates of return/private rate of return ratio, 1965-89*

Region	% of age-group enrolled in education (%)						Social rate of return/ private rate of return (%)[a]		
	Primary		Secondary		Tertiary		Primary	Secondary	Tertiary
	1965	1989	1965	1989	1965	1989			
Newly industrializing economies									
Hong Kong	103	105	29	73	5	–	–	81	49
Singapore	105	110	45	69	10	–	–	88	60
South Korea	101	108	35	86	6	38	–	87	83
Taiwan	–	–	–	–	–	–	54	97	112
Southeast Asia									
Indonesia	72	118	12	47	1	–	84	100	–
Malaysia	90	96	28	59	2	7	–	–	–
Philippines	113	111	41	73	19	28	73	85	91
Thailand	78	86	14	28	2	16	54	90	79
South Asia									
Bangladesh	49	70	13	17	1	4	–	–	–
India	74	98	27	43	5	–	88	69	82
Myanmar	71	103	15	24	1	5	–	–	–
Nepal	20	86	5	30	1	6	–	–	–
Pakistan	40	38	12	20	2	5	65	82	30
Sri Lanka	93	107	35	74	2	4	–	–	–
China	89	135	24	44	0	2	–	–	–

Notes: – not available. [a] Years studied are 1976 (Hong Kong), 1978 (India), 1978 (Indonesia), 1975 (Pakistan), 1966 (Singapore), 1986 (South Korea), 1972 (Taiwan) and 1970 (Thailand).

Sources: World Bank (1992, pp. 274-5); Psacharopoulos (1994, pp. 1340-1).

A convenient measure of the social optimality of the level of educational spending is the ratio of the social rate of return to the private rate of return. The lower the ratio, the less desirable is the expenditure from the country's viewpoint. Data on this measure is not easily available but what is available shows that the NIEs' record in ensuring that their educational spending is not socially sub-optimal is no worse than that of other countries. Table 6.8 shows that their record in secondary education is rather better.

The modernization and industrialization programmes of many developing countries have been hindered by the shortage of vocational, technical, scientific and research and development (R and D) skills. Table 6.9 presents data on the supply of such skills. At the lower end, this is measured by the share of secondary technical enrolment in total secondary enrolment. At the top end, it is measured by the number of R and D scientists and technicians per ten thousand people. In between is the number of scientists and technicians per thousand people.

The data is for the 1985-9 period only. Pre-1965 data is unfortunately not available. However, as increases in the supply of the skills concerned, especially at the top end, take a long time to generate, the data for the 1985-9 period should reflect the situation some years back, not perhaps all the way back to 1965 but very soon after.

It can be seen that the NIEs are well ahead in the supply of scientists and technicians. The lowest number of scientists and technicians per thousand people recorded for a NIE (Singapore at 23.6) is over twice that registered by the highest ranked of the other countries (Indonesia at 10.1). The NIEs are also well ahead in the supply of R and D scientists and technicians, for although data is available only for one NIE (South Korea), the supply of such highly skilled and specialized personnel is only possible with a large pool of scientists and technicians. The NIEs have much larger numbers of scientists and technicians per thousand people, from which can be inferred that they also have much larger numbers of R and D personnel per ten thousand people. The score of 21.6 R and D personnel per ten thousand people for South Korea may thus be seen as representative of the situation in the NIEs as a whole, and this score is many times higher than the highest recorded by the other countries (Malaysia at 3.7).

Table 6.9 shows that in 1987-8 the NIEs had done very well in the supply of secondary technical personnel when compared to South Asian countries and Malaysia. They had performed well compared to China and just as well compared to Thailand and Indonesia. However, it should be noted that these figures probably understate the NIEs' relative

Table 6.9 Supply of vocational, technical and R and D personnel, 1985-9

Region	Secondary technical enrolment/ total secondary enrolment (%) 1987-8	Scientists and technicians/ 1,000 people (%) 1985-9	R & D scientists and technicians/ 10,000 people (%) 1985-9
Newly industrializing economies			
Hong Kong	10.0	41.0	–
Singapore	–	23.6	–
South Korea	15.9	47.3	21.6
Taiwan	–	–	–
Southeast Asia			
Indonesia	10.6	10.1	1.7
Malaysia	1.7	–	3.7
Philippines	–	–	1.1
Thailand	16.2	1.2	1.5
South Asia			
Bangladesh	0.7	0.5	–
India	–	3.6	2.3
Myanmar	1.2	–	–
Nepal	–	0.6	0.2
Pakistan	1.6	4.1	1.3
Sri Lanka	–	–	2.0
China	7.9	8.5	–

Note: – not available.
Source: UNDP (1992, pp. 136-7 and pp. 156-7).

achievement in the supply of technical personnel at the lower level. The comparison should have been for an earlier year, such as 1965. The gap then in favour of the NIEs would have been far larger to produce the huge gap noted in their favour in 1985-9 in the supply of technical personnel at a higher level. It is not possible to have a much larger supply of scientists and technicians per thousand people in 1985-9 without a similarly much larger supply of secondary technical personnel earlier on.

It is difficult to obtain reliable data on the quality of the education and training provided. One possible indicator for which data is widely available is the primary pupil–teacher ratio. If individual teacher attention is important for the learning process, then the lower the ratio the higher the quality of primary education. In 1965 Hong Kong and Singapore each had a value of 29 for this ratio, compared to the average of 34 for Southeast Asia, 42 for South Asia and 30 for China. Thus the quality of the primary education provided by the NIEs was higher than that provided by other economies.

The World Bank (1993a) used the level of real educational expenditure per pupil as a measure of educational quality. Figures on this common but imperfect measure show that between 1970 and 1989, real expenditure per pupil at the primary level increased by 355 per cent in South Korea, while in Pakistan it went up by only 13 per cent between 1970 and 1985.

A better measure of schooling quality is the performance of children on tests of cognitive skills, standardized across economies. However, very few of such tests have been carried out but from whatever is available the World Bank has concluded that 'East Asian children tend to perform better than children from other developing regions – and even, recently, better than children from high-income economies' (1993a, p. 45).

The evidence presented by the World Bank is not comprehensive enough to conclude firmly that the quality of the education and training provided by the NIEs is superior to that provided by other Asian developing economies. For the first measure of quality, only the data for South Korea and Pakistan is given, while for the second measure, 'East Asia' includes the NIEs and Indonesia, Malaysia and Thailand. However, the evidence is at least consistent with the argument that the NIEs' quality is no worse than that elsewhere. Together with the evidence presented on the level of educational attainment and the skills needed for modernization and industrialization, it is probably safe to say that the quality of education and training provided by the NIEs is better than that provided by most other developing economies in Asia.

6.5.4 Policy performances in improving health

The health and therefore the productivity of the labour force can be improved by pursuing economic growth with equity, especially for the female section of the population; by providing a high level of health care which favours basic public health and clinical services over expensive sophisticated medical programmes; and by introducing competition into the health sector.

In Chapter 1 we saw that the NIEs have a better record than most other Asian developing economies in producing economic growth with equity. This resulted in a faster reduction in the percentage of the population living below the poverty line and a more equal distribution of income. To the extent that the poor tend to spend additional income on improving their health, the development processes in the NIEs, which promote growth with equity more successfully, would have improved the health of their labour force more effectively. In turn, this would have helped the development process.

This is especially since Section 6.5.2 of this chapter has shown that the development processes of the NIEs have resulted in greater educational opportunities for females. Traditionally women have been responsible for the health of the family. The greater knowledge and sense of fulfilment provided by the greater educational opportunities would have increased the efficiency with which they carry out this role.

Table 6.10 shows that in 1990 the NIEs spent very considerably more on health per capita. It can, of course, be argued that by 1990 the standard of living of the NIEs was so much higher than that of the rest of developing Asia that they could offer to spend more per capita on health. The high level of health spending would have been the effect, and not the cause, of economic growth. While per capita health expenditure data for an earlier year is needed to resolve this issue of the direction of the causation, it can be seen from the table that in 1981 the share of health spending in the GDP in the NIEs was higher than most. This suggests that the high expenditure on health preceded rather than followed the high standard of living.

Table 6.11 shows that in 1975 a far higher percentage of the NIEs' population had access to safe water. While data on the population's access to basic health services and sanitation is not available for 1975, it is likely that the NIEs were similarly ahead because these facilities tend to go hand in hand with the provision of safe water. Certainly the data presented for 1988-90 for access to health services and sanitation shows the NIEs to be still ahead, though clearly some of the other countries had made significant progress. Other measures of the provision of basic health programmes and clinical services, such as the population per doctor in 1960 and the number of hospital beds per hundred of the population in 1985-90, also show that the NIEs had done significantly better than other countries in the period before and after the NIEs' take-off.

*Table 6.10   Health expenditure levels and share of private sector in
total health expenditure, 1990*

Region	Total health expenditure		Private health expenditure/total health expenditure (%)
	Per capita (%)	Share of GDP (%) 1990	1981 1990
Newly industrializing economies			
Hong Kong	699	–	81
Singapore	219	4.8	42
South Korea	377	3.4	59
Taiwan	–	–	–
Southeast Asia			
Indonesia	12	2.1	65
Malaysia	67	6.4	57
Philippines	14	1.8	50
Thailand	73	3.5	78
South Asia			
Bangladesh	7	–	56
India	21	0.3	78
Myanmar	–	1.7	–
Nepal	7	1.3	51
Pakistan	12	0.5	47
Sri Lanka	18	2.4	51
China	11	–	40

Notes: – not available.
Source: World Bank (1993b, pp. 210-1).

This does not mean that the NIEs had spent a higher percentage of
their health expenditure on the provision of basic health programmes
and clinical services. However, it does suggest that, at worst, the NIEs
had spent enough on such activities to improve the health of the bulk of
their population. At best, it suggests that such activities did command a
higher share of their medical spending because it is unlikely that a
programme which concentrated unduly on expensive tertiary medical

Table 6.11 Access of population to basic health and clinical programmes, 1960-90

Region	% population with access to			Population per doctor 1960	Hospital beds/100 population 1985-90
	Health services 1988-90	Safe water 1975	Sanitation 1988-90		
Newly industrializing economies					
Hong Kong	99	97	97	2,990	42
Singapore	100	100	100	2,400	33
South Korea	94	62	99	3,000	30
Taiwan	–	–	–	2,300	–
Southeast Asia					
Indonesia	80	12	43	41,000	7
Malaysia	–	62	–	6,940	24
Philippines	–	39	91	–	13
Thailand	70	22	86	7,800	16
South Asia					
Bangladesh	45	53	–	–	3
India	–	33	–	5,800	7
Myanmar	33	17	35	9,900	6
Nepal	–	9	6	72,000	3
Pakistan	55	29	18	11,000	6
Sri Lanka	93	20	50	4,500	28
China	–	–	–	–	26

Note: – not available.
Sources: UNDP (1992, pp. 150-1); World Bank (1993b, pp. 208-9).

services would have also succeeded in providing basic services. The issue will remain unresolved until direct statistical data becomes available but the indirect evidence suggests that health spending in the NIEs had been more cost-effective.

Data on the size of the private health sector in the NIEs in the period before their economic take-off is hard to come by. Table 6.10 presents the share of private health expenditure in the total health expenditure for 1990. This shows that the private sector did not play a bigger role in the NIEs. It could have much earlier on but there is no way of knowing.

In summary, the general economic and the specific health strategies adopted by the NIEs have produced a more cost-effective health programme. The economic growth has been more equitable and has provided more educational opportunities for women. More has been spent on the health sector and the expenditure has been directed more to the provision of basic health and clinical programmes. There is no evidence that the private sector has played a more dominant role in the provision of medical services. However, given our scepticism of this aspect of the World Bank's approach to health improvement, we can discard this piece of evidence to conclude that, on balance, the NIEs have been more cost-effective than most developing countries in improving the health of their labour force. In the process they have enabled their workers to contribute more effectively to output growth.

6.5.5   Summary of Asian policy performances

Under conditions prevailing in most Asian developing economies, policies which increase the contribution of labour to output growth are those that curb population growth, promote and improve the skills essential for modernization and industrialization, and improve the health of the labour force.

The ability of Asian developing countries to introduce and implement these policies varies significantly. The NIEs have been more successful and consequently have been able to make more of the contribution of their labour force to output growth. Thus they introduced more of those policies which reduce the attractiveness of children as investment goods and backed this up with effective family planning programmes. The result was a slower rate of population growth and a lower youth dependency ratio. The former released funds for improving the skills and health of the labour force, the latter produced a higher savings rate.

The educational attainment of the NIEs was certainly higher than most, when measured by the percentage of the respective age-groups enrolled in primary, secondary and tertiary education. What little data there is on the social and private rates of return to education shows that the level of social sub-optimality in each of these levels of educational spending in the NIEs is no worse than it is elsewhere. On the other hand, they are well ahead in the supply of vocational, technical and scientific skills at all levels. There is some evidence to suggest that the quality of the education and training provided by the NIEs is superior to that provided by other Asian developing countries. The result is a more highly educated labour force, equipped with the right type and quality of skills for long-term economic growth.

The NIEs have also been more successful in introducing policies which improve the health of their labour force. Thus their development processes have produced more equity, with females benefiting from the greater educational opportunities. In their early years of development they concentrated on the provision of basic public health and clinical services.

In summary, the NIEs have introduced more of the policies that produce an appropriately sized, skilled and healthy labour force. This has enabled their labour force to contribute more effectively to output growth. Within the production function analytical framework, this contribution has come in two forms. The first is simply the increase in the number of person-hours worked, that is, the increase in the supply of the labour factor input, without any reference to its quality. The second is the increase in the productivity of the labour input, through better education, training and health. The second forms an important part of technical progress, a topic to which we now turn.

7. Economic Policies for Technical Progress

7.1 CONTRIBUTION OF TECHNICAL PROGRESS TO OUTPUT GROWTH

Production function analyses presented in Chapter 4 show that the major source of output growth in developing countries is increases in factor inputs, especially capital. The contribution of technical progress is relatively small. These findings contrast sharply with those obtained for developed countries where technical progress is much more important, which shows that in more mature economies output growth comes largely from the growing efficiency in the use of inputs rather than from their accumulation. Within the developing world, the results for the more developed economies conform more to the pattern in the developed world. Clearly technical progress assumes more importance with economic growth.

Interpreted in this way, technical progress refers to all the things, except increasing returns to scale, which increase the productivity of the factors of production and lead to a rise in 'total' productivity. It thus means more than improvements in the technology of producing goods and services, because improvements in the design, sophistication and performance in plant and equipment, which lead to higher capital productivity, are only a part of it. It also has a different meaning to technical progress used in the narrow sense of a change in the character of the technical improvement, which can be labour-saving, capital-saving or neutral.

For technical progress defined in this broad sense to contribute more to output growth, there must be increases in the productivity of labour and capital and greater economic efficiency in combining these two factors. In production function analysis, this greater contribution to output growth can be measured in two ways. First, when improvements in the quality of labour and in the technology used are not taken care of in the measurement of the two factors, it is captured by the increase in the size of the residual factor. Second, when such improvements are incorporated, it is shown directly by the greater importance of labour and capital in output growth.

In this chapter we will examine the economic policies needed to increase the productivity of capital and to combine the use of capital and labour more efficiently. This will be followed by an analysis of the ability of Asian developing counties to introduce these policies. The policies needed to increase labour productivity and the ability of Asian countries to introduce these will not be analysed because this has already been done in the last chapter.

7.2 ECONOMIC POLICIES FOR INCREASING CAPITAL PRODUCTIVITY

There are two ways of increasing the productivity of capital. By far the more important is the use of more efficient technology, in the sense of obtaining more output with the same volume of inputs or the same output with fewer inputs. This new technology is most likely to be labour-saving because most of the world's scientific and technological research takes place in developed countries where there is constant pressure to find labour-saving devices. The second is to increase the level of capital utilization.

7.2.1 Use of improved technology

The use of improved technology is only possible when there is research and invention to produce the new knowledge, and development and innovation to apply the new knowledge for production. These two categories of activities must follow one another because success in producing new knowledge does not lead anywhere unless it is taken to the commercialization stage.

Improved technology can be brought into the country through direct foreign investment. In this case, the economic policies needed are those which attract direct foreign investment. These have been identified in Section 5.3 of Chapter 5 as policies which promote economic growth. The provision of fiscal incentives has only a secondary effect.

In the absence of imported technology and personnel, technological progress in a developing country can come about only if research and invention, and development and innovation are carried out. There can be little doubt that sociological factors can be important in encouraging such activities. The role of social values in economic development will be discussed in detail in the next chapter. In the meantime, it is enough to know that cultural values may well be crucial in determining how quickly the fear of the unfamiliar is conquered, a break with custom and tradition made and risks taken, so that new ideas are generated and assimilated to produce a more efficient way of doing things.

However, there can also be little doubt that other factors matter. We have seen, in Section 6.3.3 of Chapter 6, that a socially optimum level and composition of educational expenditure are needed to produce an adequate supply of research and development expertise. The cultural values of some societies may have given them a larger potential supply of inventors, innovators and risk-takers but the extent to which such values on their own can generate significant technological progress in the modern world is limited. The talent has to be nurtured by more training for its full potential to be realized.

At the same time, this entrepreneurial spirit has to be encouraged. This requires that business be provided with appropriate market incentives, access to information and markets, and low transaction costs. These conditions have to be present simultaneously for one without the other cannot produce the desired effect.

Appropriate market incentives are created by getting price signals right, so that the prices of goods and services, and capital and labour reflect their scarcity. Entrepreneurship will be encouraged under such conditions because the economic rate of return will be higher.

Table 7.1 shows the average economic rates of return (ERRs) for different categories of projects financed by the World Bank and the International Finance Corporation (IFC) over the 1968-89 period, according to the degree of price distortion. The number of projects was 1,200, divided into public agricultural, industrial and non-tradable projects and private projects.

The ERR of an investment project measures the economic contribution of the project to the country, using the methodology of Squire and van der Tak (1975). The project's true benefits and costs are estimated by using border and shadow prices. The ERR is the discount rate at which the project's net present value of the stream of benefits and costs is equal to zero. An ERR of, say, less than 5 per cent implies that each dollar of investment produces annual economic benefits to the country of less than 5 cents.

Four indices of price distortion were used. The first is trade restrictiveness. This measures the level of tariff protection and the prevalence of non-tariff barriers and divides projects into those which have high, moderate or low trade restrictiveness. The second is the foreign exchange premium, which measures the percentage deviation of the black market rate from the official exchange rate. Deviations

Table 7.1   Economic policies and average economic rates of return for projects financed by the World Bank and the IFC, 1968-89 (%)

Policy distortion index	All projects	All public projects	Public agricultural projects	Public industrial projects	Public projects in nontradable sectors	All private projects
Trade restrictiveness						
High	13.2	13.6	12.1	a	14.6	9.5
Moderate	15.0	15.4	15.4	a	16.0	10.7
Low	19.0	19.3	14.3	a	24.3	17.1
Foreign exchange premium						
High (200 or more)	8.2	7.2	3.2	a	11.5	a
Moderate (20-200)	14.4	14.9	11.9	13.7	17.2	10.3
Low (less than 20)	17.7	18.0	16.6	16.6	19.3	15.2
Real interest rate						
Negative	15.0	15.4	12.7	12.7	17.9	11.0
Positive	17.3	17.5	17.0	17.8	17.9	15.6
Fiscal deficit b						
High (8 or more)	13.4	13.7	11.7	10.3	16.6	10.7
Moderate (4-8)	14.8	15.1	12.2	21.0	16.8	12.2
Low (less than 4)	17.8	18.1	18.6	14.1	18.2	14.3

Notes: a Insufficient number of observations (less than 10) to make inferences.
b Percentage of GDP.
Source: World Bank (1991, p. 82).

exceeding 200 per cent are said to be high, those between 20 and 200 per cent moderate, and those less than 20 percent low. The third index of price distortion is the level of the real interest rate: a positive rate indicates less distortion, a negative one more. The fourth index is the size of the government's budget deficit. A deficit of 8 per cent or more of the GDP is considered to show high distortion, one of between 4 and 8 per cent moderate distortion, and one of less than 4 per cent low distortion.

For all projects taken together, the less distorted the market the higher the ERR, regardless of the measure of price distortion. This relationship also applies within each category of projects, with the exception of public industrial projects when the index used is the size of the fiscal deficit. For such projects the highest ERR was recorded by the group with the moderate level of distortion (21 per cent), though the lowest ERR was still registered by the group with the highest level of distortion (10.3 per cent).

Thus there is very strong evidence that getting prices right increases the economic viability of a project very significantly. The World Bank has claimed that this impact can be stated even more precisely. It argues that when conditions are relatively undistorted, as measured by the foreign exchange premium, 'the probability that a project will be an extreme failure (that is, has a negative ERR) is less than 10 per cent; under more distorted conditions, the probability of failing altogether is nearly three times larger. Conversely, the probability of a very successful project (one with an ERR of 20 per cent or more) is twice as likely in an undistorted climate than for projects implemented in a more distorted one' (1991, p. 84).

There is also evidence that reducing the degree of distortion for a project that is already operating in a distorted climate can increase its ERR markedly. Table 7.2 shows that public and private sector projects which were initiated and completed under relatively undistorted conditions, as measured by a foreign exchange premium of less than 30 per cent, had a high average ERR of almost 18 per cent. Projects which began under distorted circumstances but completed under undistorted ones had the same ERR. Those which operated under a reverse sequencing of events, where the level of distortion became worse over time, had an ERR of only just over 13 per cent. These results show that it is best to operate without market distortion but that it is never too late to improve and that it does not pay to relax prematurely.

Table 7.2   *Average economic rates of return for World Bank and*
              IFC- financed projects under varying foreign exchange
              premiums, 1968-89 (%)

	ERR under varying premiums at project completion [b]	
Premiums before project start [a]	More than 30	Less than 30
More than 30	11.7	17.8
Less than 30	13.2	17.8

Notes: [a] Refers to the year of project appraisal, which is a year before
           project is implemented.
           [b] Refers to a three-year average of the premiums at about
           project completion time.

Source: World Bank (1991, p.87).

The policy implication of these findings is clear. It is that distortions in important economic areas should be reduced because it is only then that latent entrepreneurship will flourish. However, it is also important to note another point made by the World Bank. This is that even with undistorted policies the probability of having a satisfactory project, with an ERR of 10 per cent or more, is only 70 per cent, not 100 per cent. An important reason for this is that businesses have not been allowed to respond to the undistorted prices.

Studies have shown that producers in developing countries respond rationally to the economic environment. Where the supply response is low or negligible, it is because obstacles have been placed in the way of the producers, and not because they have behaved irrationally (Lim, 1975; Askari and Cummings, 1976). The same will be true of entrepreneurial response to market signals. This will be strong only if the signals can be acted upon unhindered. This requires access to information and markets, and the presence of public institutional and infrastructural support.

Entrepreneurs need to know the most appropriate technology and management to use, if they are to benefit from having undistorted prices. For example, if the government of a labour-abundant and capital-scarce developing country were to increase the relative cost of capital by reducing the number of explicit and implicit subsidies on capital, a production technique that is more labour-intensive and in line with the country's factor endowments will be chosen only if the entrepreneurs have access to information on the choice of techniques, best practice and relative factor prices. For such access, they must possess the required skills. This is where education plays such an important role. The policies needed for creating an educational system that provides such skills have been described in Section 6.3.3 of Chapter 6 and will not be repeated here.

Access to information must be accompanied by access to credit facilities, inputs and outlets for the goods and services produced. If credit facilities are inadequate and loans possible only at exorbitant rates, if inputs are not available or only available at high costs, if market outlets are poor and goods are sold in a monopsonistic environment, then the profit margin will be low and entrepreneurial zeal dampened.

Even when these obstacles are absent, there is little incentive to introduce more efficient technology if the infrastructural facilities are poor (e.g. inadequate electricity supply) and the institutional framework weak (e.g. little protection of property rights). Both increase the cost of production, the first directly because of the complementarity of private and public investment, the second indirectly because of the more uncertain business climate. Evidence from the World Bank shows that the productivity of projects increases significantly as the share of public investment in the GDP rises, though diminishing returns set in after a while (1991, pp. 85-6). The evidence also shows that a project's economic rate of return can be halved if the institutional framework is inadequate.

The best entrepreneurial response is obtained and the use of improved technology maximized when the policies are introduced and implemented as an integrated whole. The impact of undistorted markets is weakened when access to information and markets is poor and the cost of doing business high. It is a case where the impact of implementing an integrated package is greater than the sum of the individual effects.

7.2.2 Higher capital utilization

Another method of increasing capital productivity is to increase the use of existing plant and equipment, when the level of utilization is low. If capital productivity is measured by the output–capital ratio, an increase in capital utilization, assuming the required supporting resources are available, will increase the output value without increasing the fixed cost of capital plant and equipment as this remains the same whatever the utilization level.

The available empirical evidence shows that capital utilization in manufacturing in many developing countries is low (Little, Scitovsky and Scott, 1970; Winston, 1971; Kim and Kwon, 1977; Bautista et al., 1981; Phan-Thuy et al., 1981). This is so whether the measure of capital utilization used is the McGraw-Hill index of capacity utilization, the shift measure, the electricity measure or the time-and-intensity measure (Lim, 1976). The result is surprising because developing countries are almost defined as those lacking physical capital, a corollary of which is that they make full use of the little capital stock they have. The strategy these countries adopt in their development plans certainly sets out to acquire more physical capital, especially from foreign sources. The implicit assumption is that greater output can be more easily generated by having new investment. The existing capital stock does not hold out much hope, an important reason being the already high level at which it is being utilized.

In a study on the determinants of capital utilization in manufacturing in Colombio, Israel, Malaysia and the Philippines, based on data collected at the establishment level in 1972-3, variations in the results were found from country to country and among industrial groups (Bautista et al., 1981). However, there was enough consistency for the more important determinants to be identified.

A major influence is the capital intensity of operation and the relative factor costs that determine this. Capital equipment need to be used as much as possible because interest charges have to be paid whatever the utilization level and profits can be earned only if the machinery is being used. The greater the capital intensity, the more interest charges there will be, *ceteris paribus*, and the greater the incentive to work the machinery longer. If the relative factor prices encourage more capital-intensive activities, they will contribute to a higher level of capital utilization.

The scale of operation is also an important determinant. The indivisibility of equipment and management makes it easier for larger plants to achieve higher levels of capital utilization. At the same time the greater economic and political power of large firms gives them easier access to the complementary inputs needed for increasing capital utilization.

Extra payments for nightshifts, overtime and weekend work, the so-called wage premiums, seem to have some adverse impact. The larger these premiums, the higher the labour costs and the greater the reluctance to start another shift.

Export orientation is another significant influence because it requires the efficiency which leads, among other things, to a higher level of capital utilization and because it makes possible the large-scale operation which facilitates higher levels of capital utilization.

The resulting economic policies needed to increase capital utilization are unfortunately not straightforward. The positive relationship between utilization and capital intensity suggests that policies should be introduced to increase the capital intensity of manufacturing activities, through having either more capital-intensive industries or more capital-intensive techniques of production. A combination of policies which reduces the cost of capital (e.g. accelerated depreciation allowance and exemption of capital imports from tariffs and other duties) and increases the cost of labour (e.g. minimum wage legislation and wage premiums) can produce the desired effect. However, it will also produce distorted factor prices and push production into areas where the country has little or no comparative advantage. This will reduce the ability to export and therefore the chances of producing on a large scale and, with it, the opportunity to utilize its capital longer and more intensively.

There is therefore a choice to be made. On the one hand, developing countries lack physical capital and should therefore make the most of whatever capital they have. For this to happen, policies should encourage the establishment of capital-intensive techniques of production and industries, because the higher the capital intensity of operation, the higher the level of capital utilization. The granting of investment incentives which reduce the cost of capital relative to that of labour will increase capital intensity and the level of capital utilization.

On the other hand, developing countries have abundant labour and scarce capital. The factor endowment explanation by Heckscher and Ohlin of the sources or causes of comparative advantage shows that such countries will have a comparative advantage in the production of labour-intensive goods because this allows them to produce goods whose production requires intensive use of labour, the abundant factor. The introduction of policies which encourage the establishment of capital-intensive activities will therefore not lead to production along comparative advantage lines. This reduces the chances of success in the export market and therefore of tapping into a source of demand which makes possible operation on a large scale and a higher level of capital utilization.

Increasing capital intensity will increase capital utilization and capital productivity. But it will also reduce comparative advantage, the scale of operation, capital utilization and capital productivity. However, the choice is clear because the preservation or encouragement of comparative advantage is far more important. In labour-abundant and capital-scarce developing countries this is achieved by having labour-intensive manufacturing activities, itself the result of having an undistorted environment where the relative cost of capital is not made artificially low.

This choice is supported by the fact that the use of new (superior) technology is far more important than greater use of the existing (inferior) technology in increasing capital productivity. As we have seen earlier, the use of improved technology is more likely when prices are less distorted.

7.3 ECONOMIC POLICIES FOR COMBINING FACTORS EFFICIENTLY

To achieve technical progress in the way defined, economic policies are needed not only to increase labour and capital productivity separately but also to combine the use of labour and capital more efficiently. For labour-abundant and capital-scarce developing countries, this requires having labour-intensive techniques of production whenever there is a technological choice and labour-intensive industries whenever there is no such choice.

Figure 7.1 shows why. Suppose the market prices of capital and labour reflect their scarcity or shadow prices and that the desired output level is Q. For a labour-abundant and capital-scarce developing country, the relative price line will be given by AB. Output will be at N, the point of tangency between the isoquant Q and the relative price line AB, with a labour-intensive process OL. For a capital-abundant and labour-scarce developed country with a relative price line CD, output will be at M, with a capital-intensive process OK.

In practice, labour-abundant and capital-scarce developing countries do not end up using labour-intensive techniques of production whenever this is technologically feasible. An important reason for this, already mentioned, is that the prices of labour and capital are frequently distorted and result in making capital artificially cheap relative to labour. Thus wages are raised beyond their opportunity cost level by minimum wage legislation and by government support of trade union demands. Foreign owned or controlled firms from developed countries face the added pressure of being expected to pay wages that are commensurate with those they pay in their home countries (Lim, 1977). Even if this pressure is absent, when local workers take over jobs once held by foreigners, the wages are kept at their previously high levels.

Figure 7.1   Choice of techniques

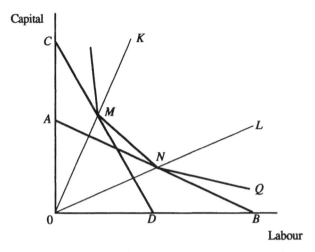

At the same time, capital is made artificially cheap by the offer of investment incentives which allow capital depreciation to be accelerated, provide tax holidays whose duration depends on the amount of capital invested, exempt the import of capital goods from duties, and place a ceiling on interest rates. Overvaluation of the domestic currency in terms of foreign exchange has the same effect.

Agell (1986) presented some estimates at the country level of the subsidy provided to capital through the granting of investment incentives in ASEAN countries. The model used assumes that firms aim to maximize their value to shareholders when planning to invest a dollar in new machinery and equipment, operate under perfect certainty and finance their investment by some exogenously determined combination of retained earnings, new issues and borrowing. The results show that the subsidy given to capital is very high for all countries. When investment is funded largely by retained earnings and the inflation rate is 5 per cent, the subsidy rate, measured by the capital subsidy as a percentage of the cost of capital without the tax incentives, is never less than 75 per cent. The highest rate was offered by the Philippines (87 per cent), the lowest by Singapore (76 per cent).

This finding is supported by a World Bank study (1988). This uses a simulation model to estimate the before-tax cashflow and the after-tax cashflow that can be expected from an investment project. The after-tax cashflow is the before-tax cashflow less any taxes paid but plus any tax credits provided by the investment incentives. The percentage difference in the rate of return generated by the before-tax cashflow and the after-tax one measures the level of capital subsidy. The larger the percentage difference, the greater will be the capital subsidy. The World Bank calls the percentage difference the marginal effective tax rate (METR). For eight of the nine East Asian developing economies analyzed, the METR was significantly lower than the statutory corporate income tax rate, when 50 per cent of the operation was financed by debt.

Thus the cost of labour has been artificially raised and that of capital artificially lowered in many developing countries. There is empirical evidence to show that capital has been substituted for labour under such conditions. A wide-ranging survey of econometric studies of factor substitution in developing countries carried out up till the middle of the 1970s concluded that 'estimates of the elasticity of substitution are, with only a few exceptions, positive, indicating ... that efficient factor substitutability is possible and that the fixed-proportions view of the world is incorrect' (White, 1978, p. 331). The studies were conducted at the total manufacturing and individual sectoral levels for single countries over time (time-series studies) and for a group of countries at a given point in time (cross-section studies). The elasticities were obtained by regressing the logarithm of value added per worker against the logarithm of the wage, with the coefficient of the latter being the desired elasticity. This indirect method of estimating the elasticity of substitution in a CES production function involving capital and labour was used because of estimation and data problems. The elasticities obtained tended to vary between 0.5 and 1.2, with the estimates obtained by cross-section studies being higher than those obtained by time-series studies.

It is possible that the causality runs the other way. The value added per worker rises with increases in capacity utilization and improvements in technology. If workers succeed in capturing some of this increase in productivity, their wages will rise. However, White (1978) believed that, on balance, the econometric evidence shows that making the relative price of capital cheaper will lead to greater capital intensity. This position is supported by the results of engineering and process-analysis studies, where technical data is used to determine the inputs needed to produce or process a given volume of products to see if there are alternative methods of producing this volume (e.g. Timmer, 1975). The elasticities were positive and often greater than one, a finding that is consistent with those gleaned from anecdotal evidence on Japan's use of capital-stretching, labour-intensive techniques in its early industrialization (e.g. Ranis, 1957).

In his survey of econometric estimates of the elasticity of substitution in manufacturing in developing countries conducted at the 2-digit level,

Morawetz (1976) found that the rankings of industries by their elasticities of substitution differ significantly from study to study, with the elasticity of substitution of an industry varying markedly between countries and in the same country over time. Thus it is not possible to describe specific industries as having high or low elasticities of substitution. However, there is no denying that factor substitution does occur, a conclusion echoed by Behrman (1982) in his study using more recent data.

A recent attempt to capture the effect of capital subsidies on capital intensity is by Lim (1992b). This is a study on Peninsular Malaysian manufacturing and differs from most other empirical studies by using data on capital intensity at the establishment level. It therefore avoids the artificial forcing of establishments from technically different production lines into the same industry group and the arbitrary use of weights in deriving variables at that level of aggregation.

The conduct of the study at the establishment level comes at a price because it is not possible to obtain reliable data on the cost of capital at that level. For example, to use the formula proposed by Agell (1986) at the establishment level requires data on establishment-specific variables, such as the depreciation rate and the percentage of the project financed by different means, which are not freely given. Other formulae used in the empirical studies require less data but the demand is still beyond the ability of most developing countries to fulfil. Take, for example, the formula proposed by Jorgenson (1967), which is given by:

$$P_k = (1/1 - t) (rp + dp - \alpha pt) \tag{7.1}$$

where P_k is the 'user' cost of capital, t the corporate tax rate, r the interest rate, p the price index of capital goods, d the real depreciation rate and α the depreciation allowance rate which is deductible before tax. It is easy enough to use this formula to estimate P_k for broad economic sectors, as done, for example, by Guisinger and Kazi (1978) for the manufacturing sector of Pakistan. It is quite another to attempt it at the industry group or establishment level because data on the rate of depreciation and on the price index of capital goods for different industry groups and establishments are not available.

Given such data constraints, a proxy measure of capital subsidy in Peninsular Malaysian manufacturing was used. Under the first investment incentive scheme, firms able to fulfil certain characteristics deemed important were granted pioneer status, which exempted them from paying the corporate income tax. As the duration of the exemption varied directly with the level of investment, the pioneer status legislation subsidized the use of capital. A dummy variable *PS* was used to capture the effect of this capital subsidy on the capital intensity of Peninsular Malaysian manufacturing. A value of 1 was given to each of the establishments which were granted pioneer status and a value of 0 to each which were not granted or did not seek pioneer status.

The analysis was carried out for 1979, the last year when data was collected on pioneer status establishments. There were 4985 manufacturing establishments and the following equation was estimated to explain the variation in capital intensity between them:

$$K/L = f (PS, F, S, I) \qquad\qquad (7.2)$$

where capital intensity was measured by K/L, in thousands of Malaysian dollars, with K the replacement value of the fixed assets and L the total number of full-time employees. If the provision of capital subsidies resulted in greater capital intensity, K/L and *PS* would be positively and significantly related.

The estimating equation has three other determinants. One is F, the degree of foreign ownership, measured by giving a value of 1(0) to each of the establishments which were (were not) foreign owned or controlled. F is expected to be positively related to K/L because foreign owned or controlled firms may have been able to obtain capital subsidies even without enjoying pioneer status, simply because of their international status.

Another determinant is S, the scale of operation, measured by the sales of the establishment in thousands of Malaysian dollars. This is expected to be positively related to capital intensity because of the lumpiness of capital which limits the scope for using capital-intensive techniques by small firms. The degree of incorporation, I, was also used as a determinant because incorporated establishments are much more likely to be granted capital subsidies and much less likely to pay below-award wages. I was measured by giving a value of 1(0) to each of the establishments which were (were not) incorporated. It is expected to be positively related to capital intensity.

The results for 1979 are given in Table 7.3. The *PS* variable came out with the expected positive sign and is statistically significant, with or without I in the analysis. The results are therefore unambiguous in showing that the provision of capital subsidies did encourage greater capital intensity in Malaysian manufacturing in 1979. The S and I variables also appeared with positive and statistically significant coefficients. As large and incorporated establishments are more likely to be granted capital subsidies, these results may be said to lend further support to the results for the *PS* variable. On the other hand, the presence of foreign ownership and control had no effect.

It was unfortunate that data on pioneer status firms was not available after 1979 so that analysis on a more recent year was not possible. In order to ensure that the results obtained for 1979 were not peculiar to that year, the same analysis was carried out for 1976 for 3995 establishments. The results, also given in Table 7.3, show quite clearly that the provision of capital subsidies had also led to greater capital intensity in manufacturing establishments in 1976. The *PS* variable came out with positive and statistically significant coefficients, as did the *F*, *S* and *I* variables. As foreign owned or controlled establishments

Table 7.3   *Linear regressions explaining capital intensity of Peninsular Malaysian manufacturing, 1976 and 1979*

Independent variables	1979		1976	
	K/L	*K/L*	*K/L*	*K/L*
Constant	9.1952 (27.1050)*	4.2156 (8.4920)*	6.4020 (17.3920)*	2.9923 (6.1880)*
PS	9.1900 (8.6500)*	6.2149 (5.8280)*	9.8665 (9.0360)*	6.7721 (6.0730)*
F	0.8834 (0.7930)	-1.1999 (-1.0850)	5.03162 (5.0250)*	3.0888 (2.9030)*
S	0.0002 (15.8390)*	0.0002 (15.3400)*	0.0003 (14.4170)*	0.0003 (13.9490)*
I		8.9580 (13.5330)*		7.6037 (10.6730)*
$\bar{R}^2$	0.0806	0.1131	0.1061	0.1307
F - ratio	146.7340	159.8640	159.029	151.1230
N	4985	4985	3995	3995

Notes: Figures in parentheses are *t* values and * denotes statistical significance at the 0.0005 level of confidence.

Source: Lim (1992b, p. 715).

are also more likely to be given capital subsidies, the appearance of *F* as a determinant adds yet more support to the hypothesis that the provision of capital subsidies encourages greater capital intensity.

The appearance of *F* as a determinant identifies another reason for the choice of capital-intensive techniques of production in labour-abundant and capital-scarce developing countries. Foreign firms from developed countries prefer using their home-based and invariably capital-intensive technology, regardless of the relative factor prices, because they are familiar with it, and foreign firms from developed countries still dominate direct foreign investment in developing countries.

The use of capital-intensive methods of production is also encouraged by the low productivity of labour, so that an abundance of labour does not necessarily lead to cheaper labour. The money wages may be lower but not the 'efficiency' wages, in the sense that the wage costs per unit of output are not lower than those in developed countries. The low level of labour productivity in developing countries also discourages labour-intensive activities because such activities require a great deal of skilled labour, whereas capital-intensive activities are 'machine-paced' and require only the presence of semi-skilled workers.

In summary, the reasons for labour-abundant and capital-scarce developing countries having capital-intensive techniques of production and industries are a distorted price system which artificially lowers the relative price of capital, the presence of large numbers of foreign firms from developed countries and high 'efficiency' wages.

The policies needed to increase the productivity of the labour force so that abundance of labour results in an abundant supply of cheap labour and low 'efficiency' wages have been described in Chapter 6 and will not be repeated here. If the presence of foreign firms from developed countries results in greater capital intensity, it does not mean that such investment should be discouraged because there are many benefits from having direct foreign investment. Other areas of action are called for. One is to improve the research and development (R and D) capacity of the host countries so that the cost to foreign firms of developing more appropriate methods of production is reduced. The development of such R and D capacity will also help the host country's own industrialization efforts. Another is to encourage greater investment from the multinational companies of developing countries. These companies are smaller and, coming from developing economies such as South Korea, Taiwan, India and Hong Kong, are more likely to either use more labour-intensive techniques of production or invest in more labour-intensive industries such as textiles, footwear, electrical and electronic goods and sporting equipment. At the moment multinational corporations from developing countries account for only a very small percentage of the total number of foreign firms operating in developing countries but they will become more important over time. The third method of encouraging foreign firms to establish more labour-intensive activities is to reduce price distortions so that capital costs do not remain artificially low and labour costs artificially high. If it is indeed true that foreign firms from rich countries tend to use more capital-intensive methods of production when this is technologically feasible, there is no point in further encouraging them in this direction by maintaining a distorted price system.

Reducing price distortions requires action on the costs of both capital and labour. As far as capital costs are concerned, this means not using investment incentives which subsidize the use of capital. An important example of such incentives is the tax holiday whose period of exemption from the prevailing corporate tax varies directly with the level of capital expenditure. Another is the accelerated depreciation allowance, where firms are allowed to write off the cost of their capital investment in a short period against their revenue. The provision of investment subsidies, where firms receive a subsidy proportional to the cost of their capital expenditure in addition to the ordinary depreciation allowance, also results in subsidizing capital but this incentive is seldom given.

In order to make the most appropriate use of a country's factor endowments, the investment incentives offered should be as neutral as possible in their effect on the use of factors of production. The most allocatively neutral incentive is the tax holiday whose duration is not tied to the level of use of any factor of production. As its value depends entirely on the ability of a firm to make a profit, it will encourage the most efficient method of production. Provided that the market prices of capital and labour are close to social prices, this will mean a method of production that makes appropriate use of the factor endowments of the country. Such a choice will be reinforced if ceilings on interest rates are not imposed and the domestic currency in terms of foreign exchange not overvalued.

On the labour side, measures which lead to artificially high wage rates should be avoided. These include the introduction of minimum wage legislation, significant premiums for night and weekend work and overtime, large severance pay, and payroll and social security taxes (Fields and Wan, 1989). Many of these have been introduced with the best of intentions to help the poor but end up benefiting mainly the small but well-organized groups of workers in the modern sector of the economy. By raising the cost of labour beyond its opportunity cost, these measures limit the ability of existing firms to employ more workers and harm the much larger group of workers they were intended to help.

The economically efficient combination of factors of production is also encouraged by the adoption of export-oriented policies. Countries have to be competitive to succeed on a sustained basis in the export market and this forces them to combine and use their resources efficiently. It is possible for a country to export with an inefficient allocation of its resources but this cannot last long. It is therefore not surprising that numerous empirical studies show that countries which are export-oriented tend to grow faster than those which are inward-looking (e.g. Balassa, 1978; Tyler, 1981; Ram, 1985, 1987; Kavoussi, 1984; Moschos, 1989; Krueger, 1978, 1980; Feder, 1983, 1985). There have been studies which challenge the theoretical and empirical validity of the positive link between exports and economic growth (e.g. Dodoro, 1991; Levine and Renelt, 1992; Sheedy, 1990; Yaghmalan, 1994), but they are far fewer in number. The export-led theory of growth still dominates and the reason is that exporting promotes and demands static and dynamic economic efficiency. In this regard, international trade also forces prices to reflect their scarcity values better, which strengthens its role in encouraging the efficient combination of factors of production.

7.4 POLICY PERFORMANCES OF ASIAN DEVELOPING COUNTRIES

7.4.1 Summary of economic policies for technical progress

As interpreted in this chapter, technical progress is seen to have occurred when the productivity of capital and labour has increased and the two factors of production combined more efficiently. Under conditions prevailing in most developing countries, the economic policies which increase labour productivity are those that curb population growth and improve the skills and health of the labour force.

Capital productivity can be increased by using improved technology. This requires getting prices right, in the sense of having factor prices which reflect their scarcity values more accurately. Investment incentives which subsidize capital expenditure, minimum wage and other legislation which push up the cost of labour, and monetary and trade policies which keep the foreign exchange rate artificially high have to be changed.

Entrepreneurs must have access to information on the market for technology, which requires that appropriate human resource development policies be in place. These must be accompanied by policies which give entrepreneurs access to credit, inputs and markets and which produce good institutional and infrastructural support.

Capital productivity can also be improved by increasing the utilization of the existing stock of capital. On the one hand, this requires economic policies which produce artificially low relative capital costs because this encourages higher capital intensity and with it higher capital utilization. On the other hand, such distortion leads to long-term inefficiency, a smaller scale of operation and ultimately lower capital utilization. As long-term efficiency is more important, economic policies must ensure that factor prices reflect their opportunity costs.

Getting prices right is also very important in ensuring that factors of production are combined efficiently because factor substitution takes place on a significant scale. Another important determinant is the adoption of export-oriented policies because international trade promotes and demands efficient combination and use of the country's factors of production.

The record of Asian developing countries in introducing economic policies which increase labour productivity was examined in the last chapter. The conclusion was that the policy performances varied markedly from country to country but with the NIEs as a group having done better in keeping their population growth under control and in improving the skills and health of their workers.

In the rest of this chapter we will examine the record of Asian developing countries in introducing the economic policies which increase capital productivity through the use of improved technology, a higher level of capital utilization and a more efficient or appropriate combination of capital and labour.

7.4.2 Policy performances in increasing capital productivity

An important policy requirement for new technology to be introduced, capital utilization increased and appropriate technology used is that distortions in the prices of capital, labour, foreign exchange and goods and services are minimized. Agarwala (1983) presents indices of distortion for foreign exchange pricing, factor pricing and product pricing for thirty-one developing countries in the 1970s. Unfortunately this study has rather limited use for our purpose because only South Korea among the NIEs has been included, though all the Southeast Asian and most of the South Asian economies were in the sample. Another problem is that the presentation of the distortion indices in three levels – low, medium and high – is far too crude for the real differences between countries to be measured meaningfully.

For what they are worth, the results for the Asian developing economies from the sample are given in Table 7.4 They show that the lowest (best) composite distortion index was recorded by Thailand (1.43). This was followed by Malaysia, the Philippines and South Korea, each with a score of 1.57. Next came Indonesia, India and Sri Lanka some distance behind at 1.86, with Pakistan and Bangladesh much further back at 2.29 and 2.57 respectively.

Table 7.4   *Distortion indices for selected Asian developing economies in the 1970s (1 = low, 2 = medium, 3 = high)*

Region	Foreign Exchange Pricing			Factor Pricing		Product Pricing		Composite Distortion Index
	EX	PM	DA	RI	RW	IN	PT	
Newly industrial-izing econ-omies:								
South Korea	1	1	3	2	1	2	1	1.57
Southeast Asia:								
Indonesia	2	2	1	2	1	2	3	1.86
Malaysia	1	1	2	2	2	1	2	1.57
Philippines	1	2	2	2	1	1	2	1.57
Thailand	1	2	1	1	1	1	3	1.43
South Asia:								
Bangladesh	1	3	2	3	3	3	3	2.57
India	1	3	2	2	2	1	2	1.86
Pakistan	2	3	2	2	3	2	2	2.29
Sri Lanka	1	2	1	2	3	2	2	1.86

Notes: EX = distortion level in exchange rate, PM = protection level for manufacturing, DA = distortion level in agricultural pricing, RI = distortion level for interest rates, RW = distortion level for wages, IN = distortion level for overall price level, and PT = distortion level for infrastructure pricing indicated by pricing of power utilities.

Source: Agarwala (1983, p. 49).

Thus at the aggregate level, South Korea is among the least distorted of the economies presented in the sample. At the sub-aggregate level, its good performance is most noticeable in the factor and product markets. As far as the overall foreign exchange pricing is concerned, it does not appear to have done any better than the other countries. This is certainly the case with the component indicator, distortion in the exchange rate (EX), where most of the countries were given the best score of one. For the component indicator, distortion in agricultural pricing (DA), South Korea had in fact come out worst and it is only for the component indicator, the protection level for manufacturing (PM), that it came out, together with Malaysia, ahead of the others.

The finding that South Korea has a poor record in keeping the level of distortion in its foreign exchange pricing under control is borne out in a study by Dollar (1992). This uses the Summers and Heston (1988) set of international prices to obtain a cross-country index of real exchange rate distortion. These prices were regressed against the factor endowments of the countries and the full-trade non-distorted price level obtained for each country, given its per capita GDP. The actual price level is then divided by this predicted price level to obtain the index of distortion. The study was carried out for the 1976-85 period and shows that the highest level of distortion was recorded by Taiwan and South Korea among the Asian developing economies.

This result could have been explained by the omission of population density as a determinant in the estimating equation. While there was no clear relationship between the relative price level and population density in the cross-country analysis, this does not mean that a positive and statistically significant relationship does not exist over time in a country. A more densely populated country is likely to face higher prices for non-tradable goods, especially houses, which would lead to a higher relative price level, and Taiwan and South Korea are densely populated economies. However, the study as it stands shows that the exchange rates of the two economies are as distorted as those in other Asian developing economies.

Against this, there is evidence to show that the protection level in manufacturing in the NIEs is lower than those in most other developing economies. Table 7.5 shows that the nominal tariff rates in the East Asian group, which is made up of two NIEs (South Korea and Taiwan) and two Southeast Asian economies (Malaysia and Thailand), are significantly lower than those in other Asian economies, except those in the oil states of West Asia. Of the other regional groupings of developing economies, only those in the Caribbean have lower protection levels.

On balance, the evidence presented here does not show that the NIEs have been any more successful than other economies in getting their prices right. The study by Agarwala (1983) covers only South Korea among the NIEs and even this does not show that the South Korean

Table 7.5   Average tariffs and para-tariffs by region, 1985 (%)

Region	Tariffs		Tariffs and para-tariffs	
	Unweighted[a]	Weighted[b]	Unweighted[a]	Weighted[b]
East Asia[c]	19	17	24	20
Other Asia	36	22	42	25
West Asian oil states	7	4	9	5
Caribbean	16	17	18	17
Central American	23	24	65	66
South America	34	38	46	51
North America	29	30	36	39
Sub-Saharan Africa	32	35	34	36
All regions	26	24	34	30

Notes: [a] Simple averages across products and economies.
  [b] Simple averages across products but across economies, averages weighted by total imports.
  [c] Malaysia, South Korea, Taiwan and Thailand, with 1981 data for Taiwan.

Sources: Erzan et al. (1989).

economy had performed better in all the three pricing areas. Thus while it just might be possible to conclude that South Korea had succeeded in introducing new technology, increasing capital utilization and using appropriate technology because it was able to avoid excessive price distortion, the same cannot be said of the other NIEs.

On the other hand, there is plenty of evidence to show that the NIEs have been more export-oriented, a factor which is instrumental in encouraging new and appropriate technology being used and capital utilization increased. It has already been shown in Chapter 5 (Table 5.9) that the NIEs' merchandise exports to GDP ratios and their shares of world exports are much higher than those of most of the other Asian developing economies. Chowdhury and Islam (1993) have also shown that the NIEs has been particularly impressive in penetrating the export markets for manufactured goods. Together they account for nearly half of the exports of manufactured products from developing countries.

8. Social and Political Values for Development

8.1 THE ANALYSIS SO FAR

In using the stepwise and backtracking framework for explaining economic growth in developing countries, we began by identifying the sources of output growth. The most important source was found to be capital accumulation, followed a long way behind by increases to labour and technical progress. It was also discovered that the relative importance of each of these sources changes with the level of economic development, with technical progress becoming more important the more de. economic policies needed for increasing domestic savings, the main determinant of capital accumulation, are those which keep the budget deficit, inflation, foreign indebtedness and the youth dependency ratio under control and the real interest rate positive. The policies needed to attract direct foreign investment, the principal form of foreign savings, are basically the same as those for increasing domestic savings. Investment incentives play only a secondary role.

The economic policies most likely to increase labour's contribution to output are those which reduce population growth in countries already densely populated, produce the appropriate level and mixture of skills and improve the health of the labour force. This is to recognize that increases in labour *per se* are not enough.

In the way in which technical progress is defined in this study, the policies required to bring it about are those which increase labour and capital productivity and the efficiency with which these two factors of production are combined. Labour productivity is increased, as we have seen already, by having an appropriately sized, skilled and healthy labour force. Capital productivity is increased by introducing improved technology and raising the level of capital utilization, with the former being far more important. These are more likely to happen with economic policies which are outward-looking, do not distort factor, foreign exchange and product prices, and provide entrepreneurs with access to information, credit, inputs and markets.

Many of the economic policies needed are not easy to implement. Take, for example, those essential for macroeconomic stability. There are strong pressures on the government of developing countries to spend. There are not enough schools and hospitals to provide basic educational and medical facilities. The roads are poor, the power supply inadequate. The list goes on. And yet the revenue needed to fund such expenditures is limited. The subsistence nature of much of the agricultural activities and the dominance of small family concerns in the urban sector make the collection of taxes difficult. Even when the operations are large and have a taxable surplus, the actual amount of taxes collected is small because of the political power of the firms and the investment incentives provided.

Under such conditions, it is easy enough for governments to run budget deficits, resort to inflationary financing, and borrow from foreign banks. Governments of rich foreign countries usually lend a helping hand by giving foreign aid. Once started on such practices, it is difficult to pull back, because financial discipline has been eroded and the beneficiaries fight to hold on to what they have got.

The economic policies needed to keep population growth under control and to produce a healthy labour force with the appropriate level and mixture of skills are also not easy to implement. Thus policies to make children less attractive as providers of current and future income are expensive, the tendency to overspend on education and on the wrong type of education strong, and the political pressure from the wealthy and well-connected urban dwellers to devote a large part of the health expenditure on expensive tertiary medical services difficult to resist.

It is also not easy to prevent price distortion. For example, most governments find it hard to resist calls to help the poor, which is why minimum wage legislation has been introduced in so many developing countries. They also find it hard to resist calls to offer capital-centred investment incentives. Most of their competitors offer incentives and it seems natural to tie these to capital expenditures because it is capital that is being sought. Unfortunately the net result of these apparently sensible policies is to artificially increase the price of labour and decrease the price of capital.

The overvaluation of the foreign exchange rate is also easy to slip into. National pride dictates that the value of the country's currency be kept high. Even if this political argument is abandoned, others can be found. One is the need to purchase capital and intermediate producer goods and an overvalued exchange rate will reduce their domestic prices. Unfortunately it will also make imported consumer goods cheaper and countries respond to this by either imposing controls on the import of such goods or operating a dual exchange rate system, with a much lower rate for consumer goods. These measures may appear sensible at the time of their introduction but promote corruption and rent-seeking very soon after. They also result in a bias towards capital-intensive activities because of the artificial cheapening of capital.

In short, most of the economic policies needed for economic growth are difficult to implement. Are there certain social values and political regimes which make the introduction of such policies easier? The NIEs have been more successful in implementing such policies and this better policy performance has been an important reason for their better development performances. Have the NIEs been blessed with social values and/or adopted political regimes which have made the implementation of the harsh economic policies easier?

8.2   ROLE OF SOCIAL VALUES

The importance of social values in economic development was recognized a long time ago. Weber (1904) saw deeply rooted attitudes inculcated by religion, and the absence of the Protestant work ethic as behind the lack of economic development in Asian countries. This theme was taken up by more recent writers. Thus Rostow (1952) and Lewis (1955) claimed that the socio-cultural values of traditional societies were preventing them from making the most of the economic and technological opportunities presented. McClelland (1961) argued that economic development must be preceded by a motivation to achieve (the n-Achievement), while Inkeles and Smith (1974) attached a great deal of importance to the role of attitudinal modernity in development. Triandis (1971, 1973) saw the diffusion of Western technology in developing countries as being critical for their development but pointed out that this required the adoption of Western attitudes and value systems.

The Weberian argument has been criticized for presenting a model of development that is too monolithic and based entirely on Western values. The case of Japan shows that to become economically successful, it is not necessary to import Western values and norms wholesale. It is possible to adapt a country's cultural values to meet the needs of imported technology and to grow rapidly as a result. From this has developed the endogenous school of thought on the role of social values in development. This sees social values as crucial but argues that these do not have to be cast off entirely in the quest for economic growth, only modified while retaining their individual character and drawing strength from their innate modes of thought and action.

Whatever the merits of the two schools of thought, it is clear that both accept that social values do impinge on economic growth. There is no shortage of case-studies on the types of social values which will affect economic growth. Thus Goh (1977), the architect of Singapore's remarkable economic growth, saw Singaporeans' grit and stamina in adversity as important for their country's economic success. Another example is the study of peasant societies in north Mexico by Foster (1962, 1965, 1967), where it was found that peasants saw their social world as a competitive one in which individual improvement could only be achieved at the expense of others. This belief discouraged them from seeking new economic opportunities for fear that this would lead to greater socio-economic inequalities and therefore conflict. It could lead to greater social harmony but also slower economic progress.

A third example is the series of studies on the impact of the religious fiesta system on capital accumulation (Nash, 1958; Wolf, 1955; Cancian, 1967). The system refers to the set of religious offices organized hierarchically and occupied on a rotating basis by men of communities in Central America and South America. Holders of these offices spend large sums of money sponsoring religious celebrations of the saints of the Catholic Church. It can be argued that the fiesta system is inimical to economic growth as it encourages economic surplus to be converted into social positions and not productive investment. But it is possible that the system legitimizes wealth differences and encourages social stratification, thereby providing the conditions for channelling economic surpluses into productive investment.

There are also many studies on the importance of management styles and work attitudes based on Confucian values to the economic success of the NIEs. Some of these have already been noted in Chapter 2. They show that there can be little doubt that the social values of hard work, diligence, loyalty and respect for education help to promote economic growth. Take, for example, the traits of hard work and diligence. These increase the tendency and the capacity of the private and public sectors to save, thereby lowering excess demand and inflationary pressures. The need to borrow from overseas sources will also be reduced. Thus three reasons for low domestic and foreign savings – a large budget deficit, a high rate of inflation and a high level of foreign indebtedness – will become less important and the level of such savings will be increased accordingly.

Loyalty raises labour productivity because it increases workers' commitment to the firm, reduces absenteeism and encourages further training. When this loyalty is reciprocated by management acting with high moral standards, then this commitment is reinforced.

The willingness to undergo further training, whether in-house or formal, is strengthened by the reverence for education. A higher level of education produces a more informed labour force which also understands better the advantages of having slower population growth. The high youth dependency ratio will be reduced and the significance of another reason for low domestic savings diminished. A more highly educated labour force will also understand better the need to spend on health and the long-term benefits that this will have on economic growth.

These characteristics are important elements of the Confucian value system, each of which has an important individual impact on the determinants of output growth. They also interact with each other to produce a collective impact. Thus a strong government and a meritocratic bureaucracy are generated to withstand sectional lobbying pressures. Team spirit and mutual respect are produced which enable or encourage government and business to work together to produce coherent economic policies for the greater good of the country. These form the basis of the concept of Japan Incorporated, seen to be largely responsible for that country's spectacular economic performance.

Cultural values which do not frown upon a break with tradition and risk-taking and which do not engender fear of the unfamiliar are more likely to produce the entrepreneurial spirit important for the introduction of improved technology. The 'process of creative destruction', seen by Schumpeter (1939, 1943) as the source of economic progress, is only possible with decision-makers who do not believe that the world is run by demonic and animistic forces and who do not fear coping with psychological tension and anxiety. Those who do cannot succeed because they resist and oppose change and refuse to adapt to modern conditions and techniques. Such people cannot be Schumpeterian agents of change.

8.3 ROLE OF POLITICAL REGIMES

It has often been argued that the introduction of correct but harsh economic policies is only possible under an authoritarian regime. The view was particularly strong in the 1960s and the early 1970s when it was widely held that strong central planning under a communist or authoritarian regime was the way to go, the way to achieve the Great Ascent (Heilbroner, 1963). In a popular introductory textbook on economic development, Bhagwati (1966) argued that development was not possible unless government had the capacity to implement policies and in this respect socialist countries with their totalitarian structures were less likely than democratic governments to cave in to opposition.

With the demise of the socialist economies, the debate moved on to the type of non-socialist governments that would manage more effectively programmes to deal with persistent balance-of-payments deficits. In this debate on the politics of economic stabilization or adjustment, the conventional wisdom is also that authoritarian regimes have an edge. Their leaders do not have to depend on popular support to survive and can therefore push through economic reforms which hurt privileged groups and the general public alike. This contrasts sharply with the position faced by democratically elected leaders, who face strong pressure to postpone taking corrective action and are tempted to give in, if this inaction leads to future economic hardship which can be blamed on external factors. In democracies distributional coalitions flourish (Olson, 1982). Only strong states can rein them in.

Proponents of the authoritarian approach to economic development also argue that in most developing countries people believe that a firm hand is needed to manage the economy and that a concentration of power results in greater autonomy for the technocrats and therefore greater coherence in the implementation programme.

Opponents of the authoritarian approach admit that the existence of a free press and open debate will make decision-making a more time-consuming and tedious process. However, the greater political legitimacy and popular support will make it easier for the government to appeal successfully for sacrifices to be made. It will not necessarily be all talk and no action, any more than having an authoritarian regime will automatically produce enlightened despots, who do not use their unbridled political power to build monuments to themselves and lay waste their countries. At the same time, democracy is better able to expose corruption and to provide the information needed for social and economic progress. It is often not realized that the more open the system, the more reliable and extensive the data collected.

There are very few empirical studies on the impact of the political regime adopted on the country's overall economic performance. An early one is the study by Dick (1974) on fifty nine developing countries over the 1959-68 period. Some of these countries had authoritarian governments, defined as those where one political party maintains control through force and/or propaganda or where there is no political party, with control under one or more persons, and elections, when held, are meaningless. Some countries had semi-competitive governments, where there is either one major and several minor political parties, with the major party winning all elections, or one political party which holds the occasional election to legitimize its rule. Some countries had competitive governments, where two or more political parties compete for votes at free and regular elections.

The results suggest that countries with authoritarian regimes had slower rates of economic growth than countries with more competitive political systems. At the very least, they show that there is no obvious choice between authoritarianism and democracy as the preferred approach to economic growth, with the choice depending on the circumstances prevailing in each country.

There are many more empirical studies on the impact of the political regime adopted on a country's ability to push through structural or stabilization programmes. Some strongly support the conventional wisdom that countries with authoritarian regimes have been more successful with these programmes. Take, for example, the study by Skidmore (1977) on Argentina, Brazil and Mexico in the 1950s and 1960s. During periods when competitive political forces were operating it was very difficult to reduce inflation once it had exceeded 20 per cent and the governments had to pay a very high political price for their efforts. All successful stabilization programmes were carried out by authoritarian or one-party governments and even then such governments had to have a high degree of internal consensus. The more recent study by Kaufman (1986) on the same three countries also concluded that an authoritarian regime was needed to reduce instability in prices and the exchange rate and to get the economy going again.

It would be difficult to generalize from the studies on Argentina, Brazil and Mexico and conclude that developing countries as a whole must adopt authoritarian regimes if they want to implement stabilization programmes effectively. Neither the economic structures of the three countries nor their ability to bargain with international creditors are typical of what can be expected of developing countries. Moreover, over the period of the analysis, the three countries had experienced very little democratic rule.

Studies which use larger samples of countries came to quite different conclusions. In a study of programmes under the International Monetary Fund's Extended Fund Facility (IMF-EFF) in a large number of developing countries, Haggard concluded that the 'conventional wisdom that an "elective affinity" exists between authoritarianism and IMF stabilization programmes is oversimplified. Authoritarian policies, both dominated by narrow clientelistic elites and those depending on broader systems of state patronage for their legitimacy, present daunting barriers to economic adjustment' (1986, p. 181). The ability of a country to pursue adjustment programmes successfully depends less on the political regime adopted than on the availability of non-IMF resources, the ideological orientation of bureaucratic elites and the strength of administrative structures.

Countries which have access to unexpected other sources of finance (e.g increased foreign aid and export earnings) tend to be less inclined or successful in implementing structural adjustment programmes because they can put off making the harsh economic decisions. A good example is Kenya in the middle of the 1970s when the dramatic rise in price of coffee led to the IMF-EFF programme being basically neglected for a couple of years. Another is Egypt in the late 1970s when the signing of the Camp David accord led to increased American aid and to a less than fulsome commitment to structural change.

If the ideology of the bureaucratic elite is against the market-oriented reforms associated with the IMF, then it is less likely that adjustment programmes will succeed, whatever the political regime adopted. For example, in periods in Mexico, India and Jamaica where structuralist explanations of poverty held sway with important sections of the economic bureaucratic, academic and intellectual communities, it would have been hard for IMF adjustment programmes to be implemented with enthusiasm.

Then there is the inability of administrative systems and personnel to implement the complex policies needed for structural adjustment programmes. This problem is worsened by the fact that administrative systems further down the line may not cooperate because they resent the central government or have fallen prey to local lobbying interest-groups.

In a study of five non-Latin American countries, Nelson (1984) also found that the type of political regime in place was less important than other factors in pushing through stabilization programmes. Important among these are the prevalence of patron-client relationships and the inability of mechanisms to keep government spending under control.

Perhaps the most detailed and convincing case against the conventional wisdom that authoritarianism is a necessary condition for economic stabilization has been put forward by Remmer (1986). The study looked at the implementation of IMF standby programmes over the 1954-84 period only in those Latin American countries which had attempted to push through at least one programme during each of their democratic and authoritarian periods. Thus the study excluded those countries which did not have any period of liberal democratic rule (e.g. Mexico, Paraguay, Cuba, Panama, Nicaragua, El Salvador, Guatemala and Haiti) and those which had implemented IMF programmes under only one type of regime (e.g. Dominican Republic, Costa Rica and Venezuela).

Remmer found that countries with democratic regimes were no more reluctant to initiate IMF standby programmes than their authoritarian counterparts. Nor were they more likely to break down under the pressure of implementing such programmes. Moreover, in testing the ability of each regime to control fiscal deficits, real government expenditures and rates of credit expansion, it was found that democratic regimes performed better than authoritarian ones. The same results were obtained for keeping real government expenditures under control when the performances of democratic and authoritarian regimes were examined on a country-by-country basis. As for the other two measures of economic performance, no significant difference could be discerned in the performances of the two political regimes. These results led Remmer to conclude that 'the implementation of stabilization programs is no more rigorous under authoritarianism than democracy. Indeed, to the limited extent that regime differences are significant, the edge appears to be with democracies' (1986, p.20).

On balance, there is little empirical evidence to show that authoritarian systems have been more successful at managing economic reforms. Countries which have authoritarian regimes on a continuous basis do no better than those with democratic regimes on a continuous basis in reducing budget deficits or slowing down monetary expansion. Only those countries which have embraced democracy recently do worse (Haggard and Kaufman, 1992). When political systems are further differentiated by the extent to which they are politically polarized, authoritarian systems are more successful in controlling rapid inflation in polarized environments but in non-polarized situations, democratic systems do better (Remmer, 1986).

The results are just as ambiguous when the impact of political rights and civil liberties on income growth is examined. Some studies (e.g. Grier and Tullock, 1989; World Bank, 1991) found no relationship. Others (e.g. Dasgupta, 1990; Scully, 1988) found the impact to be positive and real.

In summary, while there are strong intuitive reasons for believing that authoritarian regimes are better equipped to push through the policies needed for greater economic growth, there is no overwhelming empirical support for this belief. As far as the NIEs are concerned, three of them can be said to have authoritarian regimes but it would be difficult to argue that the political regime adopted has been responsible for their economic success. After all, there are many more countries with authoritarian regimes which have done dismally on the economic front. Ultimately, what matters is what political leaders do with the power they have, not the power itself. Clearly more careful empirical work has to be carried out before the debate can be settled one way or the other.

PART III

The Next Stage

9. A New Hypothesis?

9.1 DEVELOPMENT PERFORMANCES REVISITED

This book began by examining the development performances of developing countries since 1950. These performances were found to have generally matched or surpassed those of developed countries, bettered those achieved by developed and developing countries alike in the period prior to 1950, and exceeded the expectations of most observers.

It was also found that the development performances differed very significantly between countries or groups of countries. The developing economies in the northeastern part of Asia, popularly known as the newly industrializing economies, did far better, whether the indicator used is the rate of growth of the real output per head, the percentage of the population living above the poverty line or the distribution of income, or all three taken together.

The analysis also found that significant pockets of abject poverty still exist in many countries. The problem is most acute in South Asia and Sub-Saharan Africa, where in the most extreme cases people live under conditions which are worse than those that existed during the colonial era.

9.2 POPULAR DEVELOPMENT EXPLANATIONS REVISITED

The analysis then attempted to find the reasons for such diverse development performances. In order to make the task manageable, it was limited to four popular explanations of economic growth and to their ability to explain the different growth performances of the developing economies of Asia. The first argues that the newly industrializing economies have done well because they lack natural resources and so do not have to put up with the so-called Dutch disease. This is a rather ingenious hypothesis but there is not much to standing the Dutch disease on its head. Resource-poor countries have fewer policy options than resource-rich ones, unless it be to argue that having less choice is better.

If nature or rather its less than generous gifts cannot explain things, then politics might – so runs the second popular explanation. South Korea and Taiwan were lucky enough to receive massive foreign aid which must have helped to increase investment and economic growth. There is also not much to this hypothesis because what matters ultimately is what is done with the aid, not the amount of it.

The third explanation holds that the newly industrializing economies have done well because their common Confucian heritage gives them the social values essential for generating rapid economic growth. Again this hypothesis is not particularly convincing. It is based on a potted history of the role of Confucian values in the economic history of China, South Korea and Taiwan and ignores the possibility that the so-called Confucian values can be determined endogenously.

The explanation pushed by the World Bank, that economic development is enhanced importantly by the pursuit of market-friendly and internationally competitive economic policies, is theoretically plausible. However, this approach will work only if governments are strong enough to keep narrow sectional interests at bay. Even then, there is no guarantee that such political autonomy will always lead to efficient economic policies being pursued. The newly industrializing economies have strong governments but they have not always operated at arms length in economic matters.

The conclusion reached at the end of this search for an all-embracing explanation of economic growth and therefore of differences in growth performances is that none of the explanations so far is totally satisfactory. The market-friendly and internationally competitive hypothesis appears to be the most plausible but, like the other three, it still leaves too many important questions unanswered. The examination was limited to only four hypotheses but a wider search would probably have produced the same frustrating conclusion. There is enough in each of them to warrant retaining them in the search for the holy grail of development studies. But there is not enough in any of them to warrant one being placed head and shoulders above the rest and be generally accepted as *the* explanation of economic growth in developing countries. The market-friendly hypothesis may be ahead of the rest but not markedly so.

9.3 THE NEW ANALYTICAL FRAMEWORK REVISITED

It was against this background that the stepwise and backtracking framework of analysing the causes of economic growth was introduced. It was felt that the use of this new framework would enable the existing hypotheses to be presented in their best light and their strengths used more effectively to build new and more powerful hypotheses to explain economic growth.

The new analytical framework proposes a four-step approach to identifying the causes of economic growth. The first is to use production function analysis to identify the sources of output growth. The second is to identify the factors behind the sources of output growth. The third is to identify the economic policies needed to produce the necessary factors and to ensure their efficient use. The fourth is to identify the social and political systems needed to introduce the necessary economic policies.

This framework thus backtracks logically in a stepwise manner the growth sequence: from output growth to input requirements, the economic policies needed to increase input supply and the efficiency of input use, and the social and political values required for introducing the economic policies. It begins by identifying the sources of economic growth and ends by identifying the causes of it.

There must be consistency in the results across countries for the relationship specified in each of the four steps, if the framework is to be of use. The existing empirical studies show that there is such consistency in the relationships specified in the first three steps. For the first, production function studies show without fail that the most important source of output growth in developing countries is capital accumulation, followed a long way behind by increases to labour and technical progress. For the second, the major factor behind capital accumulation is domestic savings. The factors which result in the labour input making a positive contribution to output growth are a population growth rate that is under control and an appropriately skilled and healthy labour force. For technical progress, the major factors are the use of new technology and the efficient combination of capital and labour.

For the third step, there is general agreement on the economic policies needed to increase the rate of capital accumulation, curb population growth, produce a healthy and appropriately educated labour force, and encourage technical progress.

For the fourth step, there is widespread acceptance that the presence of social systems which value hard work, diligence, loyalty and education makes the introduction of the required and often unpleasant economic policies easier. Also, cultural values which do not encourage change and risk-taking tend to inhibit entrepreneurship. However, there is less agreement on the type of political regime required. The theoretical cases for authoritarian and democratic regimes are equally strong and the empirical evidence is mixed.

On balance, there is enough consistency in the results across countries on the sources of output growth, the factors behind these sources, the economic policies needed to produce these factors and to use them efficiently, and the social values conducive to the introduction of these policies, to make the stepwise and backtracking framework useful for identifying the causes of economic growth.

Its value lies in showing that while the existing explanations of economic growth on their own cannot provide all the answers, each has something useful to offer. It does this by enabling them to be presented at the appropriate level, where their strengths are shown to good effect. For example, the explanation which sees the absence of natural resources as the reason for the economic success of the newly industrializing economies may appear less silly when presented at Step 3 of the new framework. Having an abundance of riches can be a problem unless firm macroeconomic policies are pursued This may be beyond the ability of a democratically elected government to handle and the firm hand of an authoritarian regime may be needed, a possibility that is raised at Step 4 of the framework.

The hypothesis which sees the availability of foreign aid as an important cause of economic growth also makes more sense when presented in the new framework. Foreign aid increases the level of foreign savings and therefore capital accumulation, provided it is used as such. Step 2 makes this clear, while Step 3 highlights the economic conditions needed to make this happen and Step 4 the non-economic values required to introduce the economic policies.

The importance of the economic policies behind the market-friendly hypothesis is shown clearly in Step 3, while the type of social and political systems most likely to sustain the implementation of these policies is brought out in Step 4.

The stepwise and backtracking framework is also very effective in restoring the value of cultural explanations of economic growth. These are often derided when presented as all-embracing hypotheses. They raise expectations only to disappoint because they do not specify the economic policies needed. However, when presented at Step 4 they come into their own and show that development requires more than the introduction of economic policies. These are necessary but not sufficient on their own to bring about development. Cultural values are also important.

The new framework also allows political explanations of economic growth to be assessed more effectively. As all-embracing hypotheses they can, like cultural ones, be criticized for explaining everything and nothing at the same time. When introduced at Step 4, their value becomes more evident, though research on the role of political systems *per se* in economic development has produced rather mixed results.

In enabling these and other all-embracing explanations to be presented at the appropriate level, the new framework enables their contributions to form the basis of hopefully more powerful and successful hypotheses. It is not a new hypothesis itself but can provide a useful framework in the search for one.

9.4 THE NEXT STAGE

The next stage is to develop a hypothesis of economic growth which builds on the strengths of the existing ones. The literature on development economics and economic history suggests that this hypothesis may have to be multi-disciplinary and not limited to a small number of variables. The stepwise and backtracking analytical framework suggests that a multi-staged approach may be necessary.

The purpose of this book is not to provide a more powerful explanation of economic growth, only a new analytical framework to assist with the development of such an explanation. It may well be that this search will not go very far, if Jones (1981) is correct in the following conclusion, reached after an analysis of the factors behind long-term economic growth in Europe:

> In the present state of knowledge we must resist the notion that any simple model will account for the whole developmental process. We cannot model it, say, as a production function which makes modernization, eighteenth-century industrialization, or the sustained rise of real incomes, the output of a handful of stylized inputs, while hoping to retain any sense of the historical complexity involved. Too many parameters shift and dissolve; very long-term economic change was much more than the usual conception of an economic process. The model implied by the results of this enquiry resembles a giant combination lock. There is no one key. The parts fit together well enough to work, but perhaps not even in a unique combination: it is difficult to gauge retrospectively what the tolerances of the system may have been. (1981, p.238)

This theme was taken up by Riedel in his search for the reasons for the economic success of East Asian economies, when he concluded that:

> Perhaps consensus has eluded economists and other social scientists because they usually insist on finding the 'key' to things like growth and development, when in fact history suggests that human progress works more like a great combination lock for which there is no key. A number of tumblers must fall into place to unlock economic growth, but not always the same number nor always in the same combination. (1988, pp. 2-3)

Certainly this study's assessment of a number of popular explanations of economic growth shows that while each has something useful to say none on its own can reveal the whole picture. On their own, explanations which champion the cause of one factor or more than one factor within a single discipline touch but one aspect of a dynamic multi-faceted process. They are fine as far as they go but do not venture far enough in producing a consistent set of policies for sustained economic growth.

From what we know, it may well be that there is no single key to open the giant combination lock which guards the secrets of economic growth. However, the use of the stepwise and backtracking framework for identifying the causes of economic growth can help in the more systematic extension of this knowledge and in the identification of the required tumblers and the way they should fall to explain economic growth. The new framework will hopefully enable the more plausible of the existing explanations to be presented as benchmark pieces in the construction of a more powerful hypothesis to explain economic growth. Some of the clues for solving the jigsaw puzzle are already present. What is needed is a more efficient method of placing them in their slots and of looking for other pieces to fill in the remaining places. The stepwise and backtracking analytical framework is offered as a possible way of conducting the search.

Bibliography

Abramovitz, M. (1956), 'Resource and output trends in the United States since 1870', *American Economic Review, Papers and Proceedings*, **46**, 11-4.

Agarwala, A.N. and Singh, S.P. (eds) (1963), *The Economics of Underdevelopment*, New York: Oxford University Press.

Agarwala, R. (1983), 'Price distortions and growth in developing countries', *World Bank Staff Working Papers*, no. 575, World Bank: Washington D.C.

Agell, J.N. (1986), 'Subsidy to capital through tax incentives', in P. Shome (ed), *Fiscal Issues in Southeast Asia*, Singapore: Oxford University Press.

Amjad, R. (1987), 'Human resource development: the Asian experience in employment and manpower planning – an overview', in R. Amjad (ed), *Human Resource Planning: the Asian Experience*, New Delhi: International Labour Organization Asian Employment Programme.

Ando, A. and Modigliani, F. (1963), 'The life-cycle hypothesis of saving: aggregate implications and tests', *American Economic Review*, **53**, 55-84.

Arndt, H.W. (1987), *Economic Development: History of an Idea*, Chicago: University of Chicago Press.

Arndt, H.W. (1989), *Industrial Policy in East Asia*, Vienna: UNIDO.

Arndt, H.W. (1993), *50 Years of Development Studies*, Canberra: National Centre for Development Studies.

Asian Development Bank (1989), *Asian Development Outlook 1989*, Manila: Asian Development Bank.

Asian Development Bank (1990), *Asian Development Outlook 1990*, Manila: Asian Development Bank.

Asian Development Bank (1991), *Asian Development Outlook 1991*, Manila: Asian Development Bank.

Askari, H. and Cummings, J. (1976), *Agricultural Supply Response: A Survey of the Econometric Evidence*, New York: Praeger.

Axelrod, R. (1984), *The Evolution of Cooperation*, New York: Basic Books.

Balassa, B. (1978), 'Exports and economic growth: further evidence', *Journal of Development Economics*, **5**, 181-9.

Baldwin, R. and Weisbrod, B. (1974), 'Disease and labour productivity', *Economic Development and Cultural Change*, **22**, 414-35.

Bardhan, P. (1990), 'Symposium on the state and economic development', *Journal of Economic Perspectives*, **4**, 3-8.

Bauer, P.T. (1976), *Dissent and Development*, London: Weidenfeld and Nicolson.

Bauer, P.T. and Yamey, B.S. (1957), *The Economics of Underdeveloped Countries*, Cambridge: Cambridge University Press.

Baum, R. (1982), 'Science and culture in contemporary China: the roots of retarded modernization', *Asian Survey*, **1**, 1166-86.

Bautista, R., Hughes, H., Lim, D., Morawetz, D. and Thoumi, F.E. (1981), *Capital Utilization in Manufacturing*, New York: Oxford University Press.

Becker, G. (1981), *A Treatise on the Family*, Cambridge, Mass.: Harvard University Press.

Behrman, J.R. (1982), 'Country and sectorial variations in manufacturing elasticities of substitution between capital and labour', in A. Krueger (ed), *Trade and Employment in Developing Countries*, Chicago: University of Chicago Press.

Behrman, J.R. and Birdsall, N. (1983), 'The quality of schooling: quality alone is misleading', *American Economic Review*, **73**, 928-46.

Behrman, J.R. and Deolalikar, A.B. (1988), 'Health and nutrition', in H. Chenery and T.N. Srinivasan (eds), *Handbook of Development Economics ,Volume 1*, Amsterdam: North Holland.

Behrman, J.R. and Schneider, R. (1992), 'An international perspective on schooling investment in the last quarter century in some fast-growing Eastern and Southwestern countries', Background paper for World Bank, *The East Asian Miracle*, New York: Oxford University Press.

Benoit, E. (1978), 'Growth and defense in developing countries', *Economic Development and Cultural Change*, **26**, 271-80.

Berger, P.L. (1988), 'An East Asian model', in P.L. Berger and H.M. Hsiao (eds), *In Search of an East Asian Development Model*, New Brunswick: Transaction Books.

Bhagwati, J. (1966), *The Economics of Underdeveloped Countries*, London: Weidenfeld and Nicolson.

Bird, R.M. (1978), 'Assessing tax performance in developing countries: a critical review of the literature', in J.F.J. Toye (ed), *Taxation and Economic Development*, London: Frank Cass.

Bird, R.M. and Oldman, O. (eds) (1975), *Readings on Taxation in Developing Countries*, Baltimore: Johns Hopkins University Press.

Birdsall, N. (1988), 'Economic approaches to population growth', in H. Chenery and T.N. Srinivasan (eds), *Handbook of Development Economics, Volume 1*, Amsterdam: North Holland.

Black, D. (1958), *The Theory of Committees and Elections*, Cambridge: Cambridge University Press.

Bolnick, B.R. (1978), 'Tax effort in developing countries: what do regression measures really measure?' in J.F.J. Toye (ed), *Taxation and Economic Development*, London: Frank Cass.

Boserup, E. (1965), *The Conditions of Agricultural Growth*, London: Allen and Unwin.

Boskin, M.J. and Lau, L.J. (1990), *Post-War Economic Growth in the Group-of-Five Countries: A New Analysis*, Centre for Economic Policy Research Publication 217, Stanford: Stanford University, Department of Economics.

Bowles, P. (1987), 'Foreign aid and domestic savings in less developed countries: some tests for causality', *World Development*, 15, 789-96.

Bowman, M. (1964), 'Schultz, Denison and the contribution of education to national income growth', *Journal of Political Economy*, 72, 450-64.

Brown, G. (1971), 'The impact of Korea's 1965 interest rate reform on savings, investment and the balance of payments', a paper presented at the CENTO Symposium on Central Banking Monetary Policy and Economic Development, Izmir, Egypt.

Bruton, H. (1965), *Principles of Development Economics*, Englewood Cliffs, N.J.: Prentice-Hall, Inc.

Bruton, H. (1967), 'Productivity growth in Latin America', *American Economic Review*, 57, 1103-4.

Cancian, F. (1967), *Economics and Prestige in a Maya Community: The Religious Cargo System of Zinacantan*, Stanford: Stanford University Press.

Cao, D.T. and Lim, D. (1984), 'Papua New Guinea's tax performance, 1965-73', *World Development*, 12, 451-9.

Cassen, R.H. (1976), 'Population and development: a survey', *World Development*, 4, 785-830.

Chandavarkar, A. (1971), 'Some aspects of interest rate policies in less developed economies: the experience of selected Asian countries', *IMF Staff Papers*, 18, 48-112.

Chandavarkar, A. (1993), 'Saving behaviour in the Asian-Pacific region', *Asian-Pacific Economic Literature*, 7, 9-27.

Chelliah, R.J. (1971), 'Trends in taxation in developing countries', *IMF Staff Papers*, 18, 254-331.

Chelliah, R.J., Baas, H.J. and Kelly, M.R. (1975), 'Tax ratios and tax effort in developing countries, 1969-71', *IMF Staff Papers*, 22, 189-205.

Chen, E.K.Y. (1977), 'Domestic saving and capital inflow in some Asian countries: a time-series study', *Asian Survey*, 17, 679-87.

Chenery, H. and Eckstein, P. (1970), 'Development alternatives for Latin America', *Journal of Political Economy*, 78, 966-1006.

Chenery, H. and Strout, A. (1966), 'Foreign assistance and economic development', *American Economic Review*, 18, 139-65.

Chowdhury, A. and Islam, I. (1993), *The Newly Industralising Economies of East Asia*, London: Routledge.

Chung, W. (1970), 'A study of economic growth in postwar Japan for the period 1952-67: an application of total productivity analysis', mimeo., Denison University.

Clark, C. (1969), 'The "population explosion" myth', *Bulletin of the Institute of Development Studies*, 1, 19-20.

Clark, C. (1970), 'The economics of population growth and control: a comment', *Review of Social Economy*, 28, 449-66.

Coale, A.J. and Hoover, E.M. (1958), *Population Growth and Economic Development in Low-Income Countries: A Case Study of India's Prospects*, Princeton, N.J.: Princeton University Press.

Cobb, C. and Douglas, P. (1928), 'A theory of production', *American Economic Review*, 18, Supplement, 139-65.

Cochrane, S.H. (1975), 'Children as by-products, investment goods and consumer goods: a review of some microeconomic models of fertility', *Population Studies*, 29, 373-90.

Corbo, V. and Schmidt-Hebbel, C. (1991), 'Public policy and savings in developing countries', *Journal of Development Economics*, 36, 89-115.

Corden, W.M. (1984), 'Booming sector and Dutch disease economics: a survey', *Oxford Economic Papers*, 36, 825-48.

Correa, H. (1970), 'Sources of economic growth in Latin America', *Southern Economic Journal*, 37, 17-31.

Dasgupta, P. (1990), 'Well-being and the extent of its realization in developing countries', *Economic Journal*, 100, Supplement, 1-32.

Della Valle, P.A. and Oguchi, N. (1976), 'Distribution, the aggregate consumption function and the level of economic development: some cross-country results', *Journal of Political Economy*, 84, 1325-34.

Denison, E. (1962), *The Sources of Economic Growth in the US and the Alternatives before US*, New York: Committee for Economic Development, Library of Congress.

Denison, E. (1967), *Why Growth Rates Differ: Postwar Experience in Nine Western Counties*, Washington, D.C.: Brookings Institute.

Deolalikar, A.B. (1988), 'Do health and nutrition influence labor productivity in agriculture? Econometric estimates for rural south India', *Review of Economics and Statistics*, 70, 406-13.

Dick, G.W. (1974), 'Authoritarian versus nonauthoritarian approaches to economic development', *Journal of Political Economy*, 82, 817-28.

Dodoro, S. (1991), 'Comparative advantage, trade and growth: export-led growth revisited', *World Development*, 19, 1153-65.

Dollar, D. (1992), 'Outward-oriented developing economies really do grow more rapidly: evidence from 95 LDCs, 1976-1985', *Economic Development and Cultural Change*, 40, 523-44.

Domar, E. (1947), 'Expansion and employment', *American Economic Review*, 37, 34-55.

Dore, R. (1986), *Flexible Rigidities: Industrial Policy and Structural Adjustment in the Japanese Economy, 1970-80*, Stanford: Stanford University Press.

Downs, A. (1957), *An Economic Theory of Democracy*, New York: Harper and Row.

Duesenberry, J.S. (1949), *Income, Savings and the Theory of Consumer Behaviour*, Cambridge, Mass.: Harvard University Press.

Easterlin, R.A. (1967), 'The effects of population growth on the economic development of developing countries', *Annals of the American Academy of Political and Social Science*, **369**, 98-108.

Eaton, J. (1987), 'Public debt guarantees and private capital flight', *The World Bank Economic Review*, **1**, 377-95.

Ehrlich, P.R. and Ehrlich, A.H. (1990), *The Population Explosion*, New York: Simon and Schuster.

Emery, R.F. (1970), *The Financial Institutions of Southeast Asia*, New York: Praeger.

Emery, R.F. (1971), 'Interest rate policy, resource allocation and mobilization of domestic savings', a paper presented on the CENTO Symposium on Central Banking Monetary Policy and Economic Development, Izmir, Egypt.

Erzan, R., Kuwahara, K., Marchese, S. and Vossenar, R. (1989), 'The profile of protection in developing countries', *UNCTAD Review*, **1**, 29-73.

Faine, R., Annez, P. and Taylor, L. (1984), 'Defense spending, economic structure and growth: evidence among countries and over time', *Economic Development and Cultural Change*, **32**, 487-98.

Feder, G. (1983), 'On exports and economic growth', *Journal of Development Economics*, **12**, 59-74.

Feder, G. (1985), 'Growth in semi-industrial countries: a statistical analysis', in H. Chenery, S. Robinson and M. Syrquin (eds), *Industrialization and Growth: A Comparative Study*, New York: Oxford University Press.

Fields, G.S. and Wan, Jr., H. (1989), 'Wage-setting institutions and economic growth', *World Development*, **12**, 1471-83.

Foster, G. M. (1962), *Traditional Cultures: The Impact of Technological Change*, New York: Harper and Row.

Foster, G. M. (1965), 'Peasant society and the image of the limited good', *American Anthropologist*, **67**, 293-315.

Foster, G. M. (1967), *Tzintzuntzan: Mexican Peasants in a Changing World*, Boston: Little, Brown and Co.

Friedman, M. (1957), *A Theory of Consumption Function*, Princeton: Princeton University Press.

Friend, I. and Taubman, P. (1966), 'The aggregate propensity to save: some concepts and their application to international data', *Review of Economics and Statistics*, **48**, 113-23.

Fromm, G. (ed) (1971), *Tax Incentives and Capital Spending*, Amsterdam: North-Holland.

Fry, M.J. (1991), 'Domestic resource mobilization in developing Asia: four policy issues', *Asian Development Review*, 9, 15-39.

Fry, M.J. and Mason, A. (1982), 'The variable rate-of-growth effect in the life-cycle saving model: children, capital inflows, interest and growth in a new specification of the life-cycle model applied to seven Asian developing countries', *Economic Inquiry*, 20, 426-42.

Gaathon, A. (1971), *Economic Productivity in Israel*, New York: Praeger.

Gemmell, N. (1993), 'Wagner's Law and Musgrave's hypotheses', in N. Gemmell (ed), *The Growth of the Public Sector*, Aldershot: Edward Elgar.

Gersovitz, M. (1988), 'Saving and development', in H. Chenery and T.N. Srinivasan (eds), *Handbook of Development Economics, Volume 1*, Amsterdam: North-Holland.

Gillis, M., Perkins, D.H., Roemer, M. and Snodgrass, D.R. (1992), *Economics of Development*, New York: W.W. Norton and Company.

Goh, K.S. (1977), *The Practice of Economic Growth*, Singapore: Federal Publications.

Grier, K.B. and Tullock, G. (1989), 'An empirical analysis of cross-national economic growth, 1951-80', *Journal of Monetary Economics*, 24, 259-76.

Griffin, K.B. (1970), 'Foreign capital, domestic savings and economic development', *Bulletin of the Oxford Institute of Economics and Statistics*, 30, 99-112.

Griffin, K.B. and Enos, J. (1970), 'Foreign assistance: objectives and consequences', *Economic Development and Cultural Change*, 18, 313-37.

Guisinger, S.E. and Kazi, S. (1978), 'The rental cost of capital for the manufacturing sector: 1959-60 to 1970-71', *Pakistan Development Review*, 17, 385-407.

Gupta. K.L. (1970a), 'Foreign capital and domestic savings: a test of Haavelmo's hypothesis with cross-sectional data: a comment', *Review of Economics and Statistics*, 52, 214-6.

Gupta, K.L. (1970b), 'Personal saving in developing nations: further evidence', *Economic Record*, 46, 243-9.

Gupta, K.L. (1970c), 'On some determinants of rural and urban household saving behaviour', *Economic Record*, 46, 578-83.

Gupta, K.L. (1971), 'Dependency rates and savings rates: comment', *American Economic Review*, 61, 469-71.

Gupta, K.L. (1975), 'Foreign capital inflows, dependency burden and saving rates in developing countries: a simultaneous equation model', *Kyklos*, 28, 358-74.

Haavelmo, T. (1965), 'Comment on W. Leontief's "The Rates of Long-Run Economic Growth and Capital Transfers from Developed to Underdeveloped Areas"' in Pontificae Academic Scientiarum Scrips Vavia, *Study Week on the Econometric Approach to Development Planning*, Amsterdam: North-Holland.

Hagen, E.E. (1980), *The Economics of Development*, Homewood, Illinois: Richard D. Irwin, Inc.

Haggard, S. (1986), 'The politics of adjustment: lessons from the IMF's Extended Fund Facility', in M. Kahler (ed) *The Politics of International Debt*, Ithaca: Cornell University Press.

Haggard, S. and Kaufman, R.R. (1992), 'The political economy of inflation and stabilization in middle-income countries', in S. Haggard and R.R. Kaufman (eds), *The Politics of Economic Adjustment*, Princeton, N.J.: Princeton University Press.

Han, S.S. (1984), 'Of economic success and Confucianism', *Far Eastern Economic Review*, **126**, 104-6.

Harberger, A. (1981), 'In step and out of step with the world inflation: a summary history of countries, 1952-1976', in M. June Flanders and Assaf Razin (eds), *Development in an Inflationary World*, New York: Academic Press.

Harrod, R.F. (1939), 'An essay in dynamic theory', *Economic Journal*, **49**, 14-33.

Harrod, R.F. (1948), *Towards a Dynamic Economics*, London: Macmillan.

Heilbroner, R.L. (1963), *The Great Ascent*, New York: Harper and Row.

Heller, P.S. (1979), 'The underfinancing of recurrent development costs', *Finance and Development*, **16**, 38-41.

Henrekson, M. (1993), 'The Peacock-Wiseman hypothesis', in N. Gemmell (ed), *The Growth of the Public Sector*, Aldershot: Edward Elgar.

Higgins, B. (1959), *Economic Development*, London: Constable and Company.

Hill, C. (1985), 'Oliver Williamson and the M-form firm: a critical review', *Journal of Economic Issues*, **3**, 35-49.

Hill, C. (1988), 'Internal capital market controls and financial performance in multi-divisional firms', *Journal of Industrial Economics*, **37**, 72-83.

Hofheinz, R. and Calder, K.E. (1982), *The East Asia Edge*, New York: Basic Books.

Hollister, R.G. (1964), 'Economics of manpower forecasting', *International Labour Review*, **89**, 371-97.

Houthakker, H.S. (1961), 'An international comparison of personal savings', *Bulletin of International Statistical Institute*, **38**, 56-69.

Houthakker, H.S. (1965), 'On some determinants of saving in developed and underdeveloped countries', in E.A.G. Robinson (ed), *Problems in Economic Development*, New York: Macmillan and Co.

Hughes, H. (1979), 'Debt and development: the role of foreign capital in foreign growth', *World Development*', **7**, 95-112.

Immink, M. and Viteri, F. (1981), 'Energy intake and productivity of Guatemelan sugarcane cutters: an empirical test of the efficiency wages hypothesis, parts I and II', *Journal of Development Economics*, **9**, 251-87.

Inkeles, A. and Smith, D.H. (1974), *On Becoming Modern*, London: Heinemann.

Jamison, D.T. (1986), 'Child malnutrition and school performance in China', *Journal of Development Economics*, **20**, 299-309.

Johnson, C. (1982), *MITI and the Japanese Miracle: the Growth of Industrial Policy, 1925-1975*, Stanford: Stanford University Press.

Jones, E.L. (1981), *The European Miracle: Environment, Economics and Geopolitics in the History of Europe and Asia*, Cambridge: Cambridge University Press.

Jorgenson, D. (1967), 'The theory of investment behaviour', in R. Ferber (ed), *Determinants of Investment Behaviour*, New York: National Bureau of Economic Research.

Jorgenson, D. and Griliches, Z. (1967), 'The explanation of productivity change', *Review of Economic Studies*, **34**, 249-83.

Kahn, H. (1979), *World Economic Development: 1979 and Beyond*, London: Croom Helm.

Kaldor, N. (1955-6), 'Alternative theories of distribution', *Review of Economic Studies*, **23**, 94-100.

Kaufman, R.R. (1986), 'Democratic and authoritarian responses to the debt issue: Argentina, Brazil, Mexico', in M. Kahler (ed), *The Politics of International Debt*, Ithaca: Cornell University Press.

Kavoussi, R. (1984), 'Export expansion and economic growth: further empirical evidence', *Journal of Development Economics*, **14**, 241-50.

Kelley, A.C. and Williamson, J.G. (1968), 'Household saving behaviour in developing economies: the Indonesian case', *Economic Development and Cultural Change*, **16**, 385-403.

Kennedy, G. (1984), *The Military in the Third World*, New York: Scribner.

Keynes, J.M. (1936), *The General Theory of Employment, Interest and Money*, New York: Harcourt, Brace and Co.

Kim, Y.C. and Kwon, J.K. (1977), 'The utilization of capital and the growth of output in a developing economy', *Journal of Development Economics*, **4**, 265-78.

Knudsen, O. and Parnes, A. (1975), *Trade Instability and Economic Development: an Empirical Study*, Lexington, Mass.: D.C. Heath.

Knudsen, O. and Yotopoulos, P.A. (1976), 'A transitory income approach to export instability', *Food Research Institute Studies*, **15**, 91-108.

Krueger, A. (1978), *Foreign Trade Regimes and Economic Development: Liberalization Attempts and Consequences*, Cambridge: Ballinger.

Krueger, A. (1979), *The Development Role of the Foreign Sector and Aid*, Cambridge, Mass.: Harvard University Press.

Krueger, A. (1980), 'Trade policy as an input to development', *American Economic Review, Papers and Proceedings*, **70**, 288-92.

Krugman, P. (1979), 'Increasing returns, monopolistic competition and international trade', *Journal of International Economics*, **9**, 469-79.

Krugman, P. (1980), 'Scale economies, product differentiation and the pattern of trade', *American Economic Review*, **70**, 950-9.

Kuo, S.W.T. (1983), *The Taiwan Economy in Transition*, Boulder: Westview Press.

Kuznets, S. (1967), *Modern Economic Growth*, New Haven: Yale University Press.

Lampman, R. (1969), 'The sources of postwar growth in the Philippines', *Philippine Economic Journal*, **12**, 170-88.

Landau, D. (1983), 'Government expenditure and economic growth: a cross-country study', *Southern Economic Journal*, **40**, 783-92.

Landau, L. (1971), 'Saving functions for Latin America', in H.B. Chenery (ed), *Studies in Development Planning*, Cambridge, Mass.: Harvard University Press.

Landsberger, M. (1970), 'The life cycle hypothesis: a reinterpretation and empirical test', *American Economic Review*, **60**, 175-83.

Lee, C.H. (1992), 'The government financial system and large enterprises in the economic development of South Korea', *World Development*, **20**, 187-97.

Lee, C.H. and Naya, S. (1988), 'Trade in East Asian development with comparative references to Southeast Asia experience', *Economic Development and Cultural Change*, **36**, Supplement, 123-52.

Leff, N.H. (1969), 'Dependency rates and savings rates', *American Economic Review*, **59**, 886-96.

Leibenstein, H. (1974), 'An interpretation of the economic theory of fertility: promising path or blind alley?' *Journal of Economic Literature*, **12**, 457-79.

Levine, R. and Renelt, D. (1992), 'A sensitivity analysis of cross-country growth regressions', *American Economic Review*, **28**, 942-63.

Lewis, W.A. (1954), 'Economic development with unlimited supplies of labour', *Manchester School*, **22**, 131-91.

Lewis, W.A. (1955), *The Theory of Economic Growth*, London: Allen and Unwin.

Lewis, W.A. (1958), 'Unlimited supplies of labour: further notes', *Manchester School*, **26**, 1-32.

Lim, C.Y. (1991), *Development and Underdevelopment*, Singapore: Longman.

Lim, D. (1975), *Supply Responses of Primary Producers*, Kuala Lumpur: University of Malaya Press.

Lim, D. (1976), 'On the measurement of capital utilization in less developed countries', *Oxford Economic Papers*, 28, 149-59.

Lim, D. (1977), 'Do foreign companies pay higher wages than their local counterparts in Malaysian manufacturing?', *Journal of Development Economics*, 4, 55-66.

Lim, D. (1980a), 'Income distribution, export instability and savings behaviour', *Economic Development and Cultural Change*, 28, 359-64.

Lim, D. (1980b), 'Taxation policies', in J. Cody, H. Hughes and D. Wall (eds), *Policies for Industrial Progress in Developing Countries*, New York: Oxford University Press.

Lim, D. (1982/83), 'Malaysian development planning', *Pacific Affairs*, 55, 613-39.

Lim, D. (1983a), 'Government recurrent expenditure and economic growth in less developed countries', *World Development*, 11, 377-80.

Lim, D. (1983b), 'Fiscal incentives and direct foreign investment in less developed countries', *Journal of Development Studies*, 19, 207-12.

Lim, D. (1983c), 'Another look at growth and defence in less developed countries', *Economic Development and Cultural Change*, 31, 377-84.

Lim, D. (1991), *Export Instability and Compensatory Financing*, London: Routledge.

Lim, D. (1992a), 'Recent trends in the size and growth of government in developing countries', in N. Gemmell (ed), *The Growth of the Public Sector*, Aldershot: Edward Elgar.

Lim, D. (1992b), 'Capturing the effects of capital subsidies', *Journal of Development Studies*, 28, 705-16.

Lim, D. (1993a), 'Relevance of East Asian development experiences to the South Pacific', in R.V. Cole and S. Tambunlertchai (eds), *Pacific Islands at the Crossroads?*, Canberra: National Centre for Development Studies.

Lim, D. (1993b), 'The economic impact of AIDS on Malaysia', in D.E. Bloom and J.V. Lyons (eds), *Economic Implications of AIDS in Asia*, New Delhi: UNDP.

Lim, D. (1994), 'Explaining the growth performances of Asian developing economies', *Economic Development and Cultural Change*, 42, 829-44.

Little, I., Scitovsky, T. and Scott, M. (1970), *Industry and Trade in Some Developing Countries*, London: Oxford University Press.

Little, I. (1979), 'An economic reconnaissance', in W. Galenson (ed), *Economic Growth and Structural Change in Taiwan*, Ithaca: Cornell University Press.

Lotz, J.R. and Morss, E.R. (1967), 'Measuring "tax effort" in developing countries', *IMF Staff Papers*, 14, 478-99.

Maddison, A. (1970), *Economic Progress and Policy in Developing Countries*, London: Allen and Unwin.

Maizels, A. and Nissanke, M. (1986), 'The determinants of military expenditures in developing countries', *World Development*, 14, 1125- 40.

Malenbaum, W. (1970), 'Health and productivity in poor areas', in H.E. Klarman (ed), *Empirical Studies in Health Economics*, Baltimore: Johns Hopkins University Press.

Mason, E. et al. (1980), *The Economic and Social Modernization of the Republic of Korea*, Cambridge, Mass.: Harvard University Press.

Massell, B.F. (1961), 'A disaggregated view of technical change', *Journal of Political Economy*, 69, 547-57.

McClelland, D.C. (1961), *The Achieving Society*, New York: Van Nostrand.

Meier, G.M. (ed) (1990), *Leading Issues in Development Economics*, New York: Oxford University Press.

Mikesell, R.F. and Zinser, J.E. (1973), 'The nature of the savings function in developing countries: a survey of the theoretical and empirical literature', *Journal of Economic Literature*, 11, 1-26.

Mincer, J. (1974), *Schooling, Experience and Earnings*, New York: Columbia University Press.

Moock, P.R. and Leslie, J. (1986), 'Childhood malnutrition and schooling in the Terai region of Nepal', *Journal of Development Economics*, 20, 33-52.

Morawetz, D. (1976), 'Elasticities of substitution in industry: what do we learn from econometric estimates?', *World Development*, 4, 11-5.

Morawetz, D. (1977), *Twenty-five Years of Economic Development 1950 to 1975*, Washington, D.C.: The World Bank.

Morishima, M. (1982), *Why has Japan Succeeded? Western Technology and the Japanese Ethos*, Cambridge: Cambridge University Press.

Morss, E. (1968), *Fiscal policy, savings and economic growth in developing countries: an empirical study*, IMF, Departmental Memoranda DM/68/43.

Moschos, D. (1989). 'Export expansion, growth and the level of economic development', *Journal of Development Economics*, 30, 93-102.

Mosley, P. (1980), 'Aid, savings and growth revisited', *Oxford Bulletin of Economics and Statistics*, 42, 79-91.

Musgrave, R.A. (1969), *Fiscal Systems*, New Haven: Yale University Press.

Musgrove, P. (1980), 'Income distribution and the aggregate consumption function', *Journal of Political Economy*, 88, 504-25.

Myint, H. (1967), 'Economic theory and development policy', *Economica*, **34**, 117-30.

Myrdal, G. (1957), *Economic Theory and Underdeveloped Regions*, London: Gerald Duckworth.

Nadiri, M. (1972), 'International studies of factor inputs and total factor productivity: a brief survey', *Review of Income and Wealth*, **18**, 129-155.

Nash, M. (1958), 'Political relations in Guatemala', *Social and Economic Studies*, **7**, 65-75.

Needham, J. (1954), *Science and Civilization in China*, Cambridge: Cambridge University Press.

Nelson, J.M. (1984), 'The politics of stabilization', in R.E. Feinberg and V. Kalab (eds), *Adjustment Crisis in the Third World*, New Brunswick: Transaction Books.

Nelson, R. (1964), 'Aggregate production functions and medium range growth projections', *American Economic Review*, **54**, 575-606.

Nerlove, M. (1974), 'Household and economy: toward a new theory of population and economic growth', *Journal of Political Economy*, **82**, Supplement, 200-18.

Niskanen, W.A. (1968), 'Non-market decision making: the peculiar economics of bureaucracy', *American Economic Review*, **58**, 293-305.

Nurkse, R. (1953), *Problems of Capital Formation in Underdeveloped Countries*, Oxford: Oxford University Press.

OECD (1993), *Development Cooperation: Efforts and Policies of the Members of the Development Assistance Committee*, Paris: OECD.

O'Malley, W.J. (1988), 'Culture and industrialization', in H. Hughes (ed), *Achieving Industrialization in East Asia*, Cambridge: Cambridge University Press.

Okimoto, D. (1989), *Between MITI and the Market: Japanese Industrial Policy for High Technology*, Stanford: Stanford University Press.

Olsen, R.J. (1983), 'Cross-sectional methods for estimating the replacement of infant deaths', Ohio State University, mimeo.

Olson, M. (1982), *The Rise and Decline of Nations: Economic Growth, Stagflation and Social Rigidities*, New Haven: Yale University Press.

Pang, E.F. (1988), 'The distinctive features of two city states' development: Hong Kong and Singapore', in P.L. Berger and H.M. Hsiao (eds), *In Search of an East Asian Development Model*, New Brunswick: Transaction Books.

Papanek, G. (1972), 'The effect of aid and other resource transfers on savings and growth in less developed countries', *Economic Journal*, **82**, 934-50.

Papanek, G. (1988), 'The new Asian capitalism: an economic portrait', in P.L. Berger and H.M. Hsiao (eds), *In Search of an East Asian Development Model*, New Brunswick: Transaction Books.

Park, Y.C. (1990), 'Growth, liberalization and internationalization of Korea's financial sector, 1970-89', a paper presented to the *Conference on Financial Development in Japan, Korea and Taiwan*, Taipei: Institute of Economics, Academia Sinica.

Peacock, A.T. and Wiseman, J. (1961), *The Growth of Public Expenditure in the United Kingdom*, Princeton, N.J.: Princeton University Press.

Phan-Thuy, N., Betancourt, R., Winston, G. and Kabaj, M. (1981), *Industrial Capacity and Employment Promotion*, Westmead: Gower.

Please, S. (1967), 'Savings through taxation: reality or mirage?' *Finance and Development*, 4, 24-32.

Please, S. (1970), 'The Please effect revisited', IBRD, Economics Department Working Paper, No. 82.

Prest, A.R. (1962), 'The sensitivity of the yield of personal income tax in the United Kingdom', *Economic Journal*, 72, 576-96.

Psacharopoulos, G. (1969), 'The anatomy of a rate of growth: the case of Hawaii 1950-60', Economic Research Center, University of Hawaii.

Psacharopoulos, G. (1984), 'Assessing training priorities in developing countries: current practice and possible alternatives', *International Labour Review*, 123, 569-583.

Psacharopoulos, G. (1985), 'Returns to education: A further international update and implications', *Journal of Human Resources*, 20, 583-604.

Psacharopoulos, G. (1988), 'Education and development: a review', *World Bank Research Observer*, 3, 99-116.

Psacharopoulos, G. (1994), 'Returns to investment in education: a global update', *World Development*, 22, 1325-43.

Pye, L. (1988), 'The new Asian capitalism: a political portrait', in P.L. Berger and H.M. Hsiao (eds), *In Search of an East Asian Development Model*, New Brunswick: Transaction Books.

Rahman, M.A. (1968), 'Foreign capital and domestic savings: a test of Haavelmo's hypothesis with cross-country data', *Review of Economics and Statistics*, 50, 137-8.

Ram, R. (1985), 'Export and economic growth: some additional evidence', *Economic Development and Cultural Change*, 33, 59-74.

Ram, R. (1986), 'Government size and economic growth: a new framework and some evidence from cross-section and time-series data', *American Economic Review*, 76, 191-203.

Ram, R. (1987), 'Exports and economic growth in developing countries: evidence from time-series and cross-section data', *Economic Development and Cultural Change*, 35, 51-70.

Ram, R. and Schultz, T.W. (1979), 'Life span, savings and productivity', *Economic Development and Cultural Change*, 3, 394-421.

Ramanathan, R. (1969), 'An econometric exploration of Indian saving behaviour', *Journal of the American Statistical Association*, 64, 90-101.

Ranis, G. (1957), 'Factor proportions in Japanese economic development', *American Economic Review*, **47**, 594-607.

Ravallion, M., Datt, G. and Chen, S.H. (1992), 'New estimates of aggregate poverty measures for the developing world 1958-89', *World Bank, Population and Human Resources Department*: Washington D.C.

Reddaway, W.B. (1963), 'The economics of underdeveloped countries', *Economic Journal*, **73**, 1-12.

Remmer, K.L. (1986), 'The politics of economic stabilization: IMF standby programs in Latin America, 1954-1984', *Comparative Politics*, **19**, 1-24.

Ricardo, D. (1951), *On the Principles of Political Economy and Taxation*, Third Edition (ed) Piero Sraffa, Cambridge: Cambridge University Press.

Riedel, J. (1988), 'Economic development in East Asia: doing what comes naturally?', in H. Hughes (ed), *Achieving Industrialization in East Asia*, Cambridge: Cambridge University Press.

Riedel, J. (1991), 'Intra-Asian trade and foreign direct investment', *Asian Development Review*, **9**, 111-46.

Richter, L. (1984), 'Manpower planning in developing countries: changing approaches and emphases', *International Labour Review*, **123**, 677-92

Robinson, S. (1971), 'The sources of growth in less developed countries: a cross-section study', *Quarterly Journal of Economics*, **85**, 391-408.

Rosenstein-Rodan, P. (1961), 'International aid for underdeveloped countries', *Review of Economics and Statistics*, **43**, 107-38.

Rosenzweig, M.R. and Schultz, T.P. (1982), 'Child mortality and fertility in Colombia: individual and community effects', *Health Policy and Education, 2*, Amsterdam: Elsevier Scientific Publishing Co.

Rostow, W.W. (1952), *The Process of Economic Growth*, New York: Norton.

Rostow, W.W. (1960), *The Stages of Economic Growth*, Cambridge: Cambridge University Press.

Rubinson, R. (1977), 'Dependency, government revenue and economic growth, 1955-70', *Studies in Comparative International Development*, **12**, 3-28.

Sahota, G.S. (1961), *Indian Tax Structure and Economic Development*, London: Asia Publishing House.

Sato, K. (1971), 'International variations in the incremental capital–output ratio', *Economic Development and Cultural Change*, **19**, 621- 40.

Schultz, T.P. (1978), 'Fertility and child mortality over the life cycle: aggregate and individual evidence', *American Economic Review*, **68**, 208-15.

Schultz, T.W. (1961), 'Investment in human capital', *American Economic Review*, **51**, 1-17.

Schumpeter, J. (1939), *The Theory of Economic Development*, Cambridge, Mass.: Harvard University Press.

Schumpeter, J. (1943), *Capitalism, Socialism and Democracy*, London: Allen and Unwin.

Scott, M.F. (1979), 'Foreign trade', in W. Galenson (ed), *Economic Growth and Structural Change in Taiwan*, Ithaca: Cornell University Press.

Scully, G.W. (1988), 'The institutional framework and economic development', *Journal of Political Economy*, **96**, 652-62.

Sen, A.K. (ed) (1970), *Growth Economics*, Harmondsworth: Penguin Books.

Shah, S.M.S. and Toye, J. (1978), 'Fiscal incentives for firms in some developing countries: survey and critique', in S.M.S. Shah and J. Toye (eds), *Taxation and Economic Development*, London: Frank Cass.

Sheedy, E. (1990), 'Exports and growth: a flawed framework', *Journal of Development Studies*, **27**, 111-6.

Simon, J.L. (1981), *The Ultimate Resource*, Princeton, N.J.: Princeton University Press.

Simon, J.L. (1986), *Theory of Population and Economic Growth*, Oxford: Basil Blackwell.

Singh, S.K. (1975), *Development Economics: Theory and Findings*, Lexington, Mass.: D.C. Health.

Skidmore, T.E. (1977), 'The politics of economic stabilization in postwar Latin America', in J.M. Malloy (ed), *Authoritarianism and Corporatism in Latin America*, Pittsburgh: University of Pittsburgh Press.

Smith, R.P. (1980), 'The demand for military expenditure', *Economic Journal*, **90**, 811-20.

Snyder, D.W. (1974), 'Econometric studies of household saving behaviour in developing countries: a survey', *Journal of Development Studies*, **10**, 139-53.

Snyder, D.W. (1990), 'Foreign aid and domestic savings: a spurious correlation?', *Economic Development and Cultural Change*, **39**, 175-81.

Solow, R. (1957), 'Technical change and the aggregate production function', *Review of Economics and Statistics*, **39**, 312-20.

Solow, R. (1960), 'Investment and technical progress', in K.J. Arrow, S. Karlin and P. Suppes (eds), *Mathematical Methods in the Social Sciences*, Stanford: Stanford University Press.

Squire, L. and van der Tak, H.G. (1975), *Economic Analysis of Projects*, Baltimore, Johns Hopkins University Press.

Stewart, F. (1971), 'Foreign capital, domestic savings and economic development: comment', *Bulletin of the Oxford Institute of Economics and Statistics*, **33**, 138-49.

Strauss, J. (1986), 'Does better nutrition raise farm productivity?', *Journal of Political Economy*, **94**, 297-320.

Summers, R. and Heston, A. (1988), 'A new set of international comparisons of real product and price levels: estimates for 130 countries, 1950-1985', *Review of Income and Wealth*, **34**, 1-24.

Summers, R. and Heston, A. (1991), 'The Penn World Table (Mark 5): an expanded set of international comparisons, 1950-1988', *Quarterly Journal of Economics*, **106**, 327-68.

Tait, A. Gratz, W. and Eichengreen, B. (1979), 'International comparisons of taxation for selected developing countries 1972-76', *IMF Staff Papers*, **26**, 123-56.

Tan, T.W. (1988), 'Management of resource-based growth in different factor endowment conditions', in M. Urrutia and S. Yukawa (eds), *Economic Development Policies in Resource-Rich Countries*, Tokyo: United Nations University.

Thirlwall, A.P. (1972), 'A cross-section study of population growth and the growth of output and per capita income in a production function framework', *Manchester School*, **40**, 339-56.

Thirlwall, A.P. (1974), 'Inflation and the savings ratio across countries', *Journal of Development Studies*, **10**, 154-74.

Thirlwall, A.P. (1983), *Growth and Development*, London: Macmillan.

Thirlwall, A.P. (1994), *Growth and Development*, London: Macmillan.

Timmer, C. P. (1975), 'The choice of technique in Indonesia', in C.P. Timmer, et al., *The Choice of Technology in Developing Countries*, Cambridge, Mass.: Harvard University Press.

Todaro, M.P. (1994), *Economic Development*, New York: Longman.

Triandis, H.C. (1971), 'Some psychological dimensions of modernisation', *Proceedings of the 17th International Congress of Applied Psychology*, Brussels, **2**, 56-75.

Triandis, H.C. (1973), 'Subjective culture and economic development', *International Journal of Psychology*, **8**, 163-80.

Tyler, W. (1981), 'Growth and expansion in developing countries', *Journal of Development Economics*, **9**, 121-30.

UNCTAD (1985), *Compensatory Financing of Export Earnings Shortfalls*, New York: UNCTAD.

United Nations Development Programme (1991), *Human Development Report 1991*, New York: Oxford University Press.

United Nations Development Programme (1992), *Human Development Report 1992*, New York: Oxford University Press.

Vogel, E. (1979), *Japan as Number One*, Cambridge, Mass.: Harvard University Press.

Voloudakis, E. (1970), 'Major sources of the postwar growth of the Greek economy', mimeo., Athens.

Wade, R. (1988), 'The role of government in overcoming market failure: Taiwan, Republic of Korea and Japan', in H. Hughes (ed), *Achieving*

Industrialization in East Asia, Cambridge: Cambridge University Press.

Wade, R. (1990), *Governing the Market: Economic Theory and the Role of Government in East Asian Industralization*: Princeton, N.J.: Princeton University Press.

Wagner, A. (1883), *Finanzwissenschaft*, Leipzig. Partly translated and reprinted in R.A. Musgrave and A.T. Peacock (eds) (1958), *Classics in the Theory of Public Finance*, London: Macmillan.

Walters, A.A. (1968), *An Introduction to Econometrics*, London: Macmillan.

Weber, M. (1904), *The Protestant Ethic and the Spirit of Capitalism*, translated by T. Parsons, 1930, London: Allen and Unwin.

Wheeler, D. (1980), 'Basic needs fulfillment and economic growth: a simultaneous model', *Journal of Development Economics*, 7, 435-51.

White, L.J. (1978), 'The evidence on appropriate factor proportions for manufacturing in less developed countries: a survey', *Economic Development and Cultural Change*, 27, 27-60.

Williamson, J. (1991), 'The debt crisis: lessons of the 1980s', *Asian Development Review*, 9, 1-13.

Williamson, J.G. (1968), 'Personal saving in developing nations: an inter-temporal cross-section from Asia', *Economic Record*, 44, 194-210.

Williamson, O. (1975), *Markets and Hierarchies: Analysis and Anti-trust Implications*, New York: Free Press.

Williamson, O. (1985), *The Economic Institutions of Capitalism*, New York: Free Press.

Winston, G. (1971), 'Capital utilization in economic development', *Economic Journal*, 81, 36-60.

Wolf, E.R. (1955), 'Types of Latin American peasantry: a preliminary discussion', *American Anthropologist*, 57, 452-71.

Wolgemuth, J.C., Latham, M., Hall, A., Chesher, A. and Crompton, D. (1982), 'Worker productivity and the nutritional status of Kenyan road construction laborers', *American Journal of Clinical Nutrition*, 36, 68-78.

World Bank (1976), *World Tables 1976*, Baltimore: Johns Hopkins University Press.

World Bank (1980), *World Development Report 1980*, New York: Oxford University Press.

World Bank (1983), *World Tables*, Baltimore: Johns Hopkins University Press.

World Bank (1984), *World Development Report 1984*, New York: Oxford University Press.

World Bank (1988), *Malaysia: Matching Risks and Rewards in a Mixed Economy*, World Bank: Washington D.C.

World Bank (1991), *World Development Report 1991: The Challenge of Development*, Oxford: Oxford University Press.

World Bank (1992), *World Development Report 1992: Development and the Environment*, Oxford: Oxford University Press.

World Bank (1993a), *The East Asian Miracle*, Oxford: Oxford University Press.

World Bank (1993b), *World Development Report 1993: Investment in Health*, New York: Oxford University Press.

Yaghmalan, B. (1994), 'An empirical investigation of exports, development and growth in developing countries: challenging the neoclassical theory of export-led growth', *World Development*, 22, 1977-95.

Yukawa, S. (1988), 'Constraints on the development of resource-rich countries: a comparative analysis', in M. Urrutia and S. Yukawa (eds), *Economic Development Policies in Resource-rich Countries*, Tokyo: United Nations University.

Zysman, J. (1983), *Government, Markets and Growth: Financial Systems and the Politics of Industrial Change*, Ithaca: Cornell University Press.

Index